While serving in the army for twenty years (1987-2007), the author served with the Australian Army Psychology Corps (AAPSYCH) after completing a psychology degree at Queensland University of Technology with elective subjects on writing, including screenwriting under screenwriting & playwriting icon David Williamson. In 2006, he worked as a journalist on the Army Paper. He completed a BA in Writing, English and History at the University of Queensland (2013-15), where he studied under respected Australian authors such as Dr Kim Wilkins, Venero Armmano, Charlotte Nash, Kari Gislason, and Michael Robotham.

He also attended writing courses at the New York Film Academy (2009), studying film and TV writing; at the American Comedy Institute (ACI) for comedy writing (2010); Allen & Unwin's Faber Academy Novel Writing (2012) under Kathryn Heyman and James Bradley, with guest authors such as Delia Falconer, Michael Robotham, Charlotte Wood, David Malouf and Markus Zusak whose bestselling novel, *The Book Thief,* is set in WWII.

While living in the USA from 2009-11, he attended various institutions, such as the Gotham Writers Workshops (NYC) and Write Your Free (Connecticut), where he studied with Dr Patrick McCord. He attended workshops with authors such as Colin Broderick (IRE), Heather Swain, and Patricia Riley Giff. One of his scripts won the Brett Ratner Award. He also volunteered at the Holocaust & Human Rights Education Center (HHREC), where he interviewed numerous Holocaust survivors. Through the HHREC, he became friends with Dr Tina Strobos, who was honoured in 1989 as Righteous Among the Nations by the Yad Vashem in Israel. Dr Strobos, as a teenager, met Marlene Dietrich (a major character in this novel) in the Swiss Alps on skiing trips before WW2.

The author lives in North Queensland with his assistant dog and best friend, Archie, a golden Labrador. *Daughters of the Fatherland* is his first novel.

# Daughters of the Fatherland

Jericho J. Johnson

Glass House Books
Brisbane

*Daughters of the Fatherland*

Glass House Books
an imprint of IP (Interactive Publications Pty Ltd)
Treetop Studio • 9 Kuhler Court
Carindale, Queensland, Australia 4152
sales@ipoz.biz
http://ipoz.biz/shop
First published by IP in 2024
© 2024 Keith Whalley (text); IP (design)

Printed in 14 pt Avenir Book on Caslon Pro 12 pt.

ISBN: 9781922830784 (PB) 9781922830791 (eBook)

A catalogue record for this book is available from the National Library of Australia

This book is dedicated to the Roma, Romani, Sinti, Gypsy or Travellers of Europe who were persecuted by the Nazis in the Romani or Gypsy Holocaust called the Porajmos (devouring).

*There is no reason in the whole world for any war. Think what you will, this will not be a war fought on the front. This will be a war on women and children.*

– Erich Maria Remarque, *All Quiet on the Western Front*

# Acknowledgements

*Cover image:* Betty Martinez, Reedsy.com
*Author photo:* Liz Andrews Photography
*Book design:* David P Reiter

Firstly, I need to acknowledge my publisher, Dr David Reiter, for helping me get this very important story out into the 'story-verse'. Secondly, I'm fortunate to acknowledge the people directly involved in the various aspects of the development of this novel: Lauren Elise Daniels, Nadine Davidoff, Sienna Brown, Irina Dunn, Emma-Clare Daly, Cherie Reiter, and Betty Martinez. Over the years, people, places, and writing institutions have all helped me on my writer's journey, too numerous to name. I acknowledge and deeply appreciate the people and organisations that have helped me shape this story in particular, such as Donna Cohen, the then-CEO of the Holocaust and Human Rights Education Center in White Plains, NY, and her volunteers, Holocaust survivors and heroes, who were all very generous with their time and shared their honest and unfiltered stories with me. I need to give a special mention to Luana Giordano, the first cheerleader for me and my novel and pivotal in giving us both that final push on this long path to publication. Finally, and most importantly, as this book has a strong theme of mothers and motherhood, I have to thank my Mum, Beverley Ann Whalley (nee Johnson), who always urged her dreamful son to pursue his dreams.

# Contents

# Daughters of the Fatherland

# Keith Whalley

## Map of Europe: World War II

# Chapter 1

## 31 August 1939 (Thursday)

*Nazi Germany, somewhere east of Cologne*

Little Rosa sat on the back steps of her horse-drawn wagon, as it ambled through the German villages perched alongside the great Rhine River. Hers was the last of the more-than-twenty Romani wagons—Rosa stopped counting at twenty because she couldn't count any higher—but last night, she'd heard her father say that there were now thirty-five wagons. She could tell her father was worried about the number of wagons by the number of wrinkles in his very wrinkly brow—way more than twenty.

When they'd set out, there were only seven, with the wagons looking like a giant wooden barrel had been cut in half to provide a rounded top and sides. And, although these didn't have any windows, they were robust in all forms of extreme weather. But now, with all the additional Romani, their wagons came with a lot of variety, such as open-top wagons, some with a makeshift tent to keep out the sun and rain. Others were square and were probably used in previous centuries but had long-since been abandoned, only to be claimed and repurposed by the passing Romani. Most had two horses pulling, but the smaller ones had only one, with spare horses trailing behind. In between were Romani of various ages walking with the occasional horse rider. But the Romani caravans had one thing in common: they were all painted with bright colours, some with intricate patterns, and some had flower pots hanging at the front and back to add even more colour.

Rosa turned the well-worn pages of her book. *Little Red Riding Hood* and Rosa had so much in common: they both loved their grandmothers, and, just as the heroine's grandmother had given her the red hood, so too Rosa's grandmother had given her this *Brother's Grimm Book of Fairy Tales* along with her now favourite red scarf. When Little Red Riding Hood met the wolf on the path, she wasn't scared, nor had Rosa been scared a few years ago when she ran into her first wolf while collecting firewood one day in the woods of Romania. The she-wolf stared into Rosa's eyes for a long moment before disappearing back into the forest. Rosa knew that the she-wolf would never have eaten a fellow wood spirit. They were both sisters of the woods, as she'd told her father about this encounter afterwards. Her father had laughed it off and told her the wolf must have decided that Rosa was all skin and bones, no meat, so she wasn't worth the effort. But that meeting with her forest sister had filled Rosa with an exhilarating sense of confidence.

Rosa often imagined the evil, story-book wolf, satisfied with his trickery and a full belly, sleeping with a contented smile. All of a sudden, his eyes would flash open, and he would howl so loudly that the full moon would hide from fright. Looking down, the wolf would see something sticking out of his furry stomach: a small hand holding a large pair of shiny scissors, which Red Riding Hood had hidden in her apron. And Rosa imagined that if she had killed the wolf, like in the children's tale, she would have made a cloak from the wolf's fur. And from that day onwards, she would forever be known as the Wolf Slayer, but they would only whisper that name, as no one would dare say it aloud to Rosa's face. She knew the original story was meant to frighten children, so they wouldn't wander off the path to pick flowers. But she would write her own story, and, as the Wolf Slayer, she could make her own path and pick and smell all the flowers she wanted.

Rosa stopped reading as she watched the uniformed boys on bicycles stalking her Romani caravan. The boys rode in perfect formation, their handlebars and polished tire spokes gleaming. She was familiar with their uniforms; according to her father, they were the Hitler Youth or Hitler wolf-pups, very dangerous, to be avoided at all costs. Rosa found herself mesmerised by the spectacle of six blue-eyed boys cycling towards her, their chocolate-brown ties flowing in the breeze.

From out of nowhere, something flew at her. She ducked as the object slammed against the back door of her caravan and landed on the step beside her. She picked it up and stared at the hefty rock. She looked at the boys, identifying the rock thrower by his broad, toothy grin. She stood up on the back steps and, with both hands, slung it up in a high arc, throwing it back at her attacker. He let out a yelp as it narrowly missed him. The boys stopped their bicycles and glared at her.

"How dare you?" the leader shouted at her. "You dirty little Gypsy. We'll teach you a lesson." Then he lifted his front wheels, turning and speeding away in the opposite direction. His mustard-shirted friends followed him.

She watched as their blonde-haired heads disappeared behind the long grass. *Good riddance.*

She felt light-headed from this attack out of nowhere and sat back down on the steps. She felt the blood return to her body as what happened began to sink in. She hadn't meant to throw the rock at the boys, who were all about her age—ten. She'd promised her mother there would be no more fighting with other kids. But Rosa's promise only extended to the children from her own tribe, not outsiders. She fingered the scuff marks on her knees and her bruised calves. It wasn't her fault she got into so many fights. She had to defend herself, didn't she, when the other children accused her of not being a real Romani? She did her best to ignore their taunts, but eventually, her resolve would crack, and she would answer her accusers with loud thunderous fists.

She could feel her anger rising, so she picked up her book and paused to look at the front cover before opening it. She didn't understand why, but reading was the only way to make her anger disappear. Perhaps, for a short while, while she was reading anyway, she wasn't Rosa. She was somebody else—anybody but herself.

Rosa was startled by a bang followed by a loud crack. The tired and worn wagon suddenly bucked and jolted like a young bull. The wagon's steel-rimmed wheels had lurched over a large pothole, and then her house-on-wheels groaned stubbornly onwards. The wagon righted itself as it ambled along. Over the grumbling of wheels, Rosa heard someone moving inside the laden wagon, attempting to settle the disturbed, caged and tethered animals.

She stiffened.

"Rosa?" her mother yelled from inside the patchwork-painted rear door. "You better not be reading again instead of doing your chores!"

Rosa always hid her threadbare library—nine books and a tattered old Lutheran Bible, all inherited from her grandmother—so her mother wouldn't use them as kindling again. She closed the book. "No, Mama."

Her mother opened the top half of the wagon's rear door and emptied a bucket of water without looking down at Rosa. "You lazy little thing," her mother said. "You'd let your father go hungry? Get in here and cook his breakfast."

Rosa slid the book discreetly into a loose wall panel and stood to attention on the wagon's back steps. "I'm sorry, Mama, I'm coming—"

"Don't bother, little one," her father's deep voice boomed from the front of the wagon. "I'm not hungry."

"I guess that means I'll have to do it," her mother said from inside. "You'd better have your scarf on."

Rosa's hands reached her head and touched her red headscarf. She always felt like her favourite, wolf-defeating heroine when she wore it. "Yes, Mama."

"At least you can do that right," her mother said with her usual gruffness, especially whenever Rosa had done something wrong, which seemed to be all the time.

Rosa heard the stove door creak open. She'd forgotten to fill it with firewood as part of her morning chores. Her heart skipped a beat, remembering her mother's furious hands for the slightest of mistakes. She was really in for it now if there wasn't enough wood left for her father's breakfast. Her mother clanged some pots and pans, but nothing more was said.

Rosa stopped holding her breath. She silently thanked her beloved grandma, who must have been looking out for Rosa.

All Rosa could think of was that her father must have done it for her when he saw the freshly cut wood lying next to the stove. He was always looking out for her. He hated it when his family fought. Her father had said her mother punished Rosa out of an act of love designed to teach Rosa right from wrong. But it had taken Rosa a long time to learn that 'wrong' really meant anything that lowered their standing amongst the other families. But Rosa didn't care what the other families or anybody else thought about her.

Rosa heard her father yell at the two horses pulling their wagon. She removed her shoes and climbed up the rusty ladder that led from the wagon's rear to the roof. She could already feel the chill of the early autumn air on her cheeks. She inhaled the fragrant pine aroma but winced when the breeze changed direction. All thirty-five horse-drawn wagons were loaded with livestock, straw and hay. The caravan was a farm on wheels, and it smelt like one.

No two wagons in the caravan looked alike in shape or colour. It was a haphazard collection of wooden structures on wheels of various sizes, some with wooden spokes, some spoke-less as if they had been cut from a tree trunk, and a hole cut out in the middle to allow for the axle. She tiptoed along the blood-coloured curved roof, skipping over the covered chimney, which began to billow smoke as her mother lit a fire to prepare breakfast.

Rosa, an expert at balancing against the swaying motion of a moving wagon, stood on the wagon's roof and looked down at her father, who was holding the reins of their horses, Kizzy and Lala. The curved roof extended over the back steps and the driver's seat.

Her father looked upwards to face her with a worried expression on his broad face.

She clambered down from the roof and hugged her father before sitting next to him. "What's wrong, Papa?"

"Our leader is going to get us killed; that's what is wrong."

"Killed? Why?"

He looked startled and turned to face her. "I'm sorry, Rosa, I shouldn't have said that. But even you young ones can tell we live in dark times, and our tribe has survived all these generations because we've always been careful. But now, as dark clouds hang over Europe, we need to be extra careful, and our new, young *leader* is being reckless with our lives."

"I like Manfri," Rosa said. "He has kind eyes. Mama says his name means 'man of peace'."

"Well, in times like these, we don't need a man-of-peace, but a man o' war," her father replied.

Rosa looked up at him quizzically at his use of a new word.

"*Man 'O' War* was an olden-day warship so-called because of all the guns it carried on its two or three decks," he explained.

"Grandma used to say that our wagons are like the land ships of Europe."

"She was a very wise woman, your grandmother. So wise, she wouldn't have tried to sneak across from Romania to Holland through Austria and Germany. We should have taken the safer route of Italy, through France, then up to Holland."

"What's so bad about Germany?" Rosa wondered aloud. "Mama says that our tribe belongs to the River Romani, where we live and travel along the great river systems of Europe, such as the Rhine River."

Her father laughed. "Make no mistake, I love the rivers, the real lifeblood of Europe, and I'm sure our tribe has the Rhine River flowing through our veins, including yours. But Germany is no longer safe, especially since the Führer annexed his birthplace, Austria, as well as Sudetenland in Czechoslovakia and Lithuania to make one grand Germany. And in my experience with those in charge of nations, once you get a taste for expansion, you can't stop, and you can bet Adolf Hitler won't stop there."

"But Manfri said this way was twice as fast."

"Fast is not necessarily safer, little one, especially in this case—for a stupid wedding, no less. This is no time for celebrations."

"But Mama said, in these dark times, this is exactly when we need to have—good times, like a big Romani wedding. And besides, it's family. The eldest Heigl girl is getting married, so we must be there."

Her father laughed. "When you're Romani in Europe, we're *all* family; everybody is related to some other tribe in some way. And that's not by accident. But your mother is forever the diplomat."

"Mama said that was her full-time job when you were our tribe leader. Why did you stop, Papa? I liked it when you were the boss-man. Everyone left me alone back then."

"Being the boss-man is a young man's game. Martha and I are way too old for games. That's why we both need your help, little one."

"I forgot my chores this morning, again. Thank you for filling the stove with wood for me."

"You are always daydreaming, but it's all right, little one; sitting up front keeping me company is chore enough. But you know the temper your mother has. She keeps me on my toes. But speaking of keeping on your toes, you'd better tiptoe back to your reading place, just in case your mother discovers your crime and decides to burn another of your books as punishment."

Rosa stood and gave him a big hug and a kiss on his shiny, clean-shaven cheek. She quietly retraced her footsteps to get back onto the roof where she turned down to face her father, who was watching her. His big grey moustache with its specks of black, which always tickled when he kissed her, curved into a smile.

She mouthed, "I love you, Papa," and blew him a kiss.

As always, he caught her flying kiss—like plucking a butterfly from the air—and put it in his pocket for later. She continued and climbed back down the ladder to nestle safely in her perfect hiding place—the rear steps of the last wagon in the caravan.

Rosa still didn't understand why they had to leave Germany. It was one of her favourite countries to travel through, the setting of all her favourite stories.

She retrieved her book and opened it at *Little Red Riding Hood.* Rays of the morning sunshine fought their way through the pine-forest canopy to splash upon her page as the wagon rumbled along the path. The trees looked like giant green soldiers lining up perfectly straight, ready for a parade inspection. She closed her eyes, tipping her face up to the warmth as the wagon swayed. As she turned to the story's final page, something slammed into her chest. The pain was so loud it was like she couldn't hear. She gasped for air. Her eyes stung. She realised her book was gone, replaced by a hefty rock, which weighed more than twice the weight of her large storybook.

Laughter. Her blonde-haired tormentors were back. But now, at least twenty boys were leaning on the handlebars of their shiny bikes, little Nazi flags attached to the metal frames.

Rosa spotted her book lying on the cobbled road, the pages flicking wildly about as if calling out to her for help. With the rock still in hand—for protection—she jumped off the slowly moving wagon and shuffled quickly forward, breathless and barefoot. She picked up the storybook and hugged it to her still-aching chest before turning back towards her wagon.

But the boys were too fast.

They cut her off, circling on their bikes. They taunted and jeered, pushing their bikes into an ever-tightening circle.

Rosa was trapped.

Her thoughts raced. She could shout for help, but was it worth unleashing the full fury of her mother's anger? She had no choice. She needed to handle this situation herself.

The leader got off his bike. His golden hair and sky-blue eyes made him look more like a church altar boy than a scoundrel. "*Was ist das?*" he asked. "It's Little Red Riding Hood, and she's lost her way."

The other boys laughed.

The leader lunged at her. She fell back onto the muddy road.

The boy held up her red scarf and then wrapped it around his head, to the amusement of the others.

But when he looked down at her, he exclaimed, "Gypsies don't have blonde hair!"

Rosa tightened her left fist around a cold, smooth rock. Bouncing to her feet, she threw the giant rock squarely at his temple. He collapsed to the ground, still clutching her red scarf.

Rosa leapt over his crumpled body and with book in hand raced back towards her wagon.

One.

Two.

Three!

She was up the wagon's back steps, turning the handle, slamming the door shut behind her.

Only once she was safely inside her wagon did she remember to breathe, inhaling cool air into her burning lungs. She peered through the curtained rear window. The boys had not given chase but were standing around the leader she'd hit. He had that same stare she had witnessed before. Her father said it was the look of people who no longer had any problems: the stare of the dead.

"Rosa! Where's your scarf?"

She swirled to face her mother's outraged eyes.

"Where is your scarf, Rosa? Tell me!"

She was feeling for it. Gone. She stammered, trying to think. "I, it wasn't my fault."

Despite her mother's enormous size, she was quickly upon her. "You promised me that you would never, ever remove your scarf! That was our deal." She grabbed Rosa's bony arm. Her mother stormed over to the rear window with her daughter in tow. Her expression darkened even further when she saw the Hitler Youth gathered around their fallen comrade. She shook Rosa. "What did you do this time?"

"I—"

Her mother slapped Rosa across her face. Rosa slammed against one of the tied-down boxes.

"You promised me never to take off the scarf. Never!" Her mother squeezed past the chicken coop and headed to the steaming stove.

Through hot tears, Rosa cried out, "Mama, I swear. It wasn't my fault!"

"It never is, Rosa."

Her mother pulled out pots and pans from the wall-mounted cupboards. "We are sick of your lies." She found what she was looking for: a big, old black pot.

Rosa's eyes widened, and she clamped her hands over her long blonde hair. "No, Mother, it won't happen again, I swear."

Her mother poured a dark, foul-smelling liquid into the pot, added some other ingredients with cold water and stirred, producing a bitter tar-like smell.

"Mother, no! Please don't. It smells, and the other kids will poke fun at me. I'll be good. It'll never happen ever again. I promise."

Her mother took a kettle off the stove and poured hot water into the pot, stirring until the disgusting thick paste became liquid. "No. It certainly won't happen again. What was I thinking? It's your father's fault. He said I could trust you this time. My head must be getting soft. Come here, girl."

The pungent smell, combined with her mother's rage, had Rosa frozen with fear.

Her mother grabbed a stick hanging by a leather strap on the wall. The stick might as well have had 'Rosa' burned onto it—it had only one purpose. The mean boys Rosa had just encountered were nothing compared to the pain that stick could inflict. The welts and bruises would last for days, and sometimes every breath or step she took would be agony. There was no escaping her mother. Resigned, now, with tears streaming down her face, Rosa inched closer to her mother, who was still stirring the foul-smelling pot.

Her mother thrust Rosa's head and hair into the big black pot. Rosa screamed, bucking and struggling. Ignoring her protests and yelps, her mother massaged the stinking substance into Rosa's blonde hair, steam rising.

"Stop squirming, girl."

Rosa's limp body complied. It would be over sooner if she stopped resisting. But the acrid smell was too stomach-churning, and Rosa felt like she was about to be sick.

She held her breath.

For too long.

She passed out.

***

Rosa tramped along the forest floor until her feet crunched to a halt on some dry wood. She clambered up the fallen branch, bouncing up and down until her body weight finally cracked the branch into several smaller pieces. At times like these, especially after a fight with her mother, Rosa liked to imagine her real surname.

Rosa Stavros?

No.

Rosa Shivitz?

No.

Perhaps her actual name was Rosa Heigl? But she didn't have the Heigl twins' bushy eyebrows or their big noses.

No.

Then again, she wasn't a *real* Romani: they'd found her in the big city of Berlin, after all.

Rosa Bremmer?

No.

Rosa Müller?

No.

Rosa Schmidt? *Hello, I'm Rosa Schmidt from Berlin. Erk!*

No.

None of those names sounded like her. No name ever seemed to fit her. Her parents' family name was Katka, but no one in the tribe, not even her parents, had ever called her by that name. And as far as her mother was concerned, her name may as well have been Rosa Get-Here-Right-Now! No. She didn't feel like a Katka, especially not after what had happened to her that morning.

Scooping up the wood shards, she felt a splinter stab her thumb. She let out a scream of frustration, throwing the offending stick as far as it would go.

"It's not my fault!" she shouted to herself.

"No, it's never your fault," Rosa said, mimicking her mother. "Whose fault is it, then?"

"Yours!" she yelled aloud all to herself.

"I wish everybody would just leave me alone. I hate them so much! When I grow up, I'm going to live up high on a mountain somewhere, all by myself," Rosa added.

A strong wind blew the dry leaves into a whirlpool around her. She shivered as if a hairy spider had crawled up her bare leg. Not that she was scared of creepy critters like the other children seemed to be so terribly afraid of. If she was ever bitten by a poisonous snake or stung by a dangerous scorpion and died then such is life. Life is death as her father always said. But it was getting late in woods she'd never been in, so Rosa raced back toward the safety of her camp.

By the time Rosa returned to camp, darkness had fallen. The Romani caravan was well hidden in a small, grassed clearing shielded by a ring of large leafy-green oaks. Rosa noticed people moving about or quietly gathered around campfires but without the usual laughing and talking. Within the large meadow where they'd camped for the night, her tribe's seven original camped wagons were encircled by the other tribes' wagons. The other Romani never really spoke to Rosa's tribe, but whenever her tribe moved, the other tribes followed. And whenever her tribe stopped and camped for the night, so did the others. Her father had explained to Rosa that these Romani were lost sheep looking for a shepherd, and as Rosa's tribe seemed to know what they were doing, the sheep simply followed them.

As Rosa got to her tribe, she could tell from their glares that they knew about her encounter with the blonde-haired boys. The Heigl identical twins stepped in front of her, blocking her way.

"Hello," said Rosa.

"You're in *big* trouble now, Rosa," said Kizzy.

"Father always said you would bring down the tribe one day," said Lala.

"And he was right," they said in unison, as they often did, especially when picking on Rosa.

Rosa pushed between them and turned. "Do you know why I called our horses Kizzy and Lala?" she asked.

The twins shook their heads again in perfect unison.

Rosa smiled. "It's because my horses smell just like you two, who are both full of horse poo." She pinched her nose tightly while holding her breath for added effect.

The twins stormed off.

Rosa swished her skirt, strutting back over to her wagon. At least she had one win today. When she returned to her camp, she saw a large group gathered around the fire. She recognised it was her tribe having a meeting. She saw her father standing in the middle of the group. He was angry, and in the firelight, his eyes twinkled, and he looked twenty years younger. She got closer to listen to the adults talk.

"War's coming, and not just any war," said her father, addressing the group. "The first war was called the Great War; well, this coming war in Europe will be far greater," he said. "And we don't want to be here when it starts."

Rosa could tell by the group's silence that they agreed with him.

"There are too many of us," he continued. "We will attract too much attention from the German authorities."

"Max, what do you suggest we do?" asked Manfri, the young leader of their tribe, his gentle voice matching his kind eyes. "We are all caught up in this together. We are *all* looking for a way out. We can't abandon each other, especially in times like this."

Her father said nothing as he looked at the much younger man, who had suddenly found himself the leader of this much larger group made up of all the stragglers who'd joined them along the way.

"Max, tell us what to do," Manfri asked again, his black eyes reflecting the campfire light. "You used to be our leader."

Max's stern face softened. "I'm not in charge, not anymore, not for a long time." He sat back down to light the tobacco in his short ivory pipe.

"Well, unless anybody has a better plan," Manfri said, turning to the men and women who were all facing the warmth of the crackling campfire, "I say we keep heading north until we find a crossing over the Rhine to the safety of Holland."

"Cologne."

"Who said that?" asked Manfri.

"I did." A stooped, bull-necked, bald man, Patrin, her father's best friend, shuffled his way to the front of the campfire. "Unless we can magically turn our wagons into riverboats, Cologne is our only hope."

The young man's eyes narrowed. "Patrin, are you crazy? Cologne is one of the largest cities in Germany. We are trying to evade the German authorities. We don't want to get arrested and sent to some prison in Berlin."

Max stood back up, and after puffing out tobacco smoke, he spoke. "Cologne is not only the biggest city west of Berlin but also the biggest city on the Rhine. It's so big that the Rhine River cuts it in two, and there are some thirty bridges that join the west bank to the east bank of the Rhine, exactly where we are trying to get to. Whereas thirty-something wagons in the German countryside stands out like a Nazi parade, thirty wagons spread out through the hustle and bustle of a million-strong city won't be noticed." With that said, her father sat down again.

Everyone returned to their own wagons without saying another word: all had silently agreed to her father's plan.

Rosa wasn't sure what "war" truly meant, but their serious eyes clearly indicated that it was awful. Of course, sitting around the campfires numerous times, she'd heard the not-so-great stories about the Great War, which had finished almost a decade before she was born. And although she'd seen bombed-out buildings and villages, war seemed too wretched and too awful for her to imagine properly.

By the time Rosa had finished her chores, she found her father whispering to Patrin, whom her father affectionately called 'Pat' because they had been best friends since childhood. But to Rosa, Patrin was nothing but bad news. Whenever Rosa was in trouble, he was always there. Rosa dumped the firewood onto the ground next to the fire, and Patrin turned to face her.

"Hello, Patrin," she said with her sweetest of smiles.

Patrin stood, momentarily looking at Rosa, before disappearing into the darkness.

Her father picked up a stick to stoke the fire, then used the embers at the tip of the burning stick to relight his pipe. He sat back down and smoked his pipe in the warm glow of the firelight.

"Was he here telling on me again?" she asked.

"Pat is not like that. He only has your best interests at heart," Max replied.

"Just like Mama," Rosa said, rubbing her cheek.

He spoke in a rumbling yet calming voice. "Don't be angry with your mother, little one."

"But, Papa, she blames me for everything. *Everything.* I think sometimes the only reason she took me in in the first place was that she needed someone to blame and to yell at." Rosa knelt, adding more sticks to the fire, which had a warming pot of stew hanging over it from a tripod. The smell of meat and vegetables stewing with thyme and oregano sparked her hungry belly into life. Rosa punched her stomach back into silence. She knew—evidently forgotten by her stomach—that once her chores were done, she was to go to bed without any supper—another punishment courtesy of her mother. "Papa, she just needed a slave!"

Her father chuckled. His dark eyes reflected the warmth and sparkle of the crackling firelight. "Ten years ago, our caravan was lost in the Berlin ghetto, times were tough due to the so-called Great Depression, and ghettos were everywhere back then, especially since Germany had also lost the Great War, and so Germany's suffering was great indeed—tens of millions of Germans out of work with famine and disease killing thousands of them on a daily basis. One day, we saw a Berlin street girl who couldn't have been more than fifteen or sixteen—"

"—A common German whore," Rosa interrupted, "as the other kids tell me whenever you adults aren't around to hear."

"As our wagon passed by, the young girl collapsed right there in front of us and dropped her small bundle of blankets, which rolled into the street. I wouldn't have stopped, but your mother saw something and pulled at the horse reins, the horses' hooves stopping only inches away from the bundle."

Rosa's eyes popped open upon hearing this.

"I've never told you that part before, have I?" Max laughed. "The girl died right there and then, and you know me, I didn't want any trouble with the authorities, especially the German authorities. Even back then, they hated us "Gypsies". They've never understood that for the Romani, our wagons were and *are* our home, and the world is our backyard." He stopped and looked blankly at Rosa. "Where was I?"

"You were up to the part where the bundle of rags was in front of Kizzy and Lala," Rosa reminded him.

"Our horses weren't called that, and you know your mother and I disapprove—"

"And then what happened?"

"Well, Martha jumped down and picked up the bundle and opened it up to find a beautiful baby girl, you. And you couldn't have been more than six months, but goodness knows how old you were because you were clearly dying of starvation, just like your mother. You didn't even make a sound. I wanted to leave you with the authorities. But even as a baby, you had the wild eyes of a survivor. I knew you'd make it somehow. But none of the Germans stopped to help, not even for one of their own. Berliners are a strange lot. I've always said that. Besides, your mother had other ideas, and by the look in her eyes, I knew she would have none of it. And for better or worse, we've been your family ever since. I don't mean just Martha and me. We are all your family, including Kizzy and Lala Heigl."

Max looked at the massive pile of sticks Rosa had gathered. "I'm sorry you have so much to do, little one, but your mother and I are too old. God blessed us with only daughters, who have all been married away to other tribes. You were God's gift to us both."

"I hate that woman," Rosa said. "I wish she was dead."

Rosa's father stood up suddenly and raised his hand as if to strike her.

Rosa stood in shock. She'd been slapped across the face many times but never by her father.

"Never wish that!" he cried. "She is family, and family is all we have!" He sat back down again. "I thought you, of all people, would understand that from what I just said. But you are anger wrapped up in a little girl's body. Maybe you are a true Berliner at heart?"

Rosa felt shaken at being called a Berliner—this was a much bigger insult than any of the children could have taunted her with. But when she looked into her father's eyes, she saw fear. She had never seen her father looking so scared before. Something was terribly wrong. She wrapped her little arms around his massive bulk. "I'm sorry, Papa. I won't say it ever again. From now on, I'll be a good Romani girl. Please, don't be upset with me."

He wrapped a gentle arm around her. "Little one, I had to tell them all what happened with the boys," he said. "There was a meeting while you were gone, and it seems that the *glox*, the boss man, will most certainly be after us because we hurt one of their precious children. So, it was decided that we should make our own way out of Germany."

"The tribe is abandoning us?"

"We'll meet up with them in a couple of days on the other side of the Rhine."

"It's all my fault—I'm sorry, Papa," Rosa said, her shoulders slumped and head downcast, waiting for a hug that never came.

# Chapter 2

## 1 September (Friday)

*Nazi Germany, just outside the city of Cologne*

Early next morning, while it was still dark, Rosa got up to stretch her legs and relieve herself. She stopped and stood still. The clearing was empty. The pre-morning mist washed over the ground and lapped at her knees. She saw no trace of wagon tracks nor of the dozens of fires that had been burning the evening before. The area was so well camouflaged that it was as if the other wagons had never been there. The only wagon remaining in the clearing was hers.

She looked up at the full white moon, which lit up the meadow like a searchlight. She realised it was one thing to wish to be left alone but quite another when it happened. She shivered.

Later that morning, Rosa sat by her father as the city of Cologne came into view. She looked at their wagon, which not only had a large sign plastered on the side—Max's Pots and Pans Mender— but also pots and pans hanging from the sides.

"I didn't know we had this sign and all these pots and pans," Rosa said, wondering where they had been all this time.

"They were stored in the false floor inside. It's an old Romani trick: hide in plain sight. We're no longer German Gypsies but a tradesman and his family plying his wares."

"Hiding in plain sight? Will it work?"

"We'll soon find out here in Cologne. But I don't like it, little one."

"What's wrong, Papa?"

"The streets are empty. No trucks or carts or buses or trains are running. Not even a single pedestrian. It's as if the city is dead."

Martha joined them and handed each a coat because they were shivering; however, the coats didn't stop their shaking. They travelled for another hour, slowly getting deeper into the city, the large buildings overshadowing the main street into town.

"Whoa!" Her father pulled at the reins until the wagon halted.

"What are you doing?" Rosa's mother asked. "Do you honestly think the authorities emptied the streets of Cologne just for us?"

"Something is wrong, woman," he said. "And if somebody *is* after us, how long do you think it will take them to catch up to us? Pretending to be a tinkerer's wagon only works when the city is crowded."

"Let's just get to the other side of the Rhine quickly, and then we can worry about who might be following us," Rosa's mother begged, seemingly also unnerved.

A church close by began to toll its bells. Then another church, and another. In minutes, it seemed as if all of Cologne's churches were ringing their bells.

Rosa's father pulled at the reins and turned into a side street. The furious bellringing had washed away any resolve to stay on the major roads. Rosa wondered why bells would be ringing, especially on a Friday morning.

The bellringing was careening off the sides of the buildings, like walls of water crashing through the narrow streets. The sound waves rushed past, only to encounter a fresh set of waves trying to make their escape. Rosa pressed her hands to her ears, which felt like they would burst any second now. Her parents appeared to ignore the noise, but perhaps they were too distracted to notice. The deeper they penetrated the back alleys, the more disorientated they became.

Then the fierce ringing suddenly ceased.

Silence.

With the wagon standing still in the shadows, Rosa felt worried as she watched her father trying to decide what to do next.

"We should never have left the main road," her mother said to

Rosa's father. "We would have passed through this godforsaken city by now."

"Woman, give me strength," he said.

*Ring, ring!*

Rosa swung around in a flash, her arms flapping like the floppy arms of her rag doll. There it was again. But this time she could hear the distinct sound of a bicycle bell. While her parents argued, Rosa jumped down from the wagon to investigate. Her guts twisted into a more powerful knot with each step away from the security of the wagon. But she was determined to discover where the bicycle bellringing came from.

She edged her face around the corner of the alleyway and saw nothing.

*Ring, ring!*

Rosa ducked behind a stack of empty wooden fruit and vegetable boxes and froze. She sneaked a look around and saw a boy on a bicycle stopped only feet from where she was hiding. She recognised him as one of the boys she had run into yesterday, and his grim face matched his starched, mustard-brown uniform.

*Ring, ring!*

Another bicycle bell echoed somewhere in the distance, and then another from a completely different direction, and then another and another. The ringing of bicycle bells surrounded her. The boys were looking for her, and by the sounds of things, they were closing in.

She turned but slipped on rotten cabbage leaves and bumped into the wooden crates.

The boy snapped around to face her hiding place.

She saw his intense blue eyes through the cracks. She half-turned, not daring to inhale, not daring to turn away fully, still hearing her parents babbling on to each other.

The Hitler Youth hopped off his bike.

Rosa looked for another hiding place.

Nothing.

The boy stepped closer, his hard-soled shoes clicking on the cobblestones.

There was nowhere else to hide.

She looked for a rock, stone or pebble to throw it in another direction to distract him long enough for her to get back to her wagon.

Nothing.

She saw a loose brick at the base of the brick wall behind her; she pulled at it, and it gave way, but it was too big for her little hands to use.

She slowly exhaled and thrust her hand into the hole in the wall that she'd created, her fingers searching for a piece of rock, concrete, something, anything.

The boy's hob-nailed shoes clipped closer to her until he was almost on top of her.

She looked over her shoulder and saw the boy's attention had focused squarely on her parents bickering at the front of their tinkerer's wagon.

Rosa reached further inside the breech.

Something bit her hand. She grimaced but stifled any scream of pain.

Without pausing, she reached in and grabbed the hairy rodent by its neck so that it couldn't bite her again, then swiftly pulled it out. She glared at the angry rodent before throwing it at the boy's shiny black shoes.

Jumping backwards, he let out a yelp.

Rosa put her hand back inside the hole. There *had* to be rubble that she could use.

There was more bellringing, but this time there were three rings instead of two.

The blonde youth got back on his bike, rang his bell once only and pointed his bike in the direction of the three rings before riding off.

Rosa got up and checked her hand. The rat's bite hadn't broken her skin. The rat paused to look at her before waddling back into its hole.

She bowed. "Thank you, Mr Rat. You've saved my life, good sir." She returned to her wagon where her parents were looking skyward.

She followed their gaze but could only see the sides of tall brown-brick buildings, some red-tiled roofs and the occasional pigeon.

Her father's arm shot upwards. "There it is! I can see it now!"

All Rosa could see was a very tall and pointy roof, like an upside-down ice-cream cone.

"What is it, Papa?" Rosa asked as she climbed back up to the front seat.

"It's the roof of the Cologne Cathedral. It's right next to the biggest bridge in the city."

She was confused.

"It's our way out of here." His smile disappeared when he looked at his daughter's sullen face. "What is it, Rosa?"

Her mother clutched her arm. "I swear, child, if you have done something wrong, I will—"

"Be quiet, woman!" He turned to face Rosa. "What is it, little one?"

"I saw the boys from yesterday. They're chasing us."

He thought a moment. "Did they see you?"

She shook her head.

"Good," he said. "They're probably out looking for lots of wagons, not just one. As long as they didn't see you, we should be fine. Rosa, I want you to hide inside the wagon until we get clear of the city."

She nodded.

\*\*\*

Rosa sat quietly in a little seat she had filled with soft pillows. She wished she could read one of her books, but, as the wagon was shut up tightly, there was no light, and she wasn't allowed to use a candle in case she accidentally started a fire. As the wagon rumbled along, she sat inside, eating a crunchy apple.

She knew they could cross the river on foot if they had to, but this would mean abandoning their home on wheels. These wagons weren't just a home; they were a moving family museum handed down to them over the ages.

In the darkness, Rosa felt the presence of her grandmother, who had died two years earlier. Rosa missed her. While everyone else picked on her, Grandma was always there for Rosa, listening to her complaints and ramblings. She had taught Rosa to read so Rosa was able to read to her once her grandmother went totally blind. Her grandmother also introduced her to the pain of death.

Rosa remembered their final conversation in the back of this same wagon.

*** 

Hiding gifts behind her back, an eight-year-old Rosa came in and saw her grandmother sprawled on her bed, her long white hair surrounding her pale, ghostly face. Rosa looked at the family amulet her grandmother always wore around her neck. It was a blue stone with a naturally occurring golden spiral that hung from a leather strap. The shiny blue rock was called Lapis Lazuli, which meant "sky stone" or "stone sent from heaven" in the ancient Roman tongue. It had been in the family for generations and was said to have originated in Egypt.

"What do you have in your hands, child?" her grandmother asked. "I may be blind, but I can smell cake from a mile away. And I bet you are hiding the cake behind your back again. Why do you do that when you know I can't see?"

Rosa produced a bottle of wine in one hand and a cake in the other.

"Grandma, I don't know how you do it, but you seem to see everything. I brought wine and cake to make you better, just like

Little Red Riding Hood did for her sick grandmother."

Her grandmother laughed. "I'm afraid I'm beyond wine and cake. Come, child, lie with me."

Rosa climbed upon the bed, hugged her grandmother, and stroked her wrinkles.

"How old are you, Grandma?"

"How old do you think I am, Rosa?"

"Mmm." Rosa thought seriously before answering. "Well, Papa taught me that when you cut down a tree, every one of its rings equals one year. So, you add up all the tree rings, and that is how old the tree is."

"That is true," her grandmother nodded.

"Well, then, if I count the number of wrinkles on your face, I guess you are about a thousand years old, Grandma!" Rosa deduced with a beaming smile.

Rosa's grandmother cackled until her laughter turned into a coughing fit. Once she had recovered, she continued. "I'm not quite a thousand years old, though I feel it today. But I'm not complaining. I've lived a long and happy life and all of it inside these cramped but beautiful walls. I was born here, and I dare say I was conceived here as well. I gave birth to all my children in here, and I have even had some of my children die in here."

Rosa's eyes popped open.

"Do not worry, precious one, I will join them soon enough, along with my dear husband. I just wanted you to know that all of this will one day be yours."

"I will own this wagon?"

"No, Rosa. No one can own history, but since you are the last child, one day you will be the caretaker of this wagon, and, eventually, you will pass it on to your children."

Rosa folded her arms in a show of defiance. "I'm never going to have children," she said.

"Never? Never is a very long time: the longest, in fact. Why don't you want to have children?"

"Well, I hate boys, for one thing. They think they know everything when they don't."

The old woman chuckled again. "And the other thing?"

Rosa leaned forward and whispered. "Grandma, we both know that I'm not really a Romani. So, this wagon is not really mine, you know, to take care of."

"Of course, you are a *real* Romani," Grandma responded. "How many forks in the roads did we follow to end up at that exact time and place to find you? The hand of God was guiding our reins that very day. You were meant to be here, as much as any child born in this tribe."

Rosa got up and hugged her frail grandmother.

The next morning, Grandma did not wake.

While everybody cried and wailed, including Rosa, she noticed that her grandmother had a smile on her crinkled, weathered lips. She was with her *other* family now.

They buried her in her favourite hand-made quilt in an unmarked grave on a lush green hill overlooking the Rhine River, which the river Roma called home. The place was perfect for Grandma, even though it was hundreds of miles from where they'd buried her husband and thousands of miles from the burial sites of her other loved ones: her children, siblings, parents, and grandparents. Their graves were scattered all over Europe, but it didn't matter, Europe was their home. And they were all together in the Afterlife. But this wagon was their spiritual resting place; here, they could always watch over the living, as explained by her grandmother. Indeed, in Rosa's eyes, this wagon was her grandmother.

*** 

*BANG!*

Rosa's world tumbled over. Boxes slid and shifted, ropes creaked, straining to keep them in place. Chickens clucked in a panic; baby pigs let out a high-pitched squeal. She tried to stand upright, but the wagon leaned heavily towards the front left. Rosa clambered outside the back and looked up at the big old cathedral. She joined her parents on the street, looking at the left-front wheel now snapped cleanly in half.

Her father kicked at it in frustration. "I knew it was damaged when we rode over that hole in the road yesterday, but I just didn't have enough time to stop and repair it properly."

His wife tried to comfort him. "It's not your fault, dear."

"Yes, it is, woman! We have been travelling night and day for this past week trying to pass through this accursed country. Yesterday morning, I fell asleep at the reins and didn't see the pothole. I'm getting too old."

"What can we do, Papa?" Rosa asked.

Before he could answer, several armed men in black uniforms appeared from the shadows and surrounded them. The men cocked their weapons and aimed at them.

The blue-eyed leader shouted, "Attention! You are all under arrest!" He motioned for other soldiers to grab them.

Rosa struggled against the soldier who had grabbed her. He wouldn't let go, so she stomped on his big, shiny boot, scuffing it. He swung her around, rewound his arm and struck her. She landed on the ground with a thud. Despite the pain, she got up and glared at the snickering soldier.

"Please, Rosa, you will get us all killed!" her mother cried.

Rosa looked at the soldier's early-morning shadow, which stretched out before her. She raised her foot and stomped on the head of the shadow, twisting her foot. He moved forward, blocking the sun with his enormous size, raising his arm for another blow.

The stormtrooper stopped when he saw a group of people exiting the big church. He grabbed Rosa by the scruff of her neck and hauled her over to a woman dressed all in white.

"What is happening here?" the woman asked the soldier.

"Frau Riefenstahl, we have apprehended a family of murderers."

"An old man and woman with a young child, murderers? Explain."

"According to this boy," indicating the Hitler Youth standing next to him, the same boy that Rosa almost ran into back in the alley, "this girl has murdered a boy from a nearby village."

Rosa's father spoke to the woman. "Please. My daughter didn't kill anyone. It was me. I did it."

"Papa, no!"

"Hush, child!"

"Arrest me and let my wife and child go free."

The woman barely looked at them. "Arrest them all and let the authorities sort out this mess."

"What do we do with their wagon? If we try to move it, you'll miss your plane, Frau Riefenstahl."

"We will not be late for Hitler's victorious address. Burn it!"

As this happened, people emptied out of the cathedral and into the streets. Although there were a few sombre citizens, most shouted and yelled in triumph.

"Germany has invaded Poland!" said one.

"He's done it—Adolf has declared war on the world!" shouted another.

"Victory is ours!"

"Death to Poland!"

"Long live Germany!"

An SS soldier brought up a jerrycan of gasoline and poured it over the wagon. Other armed soldiers unhitched the two horses and removed the livestock from inside. The officer moved forward and lit a match.

*WOOF!*

Within seconds, the broken-down wagon was in flames. The assembled crowd of civilians joined hands and danced around the fire. In Rosa's eyes, the people seemed to be mad with delight—rapturous. They all started singing the German National Anthem—The Song of Germany: "*Germany, Germany above all—*"

Soon the only thing that she could make out among the smouldering ruins was the black skeleton of the wagon's wheels.

Rosa looked at her parents, who were both in tears. She had caused this. If only she hadn't dropped her book, then none of this would have happened. "I'm sorry, Papa. It's all my fault!"

Her father knelt next to her and removed the sky-blue amulet from around his neck that he'd taken from his mother when she'd died. "Little one, take this family amulet, which is also a good luck charm, and promise me you will look after your mother."

Rosa was in tears.

"Promise me."

Rosa nodded.

Soldiers grabbed her father and led him away.

She ran after him. "I promise, Papa! I promise!"

The stormtrooper, who had confronted her earlier, walked up to her, raised the butt of his rifle and struck her again.

She fell to the ground, unconscious.

## Chapter 3

Christmas Day 1939 (Monday)

*Maxglan Gypsy Concentration Camp, Salzburg, Austria*

Rosa and her mother were working in the camp latrines, scrubbing the floors with stiff brushes—almost too big for Rosa to grasp.

"Rosa, why can't you keep your silly, little mouth shut?" asked her mother.

"Mama, he said that I was an ugly, stupid little girl," she replied.

"And so, you kicked him. Poor Heinrich. He has got to be at least seventy. That's a First World War uniform that he wears, the one that has all those medals."

"But, mother, it didn't fit. I just offered to fix the uniform for him so that he didn't look like a pregnant elephant in his tight-fitting, grey uniform."

"And then he called you stupid and ugly for insulting his weight. And look where we are. Again. Why won't you listen?"

"I do listen, but for some reason, it's like my tongue has a mind of its own. I swear it won't happen again."

"Please, Rosa. No more swearing that you will change. You won't change. You can't change. It's impossible for you. I can see that now. Finally."

"I'm not scared of these Nazis."

"These guys are Austrians. These guys are pussycats, Nazi wannabes, compared to the Nazis in Berlin. And that's where we'll both end up if we're not careful."

"I wonder," Rosa said, "how many people have had to build their own prison? We should have escaped back then before we put up the six-foot barbed-wire fences to trap ourselves in."

"And where would we run to?"

Rosa looked incredulously at her mother. "Anywhere is better than this godforsaken place. We'll just run to a border and cross it."

"Which border? There's a war on, don't you know? All borders are closed. And Germany just about controls everything, and what they don't control, they soon will. And you forget, in their eyes, we are no-good Gypsies."

"Whose eyes?"

"Europe's. The word "Gypsy" is more or less a swear word, and they're just as likely to arrest and imprison us as the Germans. No, a Romani's home is only with other Romani, so my home is here in this camp, with my people. For better or worse, I'm staying here with my family."

"I'm not. I hate this place. I'm escaping as soon as I get the chance."

"And what then?"

"What do you mean?" asked Rosa.

"And what will happen to us?" she said, grabbing Rosa. "They will punish us. They will punish me."

"They say they will, but they won't," Rosa said, folding her arms. "All the camp guards come to you so you can mend their uniforms."

"Child, it's time to stop thinking only of yourself. Individuals come and go. They live, and they die, but a community is forever. Living just for yourself, Rosa, is not a life, but helping others is."

Someone entered a cubicle while they continued scrubbing the cement floors, using large wire brushes with a wooden base. The Austrian camp guard passed them by.

"But it's not the camp guards that I'm worried about," Rosa's mother continued.

"You mean me, don't you?"

"The women have told me that if I don't control you, they will."

"How?"

"They didn't say, but you have to be a good girl from now on. Everyone is scared, and no one here wants to be sent to a Gypsy

Concentration Camp in Berlin. These people will do whatever they have to to survive. Remember, as far as these house dwellers are concerned, the best Gypsy—"

"—is a dead Gypsy," Rosa said.

"Exactly. Every guard here knows you by name, which is not good. And if the camp commandant gets to know you by name, then it's all over for us. We will be on the next cattle car out of here to goodness knows where. Please. You promised your father that you would look after your Mama."

The family amulet Rosa was wearing slipped out of her dress as she scrubbed in silence. She stopped cleaning to tuck the blue amulet back under her clothing being very careful that a guard didn't confiscate it. Luckily for her, it was very easy to hide it amongst the folds of her skirt or blouse. As Gypsies were seen as one step above animals, women and children weren't perceived as any threat, so they were never searched.

Rosa and her mother had not seen Max since their arrest. However, from the other captured women and children at the camp, they'd learned that most of their extended caravan had been caught at the heavily guarded western border as Germany, fearing a counterattack from France and her allies, invaded Poland in the east. They knew that most of the other captured male Romani prisoners, many from their own caravan, had been sent to Berlin, probably to the Gypsy Concentration Camp, which the Nazis had opened in 1936 to clear the streets of Gypsies ahead of the Berlin Olympic Games, which had never closed, so much so that Rosa hadn't been back in Berlin for the past several years.

"I'm sorry, Mama. I promised Father that I would look after you. I will be a good girl from now on."

A camp guard wearing an antique uniform, complete with a pointed helmet entered the stall where they were on their hands and knees scrubbing. Camp Guard Heinrich Schmidt reminded Rosa of Saint Nicholas, that the Germans celebrated every Christmas with his white hair and matching beard. Saint Nick in a German uniform, Rosa smirked to herself. He stopped in front of Rosa.

"Well, girl? Have you learned your lesson?"

"Yes, Heinrich."

"What did you call me?"

"I mean, Camp Guard Schmidt."

"I think you need a little more training. That's why I keep you here. I will break you yet, little girl. You are my project." He unzipped his pants.

Rosa's mother stopped scrubbing and looked up in horror.

Heinrich then urinated into Rosa's wooden scrub bucket. When he'd finished, he deliberately splashed some urine onto Rosa. Rosa jumped up. She picked up the wooden pail, full of dirty latrine floor mixed with Heinrich's piss. Heinrich's eyes bulged open in the realisation of what Rosa was about to do.

Heinrich and Rosa's mother raised their hands in unison as they both yelled out: "No!"

Too late.

Rosa threw the bucket's contents all over Heinrich's medal-festooned, freshly pressed and much-prized uniform. He stood there dripping wet—in his own urine—in shocked disbelief. Rosa's smile disappeared when she glanced at her mother, who looked terrified. Rosa suddenly remembered her promise she'd sworn only moments earlier.

Heinrich rummaged for something in his webbing and pulled out a pair of rusted pliers. They looked so old that Rosa thought they must have been from the Great War. He grabbed her hands and placed her little finger inside the cutting edges.

"I'll show you not to piss me off!"

Rosa's mother shuffled over to him and begged. "Please! She's just a stupid girl who doesn't know any better."

"And whose fault is that?" Heinrich shouted back. Her mother just stared back at him.

Heinrich looked down at Rosa's grim-faced determination while her finger was in the teeth of his pliers. "No. You won't learn your lesson if I take off your finger. You'll just wear it around like a badge of honour. No, I have a better idea of how to teach you a lesson. One that you'll never forget." Heinrich pushed Rosa away and grabbed Martha's hand. It took a moment for her mother to realise what was happening, but it was too late. Heinrich now held Martha's little finger pinned in the vice grip of the pliers. He looked at Rosa and squeezed while her mother screamed and howled. The ancient pliers were blunt but not blunt enough.

There was a loud crack as the rusty jaws of the pliers crunched and gnawed hungrily together. Martha let out a blood-curdling scream. Heinrich worked and wiggled the last flesh still clinging until the finger finally gave up its fight to remain with the hand. Heinrich stood in triumph. While her mother sobbed loudly, Rosa looked at the blood all over Heinrich's precious uniform.

Heinrich handed a terror-filled Rosa her mother's blood-covered finger.

As he walked towards the latrine door, he spoke over his shoulder, "Pin that to your chest."

## Chapter 4

1 April 1940 (Monday)

*Maxglan Gypsy Concentration Camp, Salzburg, Austria*

Rosa stood with the assembled Romani on the parade ground, waiting and waiting. Even though it was spring, the weather was still cool, and the winds coming down to the plateau from the surrounding Austrian Alps were cold, making her shiver. The camp commandant had assembled them an hour earlier, but he was still talking to the local dignitaries. Rosa looked up at the castle sitting high atop the crest of the large hill. She remembered the first day they had all arrived in Salzburg just months earlier via train in the cattle cars—she'd since learned that it was the Hohensalzburg Castle.

The white medieval-built castle sat perched atop the Festungsberg hill. And just as Rosa's camp was built in the shadows of the Schloss Leopoldskron on the flat ground they were now standing upon, the Schloss itself was built in the shadows of the towering castle. The once green pasturelands in front of Schloss Leopoldskron were now a confinement camp for Gypsies. However, the camp itself was little more than a collection of primitive huts surrounded by a six-foot-high, barbed-wire fence overseen by armed guards stationed in evenly spaced watchtowers.

While Rosa stood in line, ignoring the whispering around her, she looked over and saw her mother standing silently. Rosa saw the stub on her mother's hand. Heinrich had only cut half of the little finger, but because the pliers were so rusty, there had been an infection, so the local doctor was forced to amputate the remainder of the finger and some of the hand. It had healed over by now, but Rosa often saw her mother rubbing it, unsure whether it was because she was still in some pain or because her mother was remembering the hand as it used to be.

Her mother hadn't spoken a word to Rosa since the incident, and no one else in the camp had talked to her either—they all knew that Rosa was to blame for what had happened to her mother. She was used to name-calling and insults, but being totally ignored was completely different. To Rosa, it was like she was no longer a person, more like a ghost. She no longer slept with her mother, but no one would dare let her sleep near them. She often had to find a place wherever she could, but this became harder and harder with each trainload of arrivals. She'd slept in a different place almost every night.

Rosa's mother was such a busy worker; in fact, she was the busiest and best worker in the entire camp—probably the reason the two of them hadn't been deported. Not only did she work the hardest, which the camp commandant loved, but there wasn't anything her mother couldn't do. She could sew, mend pots and pans, and was the unofficial camp medical doctor for the prison inmates. Some guards paid her for treatments such as curing warts, cursing a love rival, or healing a beloved family pet. And now, with her finger amputated, her mother seemed to work twice as hard as everyone else. Rosa could see all the more clearly now: distance from her mother had given her a better vantage point. But it was all too late.

While the camp inmates stood silently in line, Camp Guard Heinrich brought in another dozen male Romani. In a women's camp, this small group of men aroused everyone's interest. Heinrich forced the men onto the end of the line next to Rosa. She instantly recognised one of them—Pat, her father's closest friend. Perhaps, he had news of where her father was.

Once these male latecomers were in position, the commandant marched out and halted in front of the assembled Romani.

"The Salzburg authorities have received complaints about the camp conditions," said the camp commandant. "And after this morning's inspection by the Salzburg police commission and invited concerned citizens of Salzburg, they have described the conditions here as appalling and in need of immediate rebuilding of inmate housing. The Salzburg Concerned Citizens Bureau representatives," he added, indicating the well-dressed, elderly men and women scattered amongst the Salzburg police uniforms standing immediately behind him, "don't feel safe in their own city." The citizens nodded vigorously in agreement to this point. "Thus, there has been an additional request for a second barbed-wire fence so that the Salzburg citizens can sleep safely at night."

Rosa overheard the whispering of one of the older ladies standing nearby. "Nothing makes anyone look guiltier than being thrown behind barbed-wire fences, but to have *two* barbed-wire fences would only make the Romani people look twice as guilty." The women around her nodded their silent agreements.

Guilty of what? Rosa wondered, but she was only eleven years old. She was sure this would all make sense to her when she was much older—perhaps thirteen or fourteen.

"Therefore," the camp commandant continued, "all work conducted outside the camp will cease immediately until this camp has complied with *all* local compliance codes. And to comply with the overcrowding regulations, those who don't pull their weight or think about escaping will automatically be sent to the Berlin Gypsy Concentration Camp. And believe me, those Berliners aren't as *cultured* as we Austrians."

The threat of being cattle-trained out to Berlin was not an empty one; this was a genuine camp-wide fear.

As soon as the parade was dismissed, Rosa raced over to her father's best friend. "Pat, Pat!" she yelled.

He turned and looked squarely at her. "Rosa? Is that really you?"

She rushed up and crashed into him with a hug.

"Where's your mother and father?" he asked.

She looked up at him. "Mother's here, but I was hoping you know where Father is."

"You mean you have no idea where your father is?"

Rosa shook her head. "We never saw him after Cologne, where we were arrested. We heard rumours he was sent to the Marzahn Gypsy Camp in Berlin along with the other captured men."

Pat shook his head. "I don't know where he is, but I can tell you he's definitely not there."

"How do you know?"

"Since '38, it's been a camp solely for Romani women and children. All the men were sent to the Sachsenhausen Concentration Camp about 30km north of Berlin. We've already been told that's where we're going next."

"You're joining my father?"

"If he's there, then I guess I am. Why?"

"Take me with you."

"I told you, it's for men only. You're a girl."

"I hate that excuse. *Girls aren't allowed.* I wish I were a man. Then nobody would ever be mean to me."

"Typical Rosa. You'll never change no matter how hard your mother and father try, especially your mother. Where is she? Take me to her."

She looked up at him. "If I do, can you do me a huge favour?"

"What favour?"

***

Rosa watched from a respectable distance as Pat reunited with her mother. Pat looked at her disfigured hand and held it, never letting it go. Pat, her father and her mother had been the best of childhood friends. The two of them spoke for a long while until she could tell that Pat brought up the subject of Rosa. Her mother turned away from Pat, crying. As Pat comforted her, he looked at Rosa, shaking his head—no. Rosa stormed off. If her mother was going to be so stubborn and not forgive her, then she didn't care.

Later that night, Rosa returned to her current hidey-hole at the bottom of a linen closet. She lit her fat stub of a candle close to an opening she'd made for an air-hole. She lay down and felt something hard beneath her pillow: her hands searched and found a small bottle of black dye. Her mother must have found out where Rosa was sleeping and put it there for her. Her hair must have been getting lighter. The black dye was only to help keep her blonde hair a secret and not get anyone else into trouble, especially her mother. Rosa didn't have to do it, but of course, she would; she didn't want her mother losing any more body parts, or worse. She would dye her hair during their next weekly bath, even though this would be the first time she would do it herself.

In the flickering dim light in the bottom of the linen closet, she unwrapped a little square piece of cloth. Inside the fabric was her mother's mummified finger. Rosa had kept holding onto her mother's still-warm and blood-wet little finger when her mother was taken away to the infirmary. Rosa didn't know what to do with it. Throwing her mother's finger away seemed wrong. She'd just assumed that the two of them would bury it together, somewhere, return the once-living to the earth from which they were born. But her mother hadn't forgiven her, and after today with Pat, Rosa realised that her mother would never forgive her. She knew the dye was only there so that her mother wouldn't get into trouble, not a sign of forgiveness. She missed her mother and was all alone in the world. Rosa couldn't hold back the tears.

"Mama, I'm so, so very sorry," she said, kissing her mother's finger.

But since meeting Pat and suspecting where her father was confined, she knew she had no choice; she would do whatever it took to join her father in Berlin.

## Chapter 5

15 April 1940 (Monday)

*Maxglan Gypsy Concentration Camp, Salzburg, Austria*

A couple of weeks later, right after morning roll call, Rosa found Pat talking to the other men he'd arrived with. She pulled him aside with some urgency. "Pat, I've heard that you're leaving soon."

"Tomorrow. We've finished putting up the second fence, but this camp is only for women and children. They're putting us men back on the cattle-car autobahn, moving us onto a men's prison camp."

"Well, I'm going with you," she announced to Pat.

"As I've already explained to you, it's a prison just for men."

But then her serious face turned into a smile. "I've thought of that, and I've decided to become a boy so that I can come with you."

"Impossible. How? Impossible," he said.

"Well, not too long ago, a boy about my age died here, so I stole his clothes."

"You stole a dead kid's clothes?"

"He didn't need them; besides, it happens all the time in this place, except I found him first."

"Why?"

"Clothes are currency. We can't exactly go into town to buy new clothes."

"I know. Sometimes, they don't even wait until the poor man is dead when he's stripped naked by men driven mad by the freezing, wet cold. But I thought you women and children would be..." he said, not finishing his sentence.

"Different? Mama taught me that men, women or children all have to find a way to survive in this mad world. He's about my size, and I will cut my hair short. When you're my age, people can only tell the difference between boys and girls by their clothes and hair. Plus, I have his cap, which I can pull down over my face, add some dirt that boys are always covered in, and no one will know I'm not a boy."

"I will know," Pat answered. "Besides, being in a men's prison is dangerous for a girl or boy, clothes or not."

"Why? It's not a real prison with real prisoners. It's for Romani, just like us. And you can look after me until I get back with my father."

"What happens if he's not there, or if he's dead, just as dead as the owner of those clothes you stole from?"

"I know he's alive. I can feel it. I still have the amulet he gave me. Grandma taught me that if a gift of love is ever lost or taken away, it means the love has gone or—"

"—the person is no longer living," Pat finished her sentence. "She taught us all. We were all children once. But then we grow up. And that's what you need to do. What if you escaped? What would happen to the people back here?"

"People have escaped before, but nothing has happened to the rest of us. They simply catch the offender and put them onto the next train out of Salzburg. Besides, they'll never think to look for me in another concentration camp, especially one in Berlin."

"I meant your mother. What about her?"

"She still hasn't spoken to me. Not since..."

"Since she lost her finger."

"She didn't lose her finger. I know exactly where it is."

Pat looked confused at her response.

"Anyway, they all hate me," she continued. "I'm sure they can't wait to see the back of me, including Mother."

"Rosa, I'm not going to tell you what to do, goodness knows we've all wasted our time doing that, but you must tell your mother. She deserves to know where you've disappeared to."

"Pat, she won't care."

"If you want my help, that's the deal."

Rosa could tell by his locked jaw that he meant it. "Okay, Pat. I'll tell her just before we go."

"No. Tell her now, today. Your mother's a stubborn woman like you. It'll take her a few hours for your crazy escape plan to sink in and realise that you actually mean it. It's the least I can do for your mother. Tell her today or find someone else to help you with your crazy escape plan."

"There is no one else. You're the only one who dares even talk to me."

Pat looked at her in stony silence.

"Okay, Pat," she relented. "But I'm telling you, she no longer cares about me. Mother truly hates me."

Pat was about to respond when they heard yelling behind them.

"Hey, you! Girl! Come here. Now!"

She turned to see Camp Guard Heinrich standing only feet away. Pat disappeared into the moving forest of camp prisoners so seamlessly that Rosa felt as if her conversation with him moments earlier was a mere dream.

"Here, now!" he yelled again at her.

Rosa stepped immediately in front of Heinrich. She didn't want anything getting in the way of her perfect escape plan, not even mean-tempered Heinrich. "Yes, Camp Guard Schmidt."

"The camp commandant has a special guest who needs attending to. He asked for a girl, and you're the first girl I've come upon, my gout is playing up, and I can't take another step. But girl, if you let me down, I'll—"

"—Camp Guard Schmidt, I've learned my lesson. You are a great teacher, the best. I'll be the best serving girl this prison has ever seen," she said, rushing off towards the commandant's office at the entrance of camp.

"Come back here. I didn't dismiss you yet," he yelled after her.

She came to a halt and sprinted back to stand immediately in front of a startled Heinrich, obviously not used to such an obedient Rosa. "Okay, you're dismissed."

Rosa ran off. When she got outside the commandant's door, she hurriedly passed by the two soldiers guarding his front door— guards in their black, full-ceremonial uniform with high-glossed helmets and ebony-shined machine guns, which only happened for the most special of special visitors. They ignored her. She quietly opened the door and slipped inside.

The commandant was doing last-minute checks of his face and uniform. Without turning, he spoke to Rosa in the reflection of his mirror.

"That was fast. You just made it. I have a special guest arriving, and I want you to be on your best behaviour. There's a lot of money involved in this tricky negotiation. How's your German?"

Rosa spoke perfect German with a slight Austrian accent—she was not only a natural at learning languages but also mastered the mimicking of accents. "My German is excellent, but my Austrian is much better," she smiled.

He stared at her in disbelief. "I didn't think you Gypsies could do anything right. I see Heinrich has chosen well. If you keep that up, girl, I'll let you take one of those sweets if there are any left over," he said, indicating the steaming pot of tea, cakes and biscuits sitting on a small serving table.

Rosa and the commandant both heard the guards at the front door snap to attention, yelling, "Heil Hitler!" One of the guards pushed the front door open.

The most special of special guests had arrived.

A confident woman in her thirties, wearing slacks and a matching jacket, strutted along the wooded boardwalk and entered the commandant's office with two smartly dressed businessmen on either side of her.

The SS commandant stood up from behind his desk and came over to shake her hand.

The short-haired brunette went to introduce the two men flanking her. "Commandant Böhmer, this is—"

"—Anton, please. And forget the formalities. I take it you have brought what I asked for?"

She held up her briefcase, placed it on his perfectly aligned desk, and opened it for him.

He pulled out the folded money and stared at it. "Is it all here?"

She nodded, "The down payment as per your request."

He returned to his desk, grabbed some formal papers from a drawer, and handed them to her.

"What is this?" the woman asked.

"Director Riefenstahl, this is a standard contract for the agreed price for hiring our Gypsy workers."

She grabbed it, reading it out loud. "*Seven Reichsmarks per Gypsy per day for the agreed dates and penalty rates if I go over.*" She stopped reading and looked up. "As I said over the phone, *Anton*, I'm not paying seven Reichsmarks for a single child," she declared, her dark eyes flashing.

Rosa had never seen a woman behave like this to a man before, and not just any man but SS Camp Commandant Anton Böhmer, no less, who was perhaps the most powerful man in the greater Salzburg area.

"Two children," he added.

"Three," she countered.

"Fraulein Riefenstahl—"

"—Director Riefenstahl."

"Of course, Director Riefenstahl, I couldn't possibly let you have three children—"

"—I was told that you were keen to help with the war effort," she said, closing the briefcase full of money. "I guess I'll have to inform the Public Enlightenment and Propaganda Ministry, Reichsminister Joseph Goebbels, that you weren't so helpful after all," she said, turning as if to leave.

The SS commandant stood in front of her, blocking her exit from his office. "Three Gypsy children it is. Besides, that means fewer mouths for me to feed."

"Well, you don't feed them very well by the looks of things. Look at this girl here," said Director Riefenstahl, pointing to Rosa.

"Plus, I saw some of the other children as I arrived, and they all look scrawny."

"Well, there's a war on, you know, and the best food goes to the frontlines and then the good citizens of Salzburg. Then the Gypsies get—"

"—What's left?"

"Exactly."

The savvy businesswoman continued reading the legal contract aloud. "*Strict isolation of the prisoners, and they must remain under armed guard and continuous observation to prevent escape attempts.* Really? Is that necessary?"

"Gypsies are the niggers of Europe. With these Gypsy scum, believe me, they will steal from you with one hand while cutting your throat with the other."

"All I want is the children."

"Especially the children! They are born with pick-pocket fingers that can slice you up more expertly than Germany's best military surgeons."

"We are a film company filming on location or in a studio, not prison guards."

"Don't worry. I have made arrangements for you in Bavaria."

"The Bavarian Mountain Corps won't guard Gypsy children. They're a highly specialised fighting unit, and all the other men are away fighting for the Fatherland."

"Who best to guard children than other children?"

"The Hitler Youth?" she asked for clarification.

"No. The Hitler Youth, aged fifteen-and-a-half to eighteen, are fighting age. You will have the Young Folk, aged twelve to fifteen-and-a-half. The Bavarian authorities have agreed to guard your prisoners day and night, and believe me, nothing will escape their notice."

"Young Folk? Great," she said with sarcasm. "It's a film set, not a school."

"Was it not Goebbels, your boss, who said that 'he who controls the youth also controls the future'?"

"Quite so," she said. "How much will the Young Folk unit cost me?"

"Nothing. They do it to prove their dedicated service to the Fatherland, and you won't hear a peep out of their parents. The Young Folk and the Hitler Youth are our best informants, so keep your nose clean on your set," he said with a wink.

She went back to the document. "*Rules and punishments are to conform with those of the camp.*"

"I have enclosed a copy of our rules."

"*And activities such as smoking and the use of latrines are under strict regulations and oversight, especially at night. They are to be housed inside barns and stables.*"

"I don't want my property getting sick and dying," said the camp commandant.

"Your property?"

"I mean Germany's property. But I am still their overseer."

"This looks all in order to me. If you don't mind, I'll have my production manager here sign the contract for me," she said, passing the contract to one of her aides.

The commandant put up his hand to intercede in the handing over of documents. "I *do* mind. This contract is between yourself and me, and you are head of the Leni Riefenstahl Film Company, as listed on the contract, so I need *your* signature, *Director Riefenstahl.*"

She looked at him. "I'd prefer not to sign anything if you don't mind. I've learned signing documents could get you into trouble later on."

"Well, I'm afraid that I require *your* signature. And once the children are safely returned, these contracts will be disposed of accordingly."

This appeared to ease her concerns as her frown softened. She and the commandant both signed the two sets of documents, and she gave her copy to one of her aides before handing the commandant the briefcase full of money.

"Well, Commandant, have you arranged my casting?"

The commandant yelled for his sergeant, who trotted in with a machine gun slung in front of him.

"Yes, my commandant?"

"Sergeant, assemble the Gypsy children, and *only* the Gypsy children."

"Yes, sir!"

The commandant turned to face Rosa. "Including her," he said, pointing.

The armed guard grabbed Rosa by her arm. The other camp guards yelled out as she was dragged to the parade ground. "Children on parade! Hurry! Hurry! Children *only* on parade!"

There was running in all directions; the exciting activity was electrified by mass confusion.

Women rushed about gathering their children to their side while the guards wrestled the younger children away from their mothers. Once the children were assembled on parade, their estranged mothers ringed the parade ground, leaning against the wire fences. Anxiety and fear filled their faces, desperate to know what was happening to their precious young. Rosa saw her mother looking just as concerned as all the other frantic parents. Pat was by her mother's side. The crowding by the women forced the camp guards to cock and point their weapons to keep the women separated from their children. Most of the children, especially the younger ones, were crying.

The camp commandant strode out with the well-dressed woman, who put on her sunglasses in the open air. The sergeant marched up to the commandant and saluted him. "Gypsy children on parade, and all 270 children present and accounted for, sir."

"Thank you, sergeant."

He was about to leave when Director Riefenstahl intercepted the sergeant. "Sergeant, I know for a fact that all the children are not accounted for," she said, pointing to a young woman holding her baby in her arms.

The sergeant looked confused. "But that is just a baby?"

"Commandant, I asked to see *all* the children, did I not?"

The commandant looked at her for just a moment before nodding to the sergeant.

The sergeant grabbed the woman and her baby, as well as any other women holding their babies, and assembled them on the parade ground along with the children.

The commandant and the woman strolled along the ranks of the children. The woman held up her hands to make a box-like shape with her thumbs and forefingers, looking at the children from different angles. Then she opened one child's mouth to check out her teeth and pushed and prodded her body to see if the child was sturdy enough until, finally, she put her hand on the child's shoulder.

"This one," Director Riefenstahl said, as two armed guards grabbed the chosen child and marched her over to one side. There was an anguished cry from the child's mother, who was watching the proceedings from afar. The child stood bewildered, tears streaming down her face, looking at her mother, who was also crying in desperate confusion.

The Commandant and Director Riefenstahl kept walking down the rows of children repeating this same process. Despite the anguish of the onlookers, there was complete silence, apart from the odd sniffling. This was all new, and none of the Romani could guess what exactly was happening.

The woman finally stood in front of Rosa, put her thumb and forefingers together, and looked at Rosa through her box-shaped hands.

"What are you doing?" Rosa asked, who didn't see the commandant's backhand hit her.

The crowd muffled their collective horror.

"How dare you talk back!" the commandant spat. "Director Riefenstahl, I apologise. This one has been trouble from the start, and if it weren't for her mother, she would have been moved on long ago."

"It's okay, Anton," said the woman.

Rosa got to her feet. She looked down. She didn't mean to get into trouble; she was genuinely fascinated by what the woman was doing, and, as always, she'd forgotten her place.

The woman and the commandant moved on, but she returned and repeated her hand gestures at Rosa. "This is an imaginary viewfinder for a camera. I'm just trying to imagine what you will look like on camera, what the audience will see."

Rosa didn't say anything. She knew better, as her bruised and bloody lip reminded her.

"Have you ever seen a film?" the woman asked Rosa.

Rosa shook her head no.

"What do you expect from these animals?" said the camp commandant. "They're not cultured like us. It's well known that Gypsies have mongrel blood. Germany's best scientists have proven it beyond a doubt. Science never lies."

The woman ignored him and continued speaking to Rosa. "You're not a very pretty girl. In fact, you are rather a plain-looking child, dull to be sure, but there is something about you. The way you stare at people. What's your name, girl?"

Rosa looked at the commandant, who nodded, allowing her to speak. "Rosa."

"Rosa? My name is Leni. It's short for Helene, which I've always hated, so I started calling myself Leni. One of my best childhood friends was called Rosa. But it's such a common name, common like you."

The woman moved past her again but kept looking back towards the downcast child until she returned to Rosa.

"Child, have we met before? And I don't mean in the commandant's office."

Rosa shook her head, but there was something strangely familiar about the woman.

"I don't know what it is about you, child, perhaps you remind me of my friend, but despite your plain looks, I think I will take you with me."

"I warn you, Director Riefenstahl, this one *is* trouble," said the commandant.

Ignoring him, the woman placed her hand on Rosa's shoulder. Two armed men grabbed her and rushed her into place with the others. In the end, Director Riefenstahl selected sixty Romani children, including one baby along with the mother.

The commandant addressed the Romani. "These children are required elsewhere for the greater good of the Fatherland. They're all leaving now, but do not concern yourselves about their welfare; they will be well looked after, and once they have finished their task, they will be returned to this camp."

The sixty Romani children were escorted out of the camp while the Romani women yelled out to their children.

Rosa's mother cried out, "Rosa, look after the children. Promise me!"

"I promise, Mother."

"And no foolhardy stuff; you'll only get them into trouble," she yelled, clearly referring to Rosa's foolish thoughts about escaping.

"I promise, Mother."

The back of an open-topped truck was dropped with a loud clang. The children were lifted into the back by camp guards.

As Rosa climbed in, her mother shouted out. "Rosa!"

"Yes, Mother!"

But as the truck roared into life, Rosa couldn't hear what her mother said. The driver slammed the truck into gear and drove off. Rosa had to yell over all the shouting from both sides of the fence. "Mother, I love you!" And she kept screaming that until the camp was no longer in sight.

They were driven to a nearby airport, loaded onto a transport plane adorned with swastikas and the words 'Junkers JU52'. It had three propeller engines, including one on the nose of the aircraft.

One of the pilots objected. "This plane can only take eighteen passengers."

Director Riefenstahl waived the Luftwaffe pilot away. "These are just children, not soldiers. They can squeeze in."

Rosa's head was in a spin. Only hours earlier, she had been discussing her escape plan, and here she was being taken to somewhere in Bavaria for goodness knows what. How could she get to Berlin to find her father now? Rosa looked at the woman who had caused so much chaos.

Rosa didn't know who this Leni woman was, but she knew that the men wearing German uniforms all took orders from her, including the feared SS Commandant Böhmer. Power in the hands of a woman seemed incomprehensible to Rosa. And, yet, that power had a name: Director Leni Riefenstahl.

## Chapter 6

August 1940 (Late Summer)

*On the set of* Tiefland: *Krün, Germany*

Rosa watched on as Director Leni Riefenstahl, dressed in the rags of a poor Gypsy dancer, looked at herself in the body-length mirror, which Rosa was holding in place.

Since arriving on the set of Director Riefenstahl's *Tiefland* being filmed in Krün, Bavaria, in the south of Germany, Rosa had learned a lot—for instance, summer in Europe was the best time to shoot outdoors. *Tiefland* was supposed to be set in the Pyrenees Mountains, but they couldn't film in Spain due to the war. However, Director Riefenstahl did go to Spain for a couple of weeks to film bullfighting. Still, the crew gossiped that her real reason for the trip to Spain was to spend time with her new lover—an officer in the local Bavarian Mountain Unit.

Apart from being great gossips, the film crew were nothing like the camp guards Rosa was used to dealing with. They would ask the children to do small tasks, but generally, they were nice to the kids, and the children were better fed and housed than they were back at the camp. For whatever reason, Director Riefenstahl had taken a shine to Rosa and appointed her the director's personal assistant. Rosa even slept on a small couch in the director's large bedroom to always be at hand.

What Rosa had learned most of all was that Director Leni Riefenstahl was always in a foul mood, which she took out on absolutely everybody—none were spared her daily, often hourly, tirades. The camp commandant and Heinrich back in Salzburg seemed like kittens compared to this lioness of a woman whose black eyes roared into life whenever something went amiss. From what Rosa could see and hear, everything was always wrong, especially when they were shooting, like today.

Director Riefenstahl twirled again, looking at herself in the mirror from all possible angles and eventually, with a turned-up nose, indicated that she was not impressed. "What is this?" she asked, holding up her ripped skirt, which stopped short of her knees by about six inches.

"It's the dress of a Gypsy dancer, Director Riefenstahl," said the costume designer, who had a measuring tape wrapped around her neck and dress pins in hand. "It is very revealing and best shows off your legs."

"I'm playing the Queen of Gypsies, not some cheap whore."

Just at that moment, the animal handler brought a mule onto the set. Rosa loved the old man who seemed to do all the odd jobs on the film set.

"What is that?" Director Riefenstahl barked at the old man.

"It's the mule you requested, Director Riefenstahl," he said, his curved pipe disappearing in the corner of his white-bearded mouth, reminding Rosa of her father, whom she sorely missed.

"I requested a *donkey*, not a mule."

The old man pulled at the rope that kept his pants from falling down and spat on the ground. "Mule? Donkey? What's the difference?"

His indifference was the tipping point. Leni's eyes flared briefly, but instead, she forced her voice to be controlled and measured. "The *difference* is that when Jesus Christ rode triumphantly into Jerusalem on Palm Sunday, it was on the back of a donkey. I want the audience to see the obvious symbolism of Gypsy Queen Martha alongside that of Jesus Christ."

The old man looked at her. "Well, lady, I couldn't find a donkey; there's a war on, you know. Who knows, maybe Jesus Christ rode on a mule?"

Some of the film crew snickered at the older man's casual indifference to Director Riefenstahl.

"Ah! Get rid of this incompetent ass," she said, pointing at the old man, "and find me a real donkey!" She tore off her rag dress and handed it to the costume lady. "And you, get me a dress fit for a queen, or I will find somebody who can." Wearing only her underwear, she stormed off the set.

***

Leni Riefenstahl, now elegantly dressed as Martha the Gypsy Queen, sat atop the donkey as she rode into the Spanish village. The street children swarmed around her, cheering and throwing flowers at her. As she slipped down off the ass to soak up the children's adulation, the front of a three-storey building in the background fell over like a tree felled in a forest. Martha and all the Gypsy children jumped and swung their heads as one to look at the source of the terrible sound. Queen Martha disappeared as Director Riefenstahl tore off her black, long-haired wig.

"Cut! Cut! Isabella! Isabella! Where is my set designer?" The film crew looked around and shrugged, with no one responding. Director Riefenstahl looked at the group of children who were surrounding her in the scene. "Rosa? Rosa, where are you?"

Rosa stepped forward from the group and spoke, "Yes, Director Riefenstahl?"

"Go find Isabella now!"

Rosa rushed down to the men working on the failed set. "Isabella?" she asked the working men who, without looking at her, pointed to the latrine block. When Rosa entered, she heard sobbing in one of the cubicles. "Fraulein Isabella?"

"Yes?" came a weak voice from behind the cubicle door.

"Director Riefenstahl requests your immediate presence."

"What's happened now?"

"One of the sets fell down while we were in the middle of a shoot," Rosa said.

"Oh no," came the response.

Rosa could hear vomiting noises coming from within the cubicle.

She wanted to reassure Isabella, one of the better people from the film crew who treated everyone kindly, but there was nothing Rosa could say. She simply stood there smelling the bile. Isabella was a nervous woman with a nervous stomach, and what little she did eat didn't seem to stay down, especially on shooting days.

The toilet flushed, and the thin gaunt-looking woman with shoulder-length auburn hair quickly exited and went to wash her face and hands. She looked at the mirror above the handwash basin and adjusted her glasses. And, speaking more to herself than to Rosa, she said, "I'm ready for the dragon lady."

Rosa and Isabella walked past the men hauling the fallen façade back into place. No worker dared look at Isabella. Director Riefenstahl sat silently in her signed 'Director's Chair' when Rosa returned with Fraulein Isabella.

"Yes, Director Riefenstahl?" said Isabella.

Director Riefenstahl stood. "Finally. Isabella, do you care to explain that?" she said, pointing at the fallen set.

"It must have been a gust of wind that knocked it down," Isabella explained.

"It fell down because of the ineptitude of your set department."

"Director Riefenstahl, we've only had a few weeks to build an entire Spanish village, and we're still building the set between takes."

"I don't want excuses. I want you to fix it! Now!"

"Yes, Director Riefenstahl," Isabella said before rushing off to the men she'd just walked past.

Rosa noticed the Gypsy children were gone, probably in the mess having dinner, as it was getting late, and the sun had already set behind the Bavarian mountains.

Harald Reinl, Director Riefenstahl's new assistant director, walked up to her with some papers. "Leni, here are the changes you requested for the script," he said, handing over the freshly typed pages, fidgeting with his thick, black-framed glasses. Rosa never saw him in a suit that fitted him. He was a skinny, fidgety man, who never seemed to eat: he only smoked cigarettes and drank black coffee.

As Riefenstahl flipped through the pages, she noticed Harald looking uncomfortable. "Do not be concerned, Harald; I'm sure your changes are adequate."

"It's not that, Leni."

She paused to look at his worried face. "Well, what is troubling you, Harald?"

"It's just that I noticed the script has only your name on it."

"Yes?" she said, folding her arms.

"It's just that you and I spent months rewriting this script."

"Yes, you helped me polish my original vision of *my* script."

"I think I did more than just *polish* it. I think I have completely transformed your original story, have I not?"

"Do you think I should add *your* name to my script?"

"I did introduce the social conflict into the story. I think I deserve some credit, actual credit."

"And I think I deserve some *actual* credit for saving you from serving on the frontlines for the greater service of the Fatherland, do I not?"

"Yes, Leni," he said, with head bowed.

The director appeared to notice that some of the nearby crew were listening in on their conversation. "Let us not argue," she smiled. "I could not find a better assistant director in all of Germany. Does it matter whose name is on the script? Is film not a collaborative art after all?"

"Yes, Leni."

"Leni? Am I not the *director* of this film as well?"

"Yes, you are."

"So, please be so kind as to address me as such."

"Yes, Director Riefenstahl."

She crumpled the papers.

"No, this is not what I asked for. This will not do."

"What is wrong with it?"

"I want more eloquent dialogue for my Martha."

"But Martha is a peasant dancer. It would be inappropriate for her to talk in such a high-born fashion."

Rosa thought about how Director Riefenstahl's Gypsy Queen shared the same name as her mother. She missed her mother, having never been separated from her before, not a single day. And hearing her mother's name several times a day only made her stomach ache all the more.

"Martha is not just any peasant," Director Riefenstahl continued. "She is a Gypsy Queen. Am I not correct?"

"Yes, Director Riefenstahl."

"You see, that is why my name is on the script. Harald, please go away and give her the dialogue of a sophisticated peasant queen."

Harald, clearly defeated, slouched away with crumpled papers in hand.

Just as Harald left, Isabella returned looking even more downcast than before.

"What is it, girl?" asked the director. "Spit it out."

"I'm sorry, Director Riefenstahl, but it's the studio again."

"I told you to take a message whenever they call. I'm too busy to talk to anybody."

"They're not on the phone; they're here."

This took Director Riefenstahl by surprise. "Who's here?"

"The studio," Isabella said, pointing to a handful of men in business suits standing next to the cameras. "They've come here from Berlin to talk to you personally."

Leni looked around. "Has Captain Jacobs arrived?"

"No. Were we expecting him?"

"No. I'm expecting him for dinner. He's out this way doing some training exercises with his Bavarian Mountain Troops, and he said he'd drop by about this time. Bring him to me as soon as he arrives. Understand! The *moment* he arrives."

"Yes, Director Riefenstahl," Isabella said, slipping away.

Rosa didn't know what to do. She was sure she wasn't meant to be around these official-looking, serious-faced men, but she knew she couldn't join the other children, talking inside the nearby mess tent. Rosa remained a respectable distance behind Director Riefenstahl, waiting to be dismissed. The camera crew pushed the camera-on-wheels away as the lighting and sound equipment was being packed up by other film crew. The shooting was finished for the day.

Director Riefenstahl stalked past the film crew towards the unwelcome guests, who had assembled just metres away. "Gentlemen, I don't appreciate this intrusion."

"If you don't return our phone calls, then I'm afraid you give us no choice," one of the men said.

"Well, gentlemen, as you can plainly see, we are experiencing some technical difficulties," she said, indicating the men trying to reassemble the building façade.

Another man, a much shorter man in spectacles, spoke up. "Director Riefenstahl, we need a delivery date for *Tiefland*. And soon."

"You gentlemen simply don't understand how films are made."

The first man spoke again. "Leni, we have over fifty years of film experience between us. And we know that films are a business and that every day you don't finish the film costs the Third Reich thousands of Reichsmarks better spent elsewhere for the war effort. And you've had more than enough time and money to finish *Tiefland*."

"Gentlemen, you have heard the Führer often speaks of Germany as a nation of poets and philosophers. And I assure you that *Tiefland* is not just any movie. This will mark a watershed moment in German cinematic history—films before *Tiefland* and films after. I simply need more time. Great works of art aren't completed to a schedule."

The short, bespectacled man looked up at her. "I'm afraid there is no more time. Goebbels himself has told us that he wants you out there filming the war effort for the newsreels back home."

"What?" her eyes fired up. "He expects the great Leni Riefenstahl, who has won awards after awards, to go out there and report the news like a common newspaper reporter?"

"That's what he's told us. And it's Reichsminister Goebbels himself demanding this release date of *Tiefland*."

"I've always hated that pig of a man. He sees Germany's actresses as little more than his personal whores."

Leni looked at the men, who appeared uneasy at this public insult of Reichsminister Goebbels. "Go ahead, tell him. I don't care. I don't answer to Goebbels; I answer only to the Führer himself, who's funding this film project personally because he's a man of vision."

Isabella walked over with a tall army officer in a camouflage uniform.

Leni introduced the well-built officer to the assembled men. "Gentleman, this is my fiancé, Captain Jacobs."

The assembled businessmen acknowledged the dashing young officer.

"Darling, have you finished your training manoeuvres for the day?" she asked.

"Yes, sweetheart, but I can return if you're busy with these gentlemen?"

"I need you to do me a favour," she said, beckoning him closer. He bent over so that she could whisper in his ear.

He stood straight up. "Are you sure?"

"I'm very sure."

"Do you want me to wait until these gentlemen go?"

"No. I'm sure these men want to see the Wehrmacht in action."

Captain Jacobs turned and yelled out to his Sergeant, who was having a cigarette with the other soldiers on set.

The sergeant came running over, putting on his helmet. He saluted Captain Jacobs. "Yes, sir?"

"Sergeant, I want you and the men to grab our equipment from the rear of our trucks and go to work on the mock village down there. These men from Berlin would like a demonstration of our boys' skills."

The sergeant smiled. "Yes, sir!" He raced back to the men and ordered them into action. The men jumped up, donning their helmets, and some of them climbed into the back of the covered truck. These men re-emerged with flamethrowers. Soon twelve soldiers had the flamethrowers on their backs as each of their seconds checked the fuel tubes. When that was completed, the seconds lit the nozzles of the flamethrowers, which woofed into life.

The men marched down onto the set. The carpenters realised what was happening, so they hurriedly left the fake buildings. The soldiers sprayed flames as streams of liquid fire poured onto the wooden structures.

As the set crackled, Leni turned to face the studio men. "As you see, gentlemen, I'm quite afraid that a deadline is impossible due to unforeseen circumstances. You can never rush true art. And I would ask you all never to interrupt me at work ever again."

As the studio suits left in a hurry, Harald came racing back to look at the fire-ridden set. "My God, what's happening?"

The fire blazed in Director Riefenstahl's black eyes. "Harald, I have bought you more time to rewrite my script. And tell Isabella that I want a better set than the crap she gave me the first time."

Leni joined Captain Jacobs, kissing him while the inferno engulfed the film set, now fully ablaze.

## Chapter 7

May 1943

*On the set of Tiefland: Krün, Germany*

Rosa walked over to Director Riefenstahl, still sleeping in her bed, and shook her awake. "Director Riefenstahl, it's midday, and you have to wake up."

"Midday? Why didn't you wake me earlier?"

Eventually, the woman dragged herself out of bed and dressed slowly with Rosa's help. After two years of serving as Director Riefenstahl's personal assistant, Rosa was used to this daily charade. Every night, Director Riefenstahl would tell Rosa to wake her up nice and early. After the Director had taken so many pills, Rosa or anyone else couldn't wake her before lunch. Director Riefenstahl had been unwell recently, but she only seemed to worsen.

They had been trying to shoot a scene of *Tiefland* when sitting in the director's chair became too much for Director Riefenstahl.

"Rosa! Get me a stretcher!"

Rosa went to the First Aid room and grabbed a folded-up stretcher.

Harald and Isabella both approached the stricken director. "Director Riefenstahl, this is getting serious," said Isabella. "You need to go to a hospital now."

"Don't be ridiculous. It's just a bladder infection, something I picked up when filming *S. O. S. Iceberg* in Greenland. And you know better than I that we can't afford for me to go to the hospital or another day in bed as the film schedule has blown out. We were originally supposed to release *Tiefland* in the spring of '41, and here we are now fast approaching the summer of '43, and we're still nowhere near finished."

Rosa unfolded the stretcher, laid some army blankets on top with a few pillows, and then helped Director Riefenstahl into it.

"Leni, you can't possibly film a movie from a stretcher," said Harald.

"Watch me. I'm becoming the laughing stock of the Berlin film industry. But Berlin doesn't understand that it's not my fault that I'm surrounded by incompetents, forcing me to do everything myself. Plus, Reichsminister Goebbels is constantly harassing me, which isn't helping. He probably caused my urinary infection because he has pissed me off so many times."

As the filming continued into the afternoon, Rosa approached Director Riefenstahl, who was sleeping between takes.

"Yes, Rosa?" she answered with her eyes still closed.

"Excuse me, Director Riefenstahl, but your brother has arrived."

"My brother, Heinz? He's here?"

"Yes."

"What does he want?"

"He said it was of the utmost importance. I told him you were in the middle of filming a scene. He is quite determined to see you, Director Riefenstahl."

"With my brother, it often is. Okay, let him in."

Leni looked at her assistant director, Harald, and nodded.

"Ten-minute break," Harald yelled to the cast and crew on set. "Everybody out of the building! Now!"

"Ten? Make it five. For Christ's sake it's only my brother, not Reichsminister Goebbels," said Leni, flinching when she laughed at her own joke.

Leni's brother was a tall slim man in a designer suit and matching wide-brimmed hat, and he shared Leni's dark good looks and teeth-perfect smile.

His angry face softened, and his abrupt walking slowed when he saw his sister lying on a stretcher. "Sister, are you ill?"

"Nothing that will kill me. I'll outlive you all, yet. Heinz, what do you want? And if you have got another young girl in trouble, I will not—"

He pulled out a letter from his shirt pocket. It looked official. He handed the Nazi document to her.

She read it. "When?" she asked, handing it back to him.

"They have given me a week to get my *affairs* in order."

"Well, what do you expect me to do about it?"

"I expect you, my *dear* sister, to get me out of it. You have so many influential friends. Couldn't you ask Albert Speer?"

"It's Reichsminister Speer to you. Why should I help you?"

"Why?" he looked at her incredulously. "Because I am the vice-president of a plumbing company, which is vital to the war effort: the Riefenstahl *family* business. The one that paid for all your acting lessons, remember? I'm not some *cannon fodder* for the Eastern Front."

Leni threw back the grey horsehair blanket, and Rosa helped the ailing director to her feet.

"Cannon fodder? Do you know where my fiancé, Major Jacobs, is right now? He is fighting for the Fatherland in Russia. I am sick with worry about him and haven't heard from him in weeks. Even now, he could be dead, but it would be because he is fighting for Germany's survival. And you? What do you do?"

"I help Father run our business," he said in a barely audible voice.

"Yes, you have a big office full of beautiful secretaries that you have extended lunches with, whom you take out every night for dining at the finest restaurants and drinking at the best nightclubs Berlin has to offer, but please do not say that you help Father. If anything, you have been a full-time job for us all, trying to keep you out of trouble. Remember, I got you out of that disastrous marriage with Ilse. It is high time you finally stood up and became a man."

Heinz couldn't hide his rage. "Leni, don't preach to me. I know what makes you tick. Just find me a job on this film set so that I can hide from the war like everyone else here!"

"How dare you? This is how we fight the war. We fight for Germany by building the people's confidence and giving them the courage to fight, defending their Fatherland. We are not hiding from anything. We bleed celluloid each and every day while you sit at home and play the playboy."

His eyes opened in horror when he seemed to realise that she was deadly serious about him fighting on the Russian front. "Leni, please, I beg you. I didn't mean to insult your fiancé, but he is a natural-born soldier, a real war hero, whereas I am a coward. Yes, I live a frivolous life, but only because I'm terribly good at it. And I am your only sibling. I swear, if you get me out of this mess, maybe one day I will be able to pay you back for your help now. There won't always be a war on, and, dear sister, I have a knack for surviving. You won't regret saving your brother. You'll see."

"You admit you are a coward? I didn't know how truly pathetic you were until this very moment. Well, you can use your survival knack to survive on the Russian Front."

"You hypocrite," her brother said in a raised voice.

"What do you mean?"

"You lie here in your 'ivory castle' filming your precious *Tiefland*. How many years is it now? Four? Five? You should be out there on the front lines filming the war to uplift German morale. Instead, you hide away in Bavaria, pretending you're part of the war effort. You are truly pathetic, sister."

She walked up to him and pushed him. "If you can't live like a real man, then you sure as hell can die like one!" The instant she touched him, she clutched at her abdomen and collapsed to the ground in pain.

"Leni, Leni, are you alright?" she heard her frantic brother ask. "You! Girl!" he said, pointing at Rosa. "Go get some help! Go!"

Rosa rushed outside as people tended to the stricken director. But as soon as she had exited the building, she stopped running, and her walk turned into a stroll towards the Nurse's Office.

As Rosa walked for help, she reflected upon her last two years working for Director Riefenstahl. It wasn't the hell of living in a concentration camp, but it was another kind of torture working for someone as crazy as Leni Riefenstahl. More than once, the director had been hospitalised for weeks at a time at the Munich Insane Asylum, being treated by Dr Theodor Morell, Adolf Hitler's personal and private physician. And when she wasn't away in Munich, she would always disappear, sometimes to be with her fiancé, who was home on leave, and at other times goodness knows where. And when she finally returned, she would try to make up for lost time by working everyone into a state of frenzied exhaustion.

Two years earlier, there had been some sixty Romani children, but as time went by Director Riefenstahl had returned any child deemed unnecessary in an effort to save money, and now only ten children remained. If they needed a scene with Gypsy children in the shot, they were on hand, as the director was always reshooting shots because she always found faults that no one else could see. But mostly, the children worked on whatever chores they were assigned. Rosa knew it was easy to leave at any time despite the useless Young Folk squad meant to guard the Romani. Still, she also knew that she would not suffer the consequences of her escape—the other children would or even perhaps her mother would be made to suffer.

Regardless, she decided that when the moment was right, she would escape and head to Berlin to find her father. She knew where her mother was and that she was still alive, but not knowing exactly where her beloved father was or if he was still alive was a nightmarish torment. She had collected maps when she could and stowed away any monies she could lay her hands on.

However, the very moment Leni fell to the floor, Rosa realised that Leni's death would solve many problems—for Rosa and everybody else on set. If nothing else, at least the Romani children would be returned and reunited with their families. Perhaps her mother would have forgiven her by now. Perhaps. Rosa stood aside as the large nurse ran by. *Someone else must have alerted her. Damn.*

# Chapter 8

16 July 1944 (Sunday)

*On the set of Tiefland: Krün, Germany*

Rosa watched as a heavy-set nurse wearing a grey cape and a heavily starched nurse's cap entered the office, where Rosa sat with Director Riefenstahl.

"Finally," said Director Riefenstahl to the nurse. "Where have you been?"

The middle-aged nurse ignored the director and laid the stainless-steel tray down on the table, revealing a stainless-steel syringe and vials of clear liquid.

"This is the best," said Director Riefenstahl, as her crossed legs bounced with anticipation. "From the Führer's own personal stock," she said, licking her lips as she watched the nurse remove the syringe from its box, filling it with a vial of clear liquid. "I don't know how I'd get through the day without this stuff. It's truly a miracle drug. I told the Führer one day that if he gave his soldiers this wonder drug, they would win the war for him in one day. Do you know what he said to me?"

Rosa shook her head.

"He said he wished I were one of his generals instead of being Germany's greatest filmmaker," she said. "You know, I think I would make a great general. Being a film director is like being a general in war because war and films have much in common. Every film is a battle, and if you win enough battles, you eventually win the war." She paused a moment before rambling on. "Did I ever tell you that I've won several international awards? I even toured America, and I was the 'toast of the town' as they say over there. Do you know, in English, the word 'war' is the exact middle of the English word 'award'? And I can tell you that you have to win a war or several wars to win your award. You have all these departments coming to you all the time, then you give the command 'action!' and all your soldiers run to battle to film your movie. Yes, yes, being a director is no different from being a general. I wish I were a general, but alas, my gifts lie in storytelling, but I have so many gifts. It's truly a curse to be blessed with so many gifts, but I bear it as best as I can for the sake of the Fatherland—Germany is the only father I've truly known. Apart from the Führer, of course."

Isabella entered the office, and Rosa moved away to allow her to sit opposite the director. "Director Riefenstahl," said Isabella, "we need to discuss the Gypsy children."

"How many do we have left?"

"We had up to sixty-eight, but we've kept ten, 'just in case', as you yourself ordered."

"Just send them all back to the Gypsy camp in Salzburg."

"As I've just told you, we can't. The local authorities closed down the Salzburg camp back in May '43."

Rosa, hearing this for the first time, had to hide her shock.

"Yes, yes. I remember you telling me, but who can remember these trivialities when you're making a movie in the middle of the war?" Director Riefenstahl asked, focusing only on the nurse, who was squirting some liquid out of the needle, removing possible air bubbles.

"We think some of the women and children were sent to the Bergen-Belsen camp, but all the rest, we think, have been sent to Auschwitz," said Isabella.

"Well, send the Gypsies to Bergen-Belsen or Auschwitz; I don't care."

"Since their camp closed down, perhaps the children could stay here as workers?"

"What?" shouted Director Riefenstahl. "Do you know how much these brats cost me every day they're here? And that's not counting the expense of feeding them, including the Young Folk from the Hitler Youth who still guard them. The sooner all the children are gone, the better."

"Director Riefenstahl," Isabella said, looking uneasy, "surely you have heard the *rumours* about Auschwitz."

"No, I haven't, and I warn you, girl, spreading hateful lies about the Fatherland will surely get you locked up or hanged."

"Please, Director Riefenstahl. Unless you directly intervene on their behalf, I fear they will be sent to Auschwitz. They're only children. If only you made a telephone call, I'm sure they could be sent elsewhere."

"Where else?"

"Anywhere but Auschwitz."

"It's too late, anyway. I've just remembered that it's all been arranged."

"It has? When?"

"Today. The SS arrived to pick up those remaining Gypsy kids while you and little Rosie were out looking for props."

Rosa stood in surprise. Isabella gently moved her hands, indicating that Rosa sit back down, which she did without Director Riefenstahl noticing. Leni had taken to call Rosa, little Rosie, as a term of affection, which Rosa hated.

"I thought I'd keep my little Rosie on. She's been so helpful, especially since I've been so sick recently. I simply could not do without her, so I told the SS that she'd died, and they seemed happy with that. I mean, what were they going to do? Question Germany's greatest director?"

"And what of the Young Folk guarding the children?"

"This latest squad will be the final squad, and they will stay with us as a security detail until they turn fifteen and a half in a few months, and then they will be sent on to one of the Hitler Youth Divisions to fight for their Fatherland."

"Fifteen-year-olds fighting a war is wrong. They should be in school."

"They are learning in the school of life: the best school."

"More like the theatre of death," Isabella mumbled.

"The Young Folk will be escorting our equipment to Prague the day after tomorrow."

"Prague? I thought we were going to Berlin next month to shoot in the Babelsberg Studios?" Isabella asked.

"That prick of a man, Goebbels, says they need it to shoot another more important project. Prick! And so, we have no choice but to go now."

"Now? When exactly?"

"We have to finish packing the day after tomorrow and move out the following morning."

"Finish packing by the day after tomorrow? I have so much to do. Why didn't you tell me?"

"Because I'm the director, and I'm telling you now."

Isabella rushed out of the room, talking to herself in anguish. "No. No. No. There's not enough time to move in three days. No. No. No."

Director Riefenstahl ignored her assistant's sudden departure as the nurse strapped a rubber hose to the director's right arm. Leni instinctively started clenching and unclenching her fist so that her vein would pop out, making it easier for the fluid in the injection to flow through her body. The nurse injected the drug.

Leni Riefenstahl's head lolled backwards as she looked dreamily around at her office walls, adorned with several film posters—mostly hers. But there was one film that was not hers, which held pride of place: it was the film *The Blue Angel* starring the "legendary" Marlene Dietrich. Rosa knew all too well that this particular film poster was there as a reminder to Leni: *The Blue Angel* was meant to be *her* film, which should have launched *her* Hollywood career, but Director Josef von Sternberg had suddenly found his new protégé singing and dancing in some dingy backroom in a Berlin nightclub. All she cared about was her stolen career—stolen by one Miss Marlene Dietrich. Whenever Director Riefenstahl was taking her medicine, she was seemingly her most honest, saying exactly what she thought about everyone and everything, especially about herself. As Leni once told Rosa that talking to a little Gypsy girl was like confessing in an empty confessional booth at church. Although Rosa had often heard this story before—whenever Leni took her medicine—she was going to retell it again...

***

## Flashback...

5 December 1929 (Thursday)

*Potsdam (24 km southwest of Berlin), Germany*
*Babelsberg Studios: The film set of* The Blue Angel

A young and spritely Leni Riefenstahl, dressed in a white overcoat, entered the illustrious Babelsberg Studios in Potsdam just outside the city of Berlin. The Babelsberg Studios were world famous because this was where Director Fritz Lang filmed his *Metropolis* in 1927. The film was set 100 years into the future and was a worldwide hit.

But today, Director Josef von Sternberg had invited Leni to watch him direct his latest movie. He was an attractive filmmaker originally from Austria. His face reminded her of photos of a young Mark Twain she'd seen. Director Josef von Sternberg, or Joe as he asked her to call him, was dashing with his thick wavy hair, which matched his equally thick and dark moustache, and even though he was thirty-five, there was not a trace of any grey hair whatsoever. Director Josef von Sternberg had made his name working in Hollywood with Charlie Chaplin, who'd asked Sternberg to write and direct *The Seagull*. However, he was now shooting his first-ever German feature film: *The Blue Angel*.

The story was about a young seductress called Lola Lola, a singer-dancer at a local cabaret called "The Blue Angel", who ends up seducing a much older and much-respected professor at the local academy. In the end, Lola Lola is the cause of the professor's downfall, who ends up back in his classroom clutching a school desk as he dies from grief. Leni had been a leading contender to play the Lola Lola character when, out of nowhere, Marlene Dietrich stole the show and what should have been Leni Riefenstahl's career-defining role.

But Director Josef von Sternberg was gracious enough to allow Leni on set, and she found that she had a genuine interest in the craft behind the camera. In the few days that she attended the shoot, she had learned an amazing amount about cinematography, lighting and the new technical marvel of sound recording. He explained to Leni why he chose Marlene over Leni. The camera absolutely loved Marlene, and, from the takes the director showed Leni, she had to agree—the camera never lies.

Director Josef von Sternberg said, "Leni, you're the complete opposite of Marlene. You're both exceptional in your own unique ways, but you are remarkably different from each other. Leni, you just haven't been discovered, yet. But trust me, just as I've shaped Marlene into this wonderful creation, I swear I'll do the same for you. Have you reconsidered coming with me to Hollywood once I'm finished with this project?"

"I can't," Leni said.

"Why?" he asked, looking perplexed, "This is an opportunity of a lifetime."

"I'm just busy, that's all. I'd love to go Hollywood but..."

"Is it because of a man?" he asked.

"No," Leni lied.

But the famous director knew there was a young man whom she was madly in love with. "Marlene uses men to get what she wants and not the other way around as it usually happens. You'd do well to take that particular page from her book, perhaps even that chapter."

Leni had to admit that the more time she spent on set, the more she grew to like Marlene Dietrich. In fact, by the end of the week, Leni idolised Marlene and wished she was more like Marlene than she even dared to admit. Marlene was fearless in a time when there was a lot to be fearful about—with a global depression hitting the entire world hard, especially Germany, which had spent four years losing the Great War only a decade earlier.

Leni watched Marlene on the cabaret stage rehearsing the scene where she sang "Falling in Love Again" on a barrel. Marlene wore a white top hat, black-singlet, knee-length short dress, black stockings and high heels with a white leather belt. The front of her skirt was tucked into her belt, exposing her white frilly-laced underwear. Marlene snapped her legs open mid-song and Leni's mouth fell open in horror—this was truly un-ladylike. Marlene noticed Leni's reaction and stormed over to Leni, who was standing beside Director Von Sternberg.

"What is she doing here?" Marlene snapped, pointing directly at Leni's face.

"She is here as my guest," Von Sternberg said, interceding. "She wants to learn more about getting behind the camera. She has some talent as a cameraman or perhaps a director."

"The only talent I see is her trying to get into your pants."

"I'm not the one spreading my legs on stage for all the world to see," Leni said, having enough of Marlene's insults.

Marlene stepped forward as if to strike Leni, who raised her arms in self-defence.

Director Josef von Sternberg stepped between the two women and grabbed Marlene's hands. "Enough!"

Marlene stood back and snarled at Leni. "Either she goes, or I do," she said, storming back to the stage. She pointed to the stage musicians and started to sing "Falling in Love Again". It was good, very good, which was precisely her point.

Von Sternberg had no choice but to ask Leni to leave the studio.

They released the movie in the USA a year later, on 5 December 1930, and the rest, as they say, is history. Marlene Dietrich was acknowledged as the leading lady of Hollywood, thus the world, and Leni Riefenstahl wasn't.

\*\*\*

16 July 1944

The hefty nurse sat beside her patient to monitor the Führer's personal medicine working its magic. The moment Director Riefenstahl finished retelling her story, she fell asleep, and in an instant the director's anguish of her stolen destiny disappeared. Once the nurse was satisfied with her patient, she spoke to Rosa.

"Child, come and get me if there's a problem. You know where to find me?"

Rosa nodded. The nurse left, leaving the door slightly ajar.

"Read to me, little Rosie," said a sleepy-sounding Leni.

Rosa walked over to a pile of books and brought them over. She laid them on the ground and picked up each book. "*Alice in Wonderland?*" she asked.

"No."

"*Aesop's Fables?*"

"No."

Rosa read the titles of the other children's books that she would read to Leni whenever she drifted off to sleep, especially after having her medicine. Leni believed that children's stories were the key to great storytelling because all movie goers were a child at heart.

"Rosa, you know the story I want to hear."

"*Siegfried and the Dragon?*"

"Yes. Siegfried inspired the great German composer Wagner, you know?"

"Yes, I believe you have told me that before," said Rosa, who was sick of reading this classic German hero's tale. There were various versions of Siegfried—Nordic, Germanic, Scandinavian—and Leni's book had all of them.

Rosa looked down; Leni was fast asleep. Rosa quietly closed the office door, walked over to the director's sizeable wooden office desk, and smoothly slid out the top drawer. The glint of the stainless-steel letter opener reflected the light from the ceiling lightbulb. This was the same sharp letter opener the director had accidentally cut herself on numerous times. She pulled it out to look at it. It was just as lethal as any knife, and Rosa had been waiting years for this very moment to kill director Riefenstahl. She'd decided the best way to kill the director was after she had taken her special medicine, and Rosa would then slice both of the director's wrists, making it look like she had taken her own life. And while everyone was in a panic, Rosa would quietly slip away and be forgotten in the confusion.

When Rosa had first met Director Riefenstahl at the Salzburg concentration camp, the business-like woman looked familiar. But it wasn't until Rosa first saw Leni shoot a film scene that she remembered where she had previously met the director. Whenever Leni was directing on set, she always wore a long, white leather coat, white gloves, and white boots that she had specially made. According to the cast and crew, this was Leni's "signature look". She was always clothed in white not only on set or in a studio but also whenever she was filming on location, whether it was the Berlin Olympic Games of 1936, a Nazi rally at Nuremberg or German soldiers fighting on the frontlines during Germany's invasion of Poland. But it wasn't until Director Riefenstahl was ordering her now-husband's flame-throwing troops around on set that Rosa realised the director was the 'lady in white' who had spoken to the SS Storm Troopers outside the Cologne Cathedral.

There was no doubt about it; Director Leni Riefenstahl was the lady in white who'd been responsible for having Rosa's family arrested outside the cathedral. Rosa could never find out exactly why Leni was in Cologne on that particular day. Rosa didn't see any cameras or cameramen, which made it all the more confusing: if not filming, why was Leni at the cathedral that day? However, at Leni's last birthday party, Rosa had learned from drunken exchanges with the crew what they were doing on the day Germany declared war on Poland. Leni stated that she had to hurriedly fly into Berlin to listen to the Führer's Reichstag Address. She never revealed where she was other than to say she was sent on a personal mission by the Führer himself.

Rosa remembered when a drunken Leni swayed to her feet and pretended to be the Führer as she stood upright and recited his speech. The only words that Rosa remembered from the Führer's address were, "I will not war against women and children".

All Rosa could understand was that, for whatever reason, Leni was sent to Cologne by order of the Führer. So, the reason that Rosa and her family were imprisoned and separated was due to them both, but, if she wasn't able to kill the Führer, she most definitely could kill Leni Riefenstahl. The time for Director Riefenstahl to die was now since the Romani children were all gone, and she was the last remaining Gypsy.

With the long-bladed letter opener, Rosa advanced on the unmoving Director Riefenstahl. The director stirred, but her eyes remained closed. "Rosa, is that my evening cup of coffee?" she asked dreamily.

Rosa stopped.

But then she took a step.

And another.

All the while, Rosa was rehearsing the fatal blow in her mind. Forget the blood. Remember, you are avenging your family and the burning of your family's precious legacy. She looked at the office door. Nothing. Rosa turned back to face Director Riefenstahl, still sleeping on her scarlet lounge chair, which had a portrait of the Führer hanging on the wall behind it.

Crash!

Rosa looked down at the ground, where she'd bumped into the silver tray with the empty syringe that the nurse had left behind.

Awoken suddenly by the noise, Director Riefenstahl stared at Rosa with the long dagger-like weapon in hand.

"What do you plan on doing with that, little one? Kill me? Why?" she asked like a confused little girl.

"Don't you dare call me little one," Rosa said, pointing the long blade at the woman not moving from the couch. "Only my father called me that, and it's because of him that I'm going to kill you now."

"I didn't kill your father or anyone else for that matter," Director Riefenstahl said in her dream-like state.

"No. You arrested us ... outside the cathedral ... in Cologne ... the day Germany invaded Poland," Rosa said, letter-knife wavering.

It was one thing to kill that boy near Cologne in self-defence, but it was another thing entirely to plan and carry out killing somebody. And now that that moment was finally here, fear struck Rosa in place as she suddenly found that she couldn't take another step toward her intended victim.

"I remember now where I've seen your face before. You were the little girl outside the Cologne Cathedral." The director motioned at the blade. "I see you have come for your revenge. Well, it's not my fault you were arrested. It was her fault," she said limply, pointing to the poster of *The Blue Angel.*

"You could say she was the reason your family was arrested that day. We were there to meet her and found ourselves near the cathedral when your wagon broke down. Yes, yes. It's all her fault. Now be a good girl and go fetch me my coffee; there's a good girl." She rolled over with her back facing Rosa.

Rosa could not take her eyes away from the woman on the poster. Was Marlene Dietrich the person responsible for destroying her family? The one thing Rosa knew about Leni was that she was incapable of speaking the truth. It wasn't a lie exactly, but rather it was Leni's version of the truth; therefore, there was always an ounce of truth in all her lies. Moreover, Leni seemed the most truthful whenever she was delirious from her medicine. Was Leni's bragging about a personal mission for the Führer really about Marlene Dietrich? Marlene Dietrich was an American citizen now and thus deemed a traitor to Germany, but she was born and bred in Berlin just like Leni Riefenstahl and Rosa. Were they childhood friends? Is that why the Führer sent Leni to Cologne?

There was a gentle knock at the door.

Rosa slipped the letter opener behind her back. She had waited too long. The longed-for moment of revenge was lost.

Another knock at the door.

She looked at the sleeping woman. Rosa could do it now, but it wouldn't look like suicide as she had originally intended. Slit wrists on a troubled Leni Riefenstahl; no one would suspect otherwise. But if she stabbed the director now, there would be repercussions: serious trouble for the other Romani trapped inside concentration camps all over Europe. And Rosa needed to find her father. She hid the letter opener behind her back.

A bespectacled young man opened the door and stepped inside, followed by Isabella and the nurse, all three looking shaken.

"Harald, you sent for us to come here?" said Isabella.

"This telegram, marked urgent, has just arrived."

"What does it say?" asked the nurse.

"The telegram is from Director Riefenstahl's mother, Bertha Riefenstahl, in Berlin. And it's bad news, terrible news, I'm afraid. Director Riefenstahl's brother has been killed in action on the Russian Front, and when her father was informed, he had a major heart attack and was rushed to Berlin's La Charita Hospital, where he later died. Both funerals will be held in Berlin this Thursday."

Harald turned to Rosa, "Rosa, you need to go and pack Director Riefenstahl's personal belongings now. We'll arrange for a flight first thing in the morning. You don't need to come back here. We'll stay with the director and get her ready to leave for Berlin."

The nurse looked at the syringe and plate lying on the floor. "What's happened here? Pick up that tray and drop it in the medical office."

"Yes, Ma'am," said Rosa, bending down and deftly holding the letter opener underneath the tray.

Rosa walked into the hallway. Should she escape now? Or could she persuade the director to take her along to Berlin? Leni usually didn't remember anything on most of the other nights she'd had her medicine. She wouldn't remember tonight's incident, or would she?

## Chapter 9

19 July 1944 (Tuesday)

*On the set of* Tiefland: *Krün, Germany*

Early in the morning, Rosa initiated her escape plan, the one that had been years in the making if all else had failed, and it had. She hadn't seen Director Riefenstahl the morning after they were informed of the deaths of the director's father and brother. Leni had been whisked away on a military flight to Berlin. Rosa didn't know if that was a blessing in disguise: Rosa couldn't accompany Director Riefenstahl to the double funeral, but neither had Rosa been accused of trying to harm the director. But today was the day the set was moving, which was an ideal time to escape. People were so used to seeing Rosa with the director that they would assume Rosa's absence was due to her meeting up with Leni. But Rosa suspected that no-one would care or even notice her disappearance.

Rosa entered the studio's empty costume department and grabbed her dress, which she'd hidden underneath a large rug. She checked the inside pocket for the money she'd accumulated and the other pocket for her map, knowing that she had a tremendous distance to cover, Berlin being so far away, some 700 km. On the shelf, several fake heads were lined up wearing various wigs for both men and women. Just like being at the Salzburg prison, she still had to hide her blonde hair on the set of *Tiefland*. However, once she was on the run having blonde hair could be a big advantage, so a few weeks earlier she shaved off all of her black-dyed hair and instead began wearing one of the black, long-haired wigs she'd stolen from the costume department. No-one missed the wig or seemed to notice she was wearing one.

But she was escaping much earlier than she expected and her

real hair looked more like a soldier's haircut fresh out of basic training, and it would take many more weeks before it was long enough. So, Rosa grabbed the long, blonde wig that had been tied into two ponytails, Bavarian-style, which she would need until her natural-blonde hair grew back fully. She put the wig into her rucksack alongside her borrowed Bavarian's beer-maid dress.

She snuck over to the film set of a fake Spanish village and entered the barn, which was off-limits to cast and crew, who had been using it as a place for their little love trysts. She felt sure she would be safe here. She hung up her dress in the corner and unbuttoned her blouse when a wolf whistle sounded from somewhere in the darkness behind her.

It was Klaus, staring at her with a devilish smile. He was one of the Young Folk security details meant to guard the film company's assets, including the Romani children.

"I've been keeping my eye on you," said Klaus, unbuttoning his grey-uniform jacket. "And today is my last day guarding this shit hole. They wanted me to stay and babysit when I said no. I should be fighting for the Fatherland, so I thought I would seek you out and we could have some fun before we leave, for a proper soldier's send-off, if you know what I mean?"

"Keep away from me," said Rosa.

He laughed, unbuttoning his shirt to expose his hairless chest. As he edged closer towards Rosa, she retreated.

Nowhere for her to run.

No-one to shout out for help.

No-one to come to her rescue.

He rushed at her, tackling her, lifting and slamming her body onto straw and hay. Once she was on the ground, he pinned her down with his arms and the full weight of his body, squeezing the air out of her lungs, moving his face closer to hers, trying to kiss her but failing as she twisted and turned her head, her lips shut tight. He head-butted her instead, dazing her until their lips finally met.

He forced his tongue inside her mouth.

She bit it.

Hard.

Both hands went to his mouth as blood trickled down his jaw. She fumbled at his sides, searching for the handle of his Hitler Youth knife. When she found it, she slid it out of the scabbard, and pressed it against Klaus' naked neck. The cold steel of the long, triangular blade pressing against his jugular seemed to get his full attention. Klaus stopped moving and eased up away from her. But then he was back on top of her again, straddling her body, fighting to get his knife back.

As they struggled, her free hand was searching for something.

Anything.

Her fingers found a chinstrap belonging to his large, steel helmet.

Knowing helmets were heavy, she wrapped one of the two leather straps around her free hand.

Klaus sat up, holding up his prized knife. He grabbed her, pulling off her black wig by mistake, the one she'd been wearing instead of dying her hair.

He stared in confusion at her short blonde hair.

Rosa took the opportunity to smash the steel helmet into the left side of Klaus' skull. He went limp and slumped off her.

She stood up and looked at his motionless body, bleeding from his temple, his blood trickling onto the yellow straw. She didn't know if he was dead or not, but she wasn't waiting around to find out.

Just then, the convoy of German army trucks roared to life.

The diesel trucks would be warming up for the next ten minutes before they pulled out for their long trek to Prague. Her brain raced with a new escape plan that had just presented itself to her.

She undressed the mostly undressed Klaus. She stopped and looked at his army jacket, lifting it, testing its weight, appraising it. She tried it on. It was large, but from what she'd seen, none of the boys had grown into their man-sized uniforms. Klaus hadn't moved since she struck him, but she didn't want to take any chances. She grabbed the chinstrap with both hands and smashed his other exposed temple with an almighty blow. He didn't move. She finished undressing him and then redressed herself in his uniform. Klaus lay almost naked, so she put her dress over him.

Outside the barn, she saw Klaus' military equipment leaning against the wall, ready to go with him when the convoy departed. She grabbed Klaus' cap and put it on with the brim hanging low over her face before attaching the helmet to the backpack like she'd seen done by the other Young Folk. She shouldered the behemoth backpack, grabbed his weapon and headed for the convoy of trucks starting to pull out.

When she flagged down the last truck, the driver stopped and angrily motioned her to the back. The tarpaulin flap was down, but a hand was thrust out to her. She handed her weapon before removing her backpack and feeding it to the proffered hand. The same hand thrust out again, fingers splayed, waiting. She grabbed the offered hand and was pulled inside.

Adjusting to the dim light, she looked around and saw several eyes staring back at her. She was standing next to a tall boy.

"My name's Peter, and that big strong oaf who lifted you in is Wolfgang."

Wolfgang nodded slightly in acknowledgement.

"This is Gunter," Peter said, indicating an oversized and overweight boy. "Next to him is Fritz, but don't worry about him; he's always reading." Fritz wore glasses and was using a military flashlight to read a book. "And over here is little Charlie." He was a boy, ten at the most, but he was in uniform for some reason. "He doesn't talk, and we don't know his real name or where he comes from, but we adopted him as our squad mascot."

"If he can't talk, how did he get the name Charlie?" she asked.

"He waddles just like Charlie Chaplin, so we call him Charlie. He seems to like it. And they're the Muller brothers," he said, indicating three boys who looked almost identical. "And, finally, Hansel."

"Hans! I hate being called Hansel," he snapped.

"This is our squad. We've just replaced a squad of older boys sent to fight the Americans invading France."

That was what Klaus was talking about. His squad was being shipped to the frontlines while being replaced by this fresh squad that he'd refused to stay and babysit.

"What's your name?" Peter asked.

"Ros-Rudolph," she said. "But you can call me Rudi. I enlisted from a village not far from here. I'm a Bavarian."

Peter looked at his equally confused squad. "We were expecting one more to make us a ten-man squad, but we were told we were getting a new squad leader to *toughen* us boys up, but I thought his name was Klaus?"

"What can I say? My name is Rudi, and I am your new squad leader."

"Okay, Rudi the Bavarian," said Peter, "welcome to your new squad."

# Chapter 10

26 December 1944 (Tuesday)

*Barandow Studios, Prague, Czechoslovakia*

"Up! Up! Up! You lazy swine! Don't you know there's a war on?"

The bank of studio lights hanging over the bunkers lined up below buzzed into life. This part of the studio had been set aside for the Young Folk. They were guarding the Barandow Studios in the Czechoslovakian city of Prague.

The boys sat up in their bunk beds, raising their arms to shield their eyes as the humming lamps warmed up. They saw an old sergeant, complete in battle uniform, standing next to Gunter, who'd been on the last shift of guard duty. The sergeant kicked the slower ones into alert wakefulness. "Get up. And form a line."

In various stages of undress and white long johns, the boys stood to attention at the end of their perfectly aligned military bunks.

The sergeant towered over the disorderly and motley group as he strode between the lines of teenagers standing at attention. "Congratulations, boys! You are no longer in the Young Folk. You have all graduated into the Hitler Youth, and, as of now, by direct orders of the Führer, you have enlisted into the army, effective immediately."

"But we have another three months left to serve in the Young Folk?" questioned Fritz.

"I'll forgive your insubordination as it's your first day in the army," he said to Fritz and looked up to speak to the squad. "The Russians have just encircled Budapest, and we will be part of a major assault to free the city."

"How far away is Budapest, Sir?" Rosa asked.

"Don't call me *Sir*, son: I work for a living. I'm a sergeant, not an officer." He looked at her for a moment, deciding whether to answer or not. All eyes were on him. "It's over five-hundred kilometres to the southwest of here. Why?"

"Sergeant, Berlin is only a few hundred km away, and we were all hoping that we would be heading north to help defend Berlin, our home."

The sergeant's face softened with this information. "It's 350 km, to be precise. And I'm from Berlin as well, son, and my family is stuck there just like yours. But our duty is to the Fatherland, which is doing as the Führer instructs us to do, and he has ordered all nearby units to break back into Budapest by January One. I have to leave you to find some vehicles, but I'll be back in an hour. I expect you all to be ready to fight. Fortress Budapest needs us."

He went to leave by the front door.

"Sergeant," Rosa said, stopping him, "what news of Berlin?"

His soldierly face could not hide his distress. "The Führer is doing all he can to save our greatest city," he said before leaving.

Rosa and the nine boys quickly dressed into their battle fatigues. Once they had made their beds and were packed and ready to go, they sat on their bunks in silence. They had avoided war long enough, but they all knew this day would come. Rosa thought about her options: she didn't want to go to Budapest; Prague was only 350 km directly south of Berlin, and she did not want to go a further 500 km in the other direction. She knew she could easily slip away from the boys and make it to Berlin by herself. She preferred that. But once she got there, what would she do? She needed the boys' local knowledge to help her get around Berlin if she had any chance of finding her father. She knew what she needed to do.

Rosa got up. "I'm going. Who's coming with me?"

They all looked at her in astonishment.

"I say, Rudi, you seem very keen to get to Budapest and die," said Gunter.

"Who says I'm going to Budapest?"

84

Wolfgang stood opposite her. "What did you just say?"

"You can't go back to Bavaria," said Peter, standing beside Wolfgang. "They'll shoot you on the spot as a deserter."

"I'm not going back to Bavaria."

"Where are you going?"

"I, like most of you, was born in Berlin, and I, like you, have family there. So, I'm going to defend Berlin."

"Berlin?" the boys said in unison as they all stood in astonishment.

"I don't know about you boys, but if I'm going to die fighting Russians, I'd rather die fighting for the Führer in Germany's capital than die in a strange place that none of us has ever been to."

"I have been to Budapest," said Gunter. "It's beautiful, and their food is delicious."

"Shut up, Gunter!" they all said as one, sick of hearing of all the places he'd been to and all the food he'd eaten before the war started.

"And I can't believe you Berliners would rather die in Hungary than your birthplace," Rosa said, taking a few paces towards the door.

"How?" Peter asked.

She turned. "How, what?"

"How are you going to do it? You heard him. Berlin is 350 km away. How will we cover that distance without getting caught or killed by the Russians, Americans or Germans?"

"I have a plan."

"Tell us your plan," Wolfgang demanded.

"No," she said.

"Why not?"

"I don't want you telling on me and getting me shot. Murderer."

Wolfgang and the other boys were shocked at this suggestion.

"Wolfy, I mean Wolfgang, is not a murderer," said Peter.

"No? Why then is he always looking at me with his murderous eyes?"

"I don't trust you, Rudi," said Wolfgang. "You appear out of nowhere and seem to know nothing about the army, which is especially strange for a squad leader. It all sounds like a big fat lie to me, and yet I'm the only person who can see it."

"Well, fine. Wolfgang, you stay behind and die in Budapest like a good little soldier, and the rest of you come with me, and we'll go to Berlin and be good sons by finding our families."

The boys looked at Wolfgang, who crossed his arms. "I'd rather die fighting as a hero in Budapest than get shot in Berlin as a traitor."

"A hero's death! Is that what you want, young man?" a voice shouted behind them.

They all turned to see an elderly man wearing his World War One uniform, complete with the old-style pointed helmet.

"Sgt Fischer, the nightwatchman," whispered one of the Muller brothers.

"I'll tell you, boys, all about a hero's death," Sgt Fischer continued. "Back in the first war, my friend Heinrich was stuck on the wire squealing like a pig all day long. My officers refused to let me go out in the daylight to help him. His guts were hanging out of his belly like red strings of spaghetti. Then the British gunners decided to use him as artillery practice. With every shell burst, they took away a piece of him, one bit at a time. A finger here, an earlobe there, and still he lived until he broke down and begged us, his comrades, to shoot him. All the while, he had one hand holding the barbed wire away from his face, with his other hand trying to repack his intestines back into his belly cavity. When it was dark, we went out to get him. I tell you, children, that his body was full of holes like blood-soaked Swiss cheese. That's what a hero's death looks like. He was my best friend, and I'll be joining him soon enough."

"You?" said Gunter. "You must be at least seventy years old."

"I turn sixty this Christmas, or I would have, but I have too been ordered to Fortress Budapest. So, young man," he said to Wolfgang, "come to Budapest with me, and we can both die like heroes together."

Wolfgang looked shocked. He didn't know what to say. Nobody did.

Rosa broke the silence. "You're right, Wolfgang. I don't know much about the military, but I know how to survive. Those who want to live and hopefully still find their family alive in Berlin, come with me. Those who want to die a hero's death, stay here with Sgt Fischer and Wolfgang."

Rosa grabbed Charlie's hand, left the Barandow Studios and entered the city of Prague.

While Rosa and Charlie walked through the medieval streets of Prague, it struck her how Romani she felt. Never knowing which road to take, Romani lived and died on the highways, dirt roads and streets of Europe; their only sanctuary was with other Romani. But she had survived, thus far, precisely because she was a Romani, and, at this moment in time, she was damned proud of it and thankful.

Her skills in disguise and acting that she had learned from Leni had helped her since she joined the boys. In Rosa's eyes, acting was simply lying with confidence. And besides, ordering around a bunch of boys was fun. Clearly, these boys were a squad of failed Hitler Youth that no one wanted. That's probably why they had been given the simple task of guarding Romani extras and the studio equipment; they were getting to the bottom of the barrel with these boys she'd thought. Rosa had been lucky with the timing of her escape. She'd learned that each of the Young Folk squads had all been born in the same month and year, and the end of the month that they turned fifteen-and-a-half, the squads were transferred to a Hitler Youth Division on the frontlines somewhere.

There had been many squads that had rotated through guarding the set, and this squad had only arrived the day before their departure from Bavaria. As such, she'd never seen this particular squad before, and more importantly, they had never seen her.

Rosa was also about their age, fifteen-and-a-half, and being taller than all the boys except Peter and Wolfgang helped with her disguise. They all seemed so relieved that the infamous 'Klaus the

Cruel' was no longer their squad leader, explaining why they so readily accepted her as their new leader.

Wolfgang was the only one who seemed to question her. He was not like the others because he was quite competent and probably didn't belong in this squad of unfortunates. But she did notice that Wolfgang was a lone wolf in that he generally kept to himself. And from what she could tell, the military looked down upon general incompetence or a loner personality with equal disdain. For whatever reason, she had managed to keep up her ruse as their squad leader, Rudi from Bavaria.

Rosa stopped to stare at the beautiful church as they passed the St. Vitus Cathedral. It reminded her of something. While she and Charlie gazed up at the spire, Peter, who was out of breath, joined them.

"Rudi, what are you looking at?" Peter asked.

"It reminds me of the Cologne Cathedral."

"I love the Cologne Cathedral," Peter said. "It's my favourite building in all of Germany. It took us hundreds of years to build it, just like Germany."

"Well, I only have bad memories of it. Anyway, it's probably been blown into a million pieces by the Americans and British," she said, stalking off again.

Peter got into step with her, with Charlie in between the two. "It doesn't matter if they have blown it up," said Peter. "Even if it takes us another hundred years, we'll build a bigger and stronger cathedral in Cologne."

She didn't respond.

"Rudi! Rudi! Wait for me!" shouted Gunter, struggling under the weight of his backpack and weapon.

By the time the four of them reached the halfway point across the Charles Bridge, the entire squad had joined them, Wolfgang following from a discernible distance behind.

"Why didn't Wolfgang, the hero, stay?" she asked Peter.

"What would he have said if he'd stayed behind alone? They

would have taken all our names, which our families would have been punished for," Peter answered, "and then they would have shot him for failing to prevent us from deserting the Fatherland."

"As long as he doesn't get in my way."

"Don't you worry about Wolfy," Peter said. "We go way back."

## Chapter 11

9 February 1945 (Friday)

*90 km south of Dresden, Germany (Grandma Schneider's farm)*

The boys' squad found Grandma Schneider an unexpected treasure when they accidentally discovered her farm in the middle of nowhere. Her husband had died in the first war, and all of her five sons had been forced into military service for this second one. While she fed, bathed and washed the boys' clothes, the boys mended her fences, fixed the thatched roof, and carried out any other odd jobs Grandma Schneider could find for them. But after almost a week, Rosa knew it was time for them to leave.

A week before arriving at the Schneider Farm, they had managed to sneak into the back of an empty truck but were forced to run when the driver discovered them while refuelling. After that, they kept away from the main roads and anyone in uniform or who looked official. At Rosa's suggestion, they all walked up to a farmhouse and told the farmers they were heading south to join the fight at Budapest. The farmers were generally kind and gave them what they could.

Rosa enjoyed the break from walking just as much as anybody, but the longer they stayed at Grandma Schneider's farm, the harder it was for her to keep her secret. Her body had been deprived of food, and as a result, she had maintained her boyish figure. Puberty had been delayed because of starvation, but now with army rations and Grandma Schneider's food, her body seemed to have finally recovered and was betraying her by developing into curves. After only a few days of Grandma Schneider's generous cooking, Rosa was now struggling to do up her pants.

One day, Grandma Schneider pulled Rosa aside. "I know your

secret, *young man*."

"What secret?"

"Well, for one thing, I can tell that you are a girl and not a boy. Nice trick. I wish I had thought of that deception—turning my sons into daughters."

Rosa protested, but Grandma Schneider interrupted her. "Don't worry, Rudi, or whatever your real name is."

"Rosa," she said, realising the futility of lying to the elderly woman who saw and knew everything, just like her own grandma did.

"I also know you are not heading to Budapest to free the city. I overheard your boys chatting the other day. Plus, you are well away from the autobahns, which would take you there. Tell me now, girl, where are you really headed? Otherwise, I'll let slip your little secret to the boys."

"Berlin. To get to our parents before the Russians come," she said.

"Berlin? Family. Women understand family, especially mothers who have lost five sons to this war. I need some more help around the farm before you leave, and I will keep both your secrets."

Rosa nodded in silent agreement.

"Tell me, girl, are you bleeding yet?"

Rosa shook her head.

"No? Well, that's one thing in your favour, I guess."

After this exchange with Grandma Schneider, Rosa was keen to keep moving. She didn't trust people who kept secrets.

A few days later, after all the jobs were nearing completion, Grandma Schneider hitched up her horse-drawn buggy from the last century, telling the boys she had to go into town for supplies.

"Now stay here, boys and finish your work for old Grandma Schneider. I always go into town on Sundays to go to church. I won't be long. And when I get back, I'll have a big surprise waiting for you."

"Apple strudel!" shouted Gunter.

"Maybe," said Grandma Schneider, whipping the old horse into action.

As soon as she left, Rosa entered the stables where they were sleeping and packed her bags.

"We're leaving now," she said. "Quickly, go pack your bags."

"But why, Rudi?" Gunter asked. "It's so nice here, and Grandma Schneider has looked after us so well."

The other boys nodded in agreement.

"We've stayed here too long as it is," Rosa argued. "And we didn't run away from Prague simply to hide out here in this middle-of-nowhere farm. Besides, Wolfgang is right."

This caught Wolfgang's attention, who was in a constant state of isolated gloom since they defied orders to go to Budapest.

"If we stay here rather than return to Berlin and save our families from the Russians, we are no better than deserters and deserve to be shot. What will you tell your grandchildren about the last days of the war defending Germany? That we hid under the skirt folds of a little old lady? We are leaving now and heading north to Dresden. And as the crow flies, Berlin is more than a hundred miles north of Dresden."

"Which is about 165 km," corrected Fritz.

Rosa grabbed little Charlie's hand and walked northwards from the farm.

First, Peter followed, then Wolfgang and the rest grabbed their belongings and followed. After a couple of hours of walking up the giant hill that overshadowed the farmhouse, Rosa and Charlie waited at the top for the remainder of the platoon to catch up. Just as the last one, Gunter, as usual, caught up, they heard diesel trucks drive up the dirt road to the farmhouse below. They all watched as a squad of German soldiers disembarked from the rear of the canopied truck, and Grandma Schneider got out of the passenger seat. The Wehrmacht searched the farmhouse and farm buildings; to no avail.

"Why Grandma Schneider?" asked an incredulous Gunter.

"Why? She was so nice."

"Nice, like the old witch in the Hansel and Gretel story," said Rosa.

"That old bitch," said Wolfgang.

"She just used us to fix her farm before reporting us," said Peter.

"Just like we used her," Rosa reminded them.

"But I don't understand," said Fritz. "She's lost five sons."

"It's because she's lost five sons," answered Rosa. "Why should our parents not suffer like her? Why should we be reunited with our families in Berlin, while she will never be reunited with her boys here on earth?"

They left in silence, heading northwards to Dresden.

## Chapter 12

13 February 1945 (Tuesday)

*12 km south of Dresden, Germany*

They'd been walking all day, and now that it was getting late, the boys were fading fast. Their early-morning forced march had slowed to a late-evening crawl.

"Rudi, can't we stop for the night?" Gunter begged. "I'm hungry."

"No. Our only chance of getting through Dresden is at night when the city sleeps."

Silence. Despite their aching tiredness, they knew she was right, and as she was their leader, no one ever argued with her—it was the German way.

She had discussed her plans with Peter during their long walk. Dresden was a further 200 km away from Berlin via the roads. However, walking for most of the 150 km from Prague to Dresden had taken them far too long. Once on the other side of Dresden, they would have to find some form of transport; otherwise, the war would be over before they got to Berlin. And to rescue her father, it was imperative to get to him before the marauding Russians arrived in Berlin.

But before worrying about Berlin, she needed to get through Dresden first. According to Peter and Wolfgang, Dresden was not only the capital city of Saxony; it was the largest city not to be bombed by the Allies. And as such, there were bound to be military units everywhere: government officials, the police, and especially the feared Gestapo.

As they trudged along, she whispered to Peter, "Are you sure there's no way around Dresden?"

Peter shook his head. "No way. Just as all roads lead to Rome, the same thing could be said about Dresden. It is a major crossroad to the west, east, north or south of Germany. Plus, it has a massive train yard because the trains also intersect here. Even if we tried to go around it, we'd still have the River Elbe to cross. There's no way around it. We need to go through Dresden to get to Berlin."

She looked behind her to see all the boys, including Wolfgang, who always tried to pretend he was superhuman, were dragging their heels. "Peter, I have to ask you one question."

"Yes?"

"Why aren't you in charge? You have a clear head, and the boys follow your lead. Except for Charlie, no one followed me out of Prague until you did."

He laughed. "Don't put yourself down, Rudi. You have more guts than the rest of us put together, Wolfgang included. You never hesitate, which is especially important in a world where a second could be the difference between life and death. You are a natural-born leader. Besides, I was a leader some years ago. When I was ten, but never again. I tried to be someone that I wasn't. Guess what my squad nickname was?"

Rosa shook her head.

"It was 'little Adolf' or 'the little Führer'."

She laughed. She could not imagine Peter shouting or hurting a butterfly. "Thanks, Peter, I needed that."

"If anyone can get us to Berlin, it's you, Rudi."

She looked out at the looming medieval city. She still didn't have a plan. Again, she knew she could get through the city if she was travelling alone. She wondered if she could take them across the city a few at a time? No way. Besides taking forever, every time she crossed the city, her chances of being caught increased. Luck is finite, and it's best to count on it when you need it most. And she could definitely use some luck right now.

She looked at the map with her torchlight. Perhaps the River Elbe was her solution and not an obstacle. They could grab a boat and float down the river until they got to Magdeburg and then head east until they arrived at Berlin.

The sirens of Dresden started wailing throughout the city. The bombers weren't above them, so the squad felt reasonably safe to continue walking. The wailing sirens and large lights searching the skies above the city of Dresden distracted them from their aches and pains. They all stopped to watch bombs rain down on the beautiful city only some minutes later. They stood on the road's crest and watched it like a fireworks show. After the bombers had left, the city was lit up like daylight as their incendiary bombs torched the numerous wooden buildings. The raging fire was everywhere and so white-hot it was as if it had scared all the shadows away. The burning city lit up the surrounding countryside, giving Rosa an idea.

"Let's hurry before the American bombers return."

"They weren't Americans," said Fritz. "They were British bombers."

"How do you know that?"

"The Americans fear the dark, so they bomb during the day. And the British are afraid of being sitting ducks for flak bombers in the day, so they bomb during the night."

"I guess that means the Germans are afraid twenty-four hours a day," she said.

"How come you don't know that, Rudi?" asked a suspicious Wolfgang. "Everyone knows that."

"I guess I figured a bomb is a bomb regardless of who drops it and when."

"I say you Bavarians are a very pragmatic people," said Gunter.

"Yes, very pragmatic," said Rosa, wondering what the word 'pragmatic' actually meant. "Boys, I know you're all tired, but we must hurry," she said. "We're going through Dresden right now. Nobody will notice us while they're rushing to put out the fires."

A couple of hours later, with the tide of south-bound Dresden refugees slowing them down, they arrived near the city's centre. They'd kept away from the firefighters, both civilian and military. Then the sirens wailed once again. They looked at her.

"This is not good," said Fritz. "The first wave has lit up the city, making it easier for the main bombing run. We have five minutes to find shelter."

She knew they couldn't risk using the sign-posted shelters around the city.

"Rudi, we have to find a bomb shelter," said Wolfgang. "And now."

"No. We have to find a bridge over the Elbe before they are all destroyed."

Just as they made their way towards the river, they heard the flak guns firing upwards at the arriving bombers, and they heard bombs hitting the ground. She could see a large bridge. It wasn't the normal typical concrete bridge that she was used to seeing. It was a military steel trestle bridge that she'd seen around, which must have been erected by a Wehrmacht engineer unit. They were almost there.

"We have to hide now!" yelled Peter over the terrible noise.

"Here!" Wolfgang yelled, standing by the door of a large building.

None of the boys waited for Rudi. She stood rooted on the spot, looking at the bridge before her. She could cross it by herself. Charlie pulled at her shirt. He was standing with her. She couldn't make it with Charlie, being too slow. She knelt and looked at him. "Charlie, you have to go with them. I'm going over that bridge."

She ran.

*Don't look back.*

*Just run away from the coming bombs.*

*Don't look back.*

But she did look back. Only to see little Charlie was chasing after her. It didn't matter. Charlie didn't matter. He was only a German. He was only getting what he deserved. They all were. He wasn't her little brother. She didn't have any siblings. The only family she had was her father. He was all that mattered. She looked again—Charlie was still following.

She bent down, picked up some rocks, and threw them at Charlie, who stopped for a second to look at her in confusion. But then he kept coming after her. One of her rocks accidentally hit Charlie square on the forehead. He fell flat on his back. He sat up, holding his head, screaming in pain, which she couldn't hear over the noise of the carpet-bombing that was coming towards them. She looked at the bridge, but Charlie just sat there unmoving, still crying. She ran onwards.

*Don't look back.*

*He's not your little brother.*

She stopped running. She couldn't help herself. She couldn't abandon Charlie.

The exploding bombs were closing, and little Charlie still hadn't moved. He was just wailing in the middle of the street. She looked back at the bridge, fearing it was her only chance at freedom. "You better still be there afterwards," she whispered.

She ran back to Charlie, carrying him over to the nearby building, which Wolfgang had found. They ran over to Peter, who was still holding the door open for Rudi and Charlie. He must have witnessed what had just happened but did not say a word, and somehow she knew he wouldn't tell the others.

She looked at the sign on the side of the building: *Schlachthof* 5.

They entered the slaughterhouse and descended the two to three flights underground into the basement. When she, Peter and Charlie got to the bottom of the stairs, the other boys were standing still at the bottom of the stairwell.

"What's wrong?" asked Peter.

"We're not alone," Gunter said.

Peter and Rosa couldn't see what the other boys could see. They made their way through the boys. "They're probably just workers," said Peter.

"They're not workers," said Gunter.

"They're American GIs," said Wolfgang.

"What's a GI?" asked Rosa.

"In English, a GI means a general infantryman," Wolfgang answered.

"But, basically, it means an American soldier," Gunter clarified.

Peter and Rosa stopped. In front of them were dozens and dozens of GIs, maybe more, who were looking back at them. The GIs moved away from the stairwell. The Hitler Youth squad moved through the human wall of olive-green uniforms and found a nearby wall to sit against. The Americans were quiet and kept away from the kids. The bombs rocked the building. They may have been enemies, but they knew that the Allied bombs didn't discriminate: the British bombs killed Americans just as easily as they did the Germans.

An hour later, the bombing seemed to ease up in their city sector.

"Who are they?" asked Gunter.

"They are POWs," said Wolfgang. "Prisoners of War," he said to Rosa.

"I know what POW stands for," Rosa said. It was impossible to spend so much time with a squad of boy soldiers and not pick up a lot of military terms, weapons handling and basic infantry tactics.

"They're all so big and tall," said Gunter, marvelling at the Americans.

"I want to know where they came from," said Rosa. "Fritz, come here."

Fritz knew a lot about a lot, but more importantly, he was educated in England until England declared war on Germany, forcing him to return to the Fatherland. She had distracted them from their aching feet by getting Fritz to teach them all English—a skill she believed would benefit them in the future.

Fritz came over to her. "Yes, Rudi?"

"We've been on the run for two-and-a-half weeks, and we don't know how the war's going. We need to find out how close the Americans are. Find out where these Americans came from."

"Okay," he said, looking at the Americans milling about the place. "Who?"

She looked at the GIs congregating against the white-tiled walls and pylons. One of the GIs ventured closer to them. "Him."

Gunter joined them.

"What?" he said, defending his curiosity. "I've never seen a GI in real life."

Fritz, Gunter and Rosa walked up to the GI, who stopped in front of them. He seemed not to notice them. It was as if he was looking through them. She was used to seeing that faraway stare from dead people, not the living. His demeanour and empty glare unnerved her. She gave Fritz a nudge.

"What?" Fritz asked her.

"Ask him his name."

Fritz spoke in English, asking the GI for his name.

"Private Kurt Vonnegut," came the response.

"Ask Private Vonnegut where he's come from."

"Indianapolis. Indiana," he answered.

"No, no," said Rosa. "Where was he captured?"

Fritz asked, and the GI responded, leaving Fritz looking confused.

"What did he say?" asked Rosa.

"It doesn't make any sense. He said the Tralfamadorians captured him."

"Tralfamadorians?" she asked. "Who are they?"

"I think I've heard of them," said Gunter. "They're a Russian unit."

"If they're Russians, why are they here in Germany?"

Gunter shrugged.

"Ask him which unit he comes from."

Fritz asked, and the GI answered. "He says he is a scout from the 106th Infantry Division."

"Good. Ask him where he was captured and how he ended up here."

Fritz looked confused again. "He says he was captured here on earth and taken away, but they brought him back here at this moment in time as punishment."

Just as she thought Fritz's English was rusty, the GI spoke in German. "We all hide in here hoping to escape death but, in the end, Father Time finds us all, and every one of us in here will die, either today, tomorrow or in fifty years, which is only a blink away. And, so it goes."

Gunter, Fritz and Rosa returned to the boys.

"What did he say?" asked Peter.

"Nothing helpful," she replied.

Gunter made a circle with his finger at his temple. "He's gone, cuckoo."

They sat back down and waited for the bombing to stop with only their thoughts for company. The trip from Prague had been long and dangerous, but they hadn't even made it halfway to Berlin. Although the Hitler Youth had taught the boys to read maps, identify planes and handle weapons, her boys lacked common sense, especially when they were on the run. When lost, they asked the nearest person and had no clue how to respond if challenged. They were good honest boys, which made for poor liars. However, they did follow her without question or complaint, to their credit. She was their leader, and they were her boys. She was almost glad that she didn't cross the bridge without them.

# Chapter 13

## 14 February 1945 (Wednesday)

*Dresden, Slaughterhouse-5*

An hour after the Dresden bomb raid, certain there would be no more air raids, Rosa woke the boys. They left Slaughterhouse-5, and even though dawn was some hours away, the city was lit up from the firebombing as if it was the middle of the day. She looked over and saw that the military bridge had been destroyed, so they walked along the south bank of the river until they came to the Augustus Bridge, which, according to Fritz, was the oldest bridge in Dresden. The swollen river from the recent thaw and rain was a raging torrent of water, too dangerous to use a small dinghy as she'd hoped to do. She could see that using the River Elbe for transportation was not a real option for this time of year.

They walked unchallenged to the northern outskirts of Dresden. As dawn broke, they saw a man working on the back of a low flatbed trailer hooked to the back of a tractor. Rosa left the road and walked over to him.

"What are you doing?" asked Wolfgang.

"We need to find out if the Russians have invaded Germany."

The boys followed her to the old man. As they got closer, they could see that the rugged old man was throwing dead bodies into a massive, football-sized trench recently dug by a bulldozer, which was parked nearby.

"Does the Führer still live?" Rosa blurted out without really thinking.

The farmer stopped to stare at Rosa.

"What news of Budapest?" asked Wolfgang before Rosa could talk again.

The old man resumed working and whistled a loud solitary note. "The news is all bad, I'm afraid. Are you sure you boys want to know?"

They all nodded.

"Our boys tried breaking through, but it was all in vain." He looked up. "What day is it today?"

"The fourteenth," said Fritz. "Wednesday."

"A couple of days ago, Saturday, I think it was, the Russians took over Buda. And by all accounts, it was terrible for the survivors, especially for the Hungarian women. Since they took the city, the Russians have been on a looting and raping spree." The old man continued his tale of horror, the horror that could have been their fate. "Priceless works of art are being carted around in baby prams, while hundreds of thousands of Russians stand in line with their trousers wrapped around their ankles, waiting their turn at the Budapest women. Colonels are standing behind privates standing behind sergeants: rape doesn't know rank, especially in an army of communists."

The boys were stunned into silence, thinking about the awful fate awaiting their mothers and sisters still trapped inside Berlin.

Rosa thought about herself. Should she still go to Berlin? Would it be any different in Berlin than it was in Budapest? Perhaps she should abandon her plan and head westwards toward the Americans. She could let the boys continue on their own while she set off by herself. She wasn't scared of death, but she didn't want to become a victim like those poor women of Budapest.

"Dirty Commies," continued the old man, spitting for added effect. "Those who own nothing take everything." He grabbed a small dead child in each of his hands and threw them into the massive pit like a fisherman throwing dead fish into a killing bin. The boys looked down at the other charred children on the trailer. They stepped back in horrified realisation.

The old man didn't seem to notice the boys' revulsion at his grizzly task. He continued his non-stop chatting while he worked.

"Isn't it funny? Germans call Germany the Fatherland, and the Russians refer to Russia as the Motherland; yet, I wonder what either parent would think of the children they've both raised?"

"Old man, you seem to know a lot for a farmer," said Wolfgang sceptically.

"True. I'm only a farmer, but my son's a radio operator right here in Dresden. So, we get the latest news every night while having dinner. He told me that despite Hitler announcing Budapest as a Fortress City, which is code for dying to the last man, about 30,000 Germans still tried busting out of Buda, but the Russians mowed them all down. About five hundred lucky bastards got through. The highest-ranking surviving officer then radioed a report to Dresden, which was forwarded onto the Führer in a bunker somewhere underneath Berlin."

"Berlin? Is it safe?" Rosa asked.

The boys were desperate to hear news about their home.

He threw more charred children in the pit as he talked. "Ivan is at the Frankfurt-on-the-River-Spree as we speak, which is just a stone's throw from Berlin."

"It's all over then," said Peter.

"We wanted to get to Berlin before the Russians," Rosa said, answering the old man's questioning look.

"Well, son, Hitler has labelled the city as Fortress Frankfurt, for all the good it did Budapest. But the Russians still have to cross the Spree, which won't be easy. And when they do, the Führer has fortified the Seelow Heights. And Hitler has everyone in Berlin turning it into Fortress Berlin. So, you can probably still make it, but why on earth would you want to?"

"Because it's our home," said Peter.

"No, it's not," said the old man. "When were you there last?"

Peter looked at his comrades. "Our parents sent us away in the summer of '43." They nodded in agreement.

"You won't recognise it," said the man. "It's being bombed almost daily. Look at Dresden. This was her first major bombing in the war. Imagine the ruins of Dresden times a thousand nights and days of bombing."

"Old man, I think you'll need a bigger pit," said Wolfgang, looking at the near-full mass grave.

"The soldiers are coming here with their flame-throwers. Germany solves all her problems with fire." He picked up some black earth. "Russia comes to soil the soil of Germany, but she comes too late. They come to burn and pillage a failed crop."

They left the old farmer, who whistled as he continued tossing in the bodies. They had covered almost a thousand yards when they saw soldiers arriving, armed with flame-throwers to torch the contents of the hole.

"The old man is crazy," said Wolfgang.

"Who won't end up mad after this crazy mixed-up war?" answered Peter.

They continued walking in silence, soaking in the shocking news about Berlin and the fate they'd avoided in Budapest. But what would be good news now, she wondered. Perhaps, the only news that any of them could hope and pray for was the announcement of Germany's surrender or Hitler's death or both.

They walked through a small village, where some reflected light caught Rosa's eye. The building was half destroyed, and bombs had cleanly removed the roof. The morning sun shone directly on the shop floor. She walked over to it. It was a bicycle shop, or it used to be. And despite the damage, several of the bikes seemed perfectly fine.

"Okay, boys, pick a bike. Our walking days are over."

They stared at her. "We can't steal them."

"Gunter, you seem to have no problem with stealing food. What's the difference?"

Gunter went up to the shop's front door and worked the doorknob. "It's locked."

She walked through the open window casing, which had been smashed in the raid. The boys laughed at Gunter. She grabbed a bike.

"Rudi, you can't ride a girl's bike," said Peter.

"Why not? A bike's a bike, isn't it?"

"But boys don't ride a girls' bicycle," he said.

"Yeah. That's just stupid," said Hans.

"A bike's a bike. Besides, I don't think the bike knows whether it's a boy or girl bike," said Rosa, taking her girls' bike out into the street.

The other boys raced inside to pick up their bikes.

Peter grabbed some boys, and they went into the rear workshop and found spare tubes, tire repair kits and tire pumps. Peter seemed to be an expert. Gunter grabbed a push-bike that had a side cart attached.

Soon enough, the boys were riding down the deserted autobahn from Dresden to Berlin, having the entire highway to themselves; no one, not even refugees, were heading into or out of Berlin. They popped wheelies, riding their brand-new bikes without a care. They were regular boys out enjoying a weekend ride together, laughing as they zigged and zagged among each other, pretending to be a fighter squadron of Messerschmitts mowing down British Spitfires, making fighter engine and machine gun noises. Even in war, these boys were play-acting war.

As for Rosa, the bikes only reminded her of the morning before her father was incarcerated in Cologne, where they'd been chased by a group of boys on bikes. The years hadn't eased her guilt. If anything, it had only strengthened. She forced herself to think about other things—the journey ahead towards her father. With young legs on brand new bikes on an empty autobahn, nothing stopped them from getting into Berlin now. They'd be there by the end of the week.

The familiar wailing sirens of Dresden snapped Rosa out of her thoughts.

They all stopped and lined up to look back in the direction of the city. They could no longer see Dresden, but they could see the smoke still smouldering from last night's fires.

They saw the bombs rain down in broad daylight and could hear the devastating bomb blasts do their work.

A fighter plane flew overhead.

"A Russian fighter, probably gone to check out the city and report back to Stalin," said Wolfgang. "They fly so low they can read the highway signs for directions."

"Come on, let's go," Rosa said. "We're losing daylight."

They peddled onwards. Suddenly, a Russian fighter—presumably, the same one they saw earlier—exploded from the treetops on the side of the autobahn and fired a gun burst at the group. They dropped their bikes and raced for the trees.

The Russian fighter circled back and fired another burst at their bicycles before heading east towards Poland.

The boys emerged from the tree line and looked at their bikes. Most had escaped damage, but a few of the bicycles had been machine-gunned to shreds. Rosa went over to the gully and looked down at the mangled, bloody mess of what was left of the Muller brothers and their blood-splattered bikes.

The boys noticed Rosa looking into the gully.

"Don't come over here!" she shouted, raising her arm. "Stay where you are. Grab what's left of our bikes and let's go. We're sitting ducks on this highway of death."

## Chapter 14

Mid-March 1945

*Somewhere south-west of Berlin*

When the squad left the smooth bitumen roads of the autobahn, their bikes deteriorated fast. Wolfgang, who turned out to be good with his hands, struggled to keep up with the constant flat and bent tires and broken bike chains. Eventually, as they lost working bikes, it forced them to double each other until, finally, the bikes succumbed, and they had to be abandoned altogether. But Wolfgang had been able to fashion a small handcart from Gunter's sidecar. It took two people to move it: one to push it and another to pull it. All took their turns pulling the cart as it was vital—it held all their food and water.

Rosa and the boys walked along the dusty dirt road. The sun was quite intense for this early springtime, but winter had come early and had ended early too. They all wore their German caps, and most had their shirts unbuttoned, while Wolfgang took off his shirt, sunning himself as he walked. Peter wore his lucky red handkerchief around his neck to catch his sweat. Most of them had long since discarded their helmets as useless extra weight, but Fritz and Wolfgang clipped theirs to their rucksacks.

Peter waited for Rosa to catch up to him. "Rudi, we need to get out of the sun and find some water," he said.

She looked around and saw a barn on the horizon. She pointed to it. "There."

They walked closer to the barn and noticed it was in the centre of a sunflower field. It was amazing. The children were dazzled as they walked through the bright rows of yellow flowers.

Rosa picked a flower and looked at it while she walked. She

thought about her version of 'Little Rosa Riding Hood: The Wolf Slayer' then said to herself, "I've picked my own path."

As they approached the barn, Charlie stopped. A German officer was leaning against a nook in the wooden fence made of saplings. Something about him looked odd. The squad could see that the motionless man wore a pilot's outfit with a matching helmet. But the man seemed to be staring at the ground.

Rosa edged closer until she saw the pilot's face, which was missing—his face was wholly gone. The man's grotesque unblinking eyeballs made her belly twist and churn in revulsion. She turned to the boys and motioned for them to hurry past. They all tiptoed past this gruesome human scarecrow.

They rounded the other side of the building and stood in front of an open-aired barn—a perfect place to hole up for the night.

"I didn't see any plane wreckage," said Wolfgang.

"He must have parachuted, and then he walked here and rested against the fence until he died still standing," Fritz said, speculating.

They dumped their stuff and collapsed onto the straw covering the floor of the barn.

"I'm so sick of walking," said Gunter. "I can't take another step."

"Where are we?" asked Hans.

"Rudi has no idea where we are, do you?" snapped Wolfgang.

"No, I don't," she said.

"It's not Rudi's fault," said Peter. "It was the right thing to do to get off the autobahn."

"But, since then, we've kept to the backroads, and now we are completely lost."

"Wolfgang, you are right. But we have been heading north, so we are getting closer to Berlin," she said, pointing to the mountains nearby. "Who knows? Berlin could be on the other side of that mountain,"

"I keep telling you all, it's the Hartz Mountains," said Hans. "We want to head north, yet the roads keep going northwest. And the Hartz Mountains are south-east of Berlin."

"I keep telling you the Hartz mountains are west of Berlin," said a clearly frustrated Fritz.

"If we are in the Harz Mountains, how far are we from Berlin?" asked Wolfgang.

"The village of Harz is about 250 km west of Berlin," answered Fritz.

"Well, let's hope we aren't in the Harz mountains," said a deflated Rosa.

"Water!" yelled Gunter, pointing to a stream about a hundred yards away.

They ran to it and drank greedily. The cold mountain water worked like nectar and revitalised their fading spirits.

Refreshed, the boys were ready for fun. They tied Wolfgang and Fritz's helmets together to make a steel ball and used their shirts as goalposts. After the three Muller brothers had been gunned down, the squad was reduced to seven, and with Fritz refereeing, it was three against three: shirts versus skins. Rosa was the captain of the shirts, and Gunter, eating some bread, was their goalie. Wolfgang was captain of the skins, determined to win, and belted the steel football with his steel-capped army boots. He scored first.

Rosa, keen to put Wolfgang in his place, was the next to score. The boys all came up and hugged her and smacked her bum in appreciation of her excellent football skills. Rosa wasn't prepared for this and had to remind herself that she was just a boy playing football with other boys, something she'd long wished for before the war.

Soon after that, she scored again, but this time she was ready for the hugging and butt-smacking. She found herself hugging Peter a little longer than she meant to. After that second celebration, Rosa was most determined to score some more goals. Rosa scored, and Peter was the first teammate to race up and hug her. Rosa kissed Peter on the mouth. Everyone stopped cheering. She'd forgotten that she was meant to be a boy for a moment.

"That's how we celebrate a goal in Bavaria," said Rosa.

Gunter yelled out from the goalposts, "I told you them Bavarians are cuckoo!"

Peter scored next, and Wolfgang argued with Fritz that Peter was offside. Fritz, with his annoying way, dismissed the protest. Wolfgang went up to Peter and punched him. Without thinking, Rosa went up to Wolfgang and kneed him in the balls. Wolfgang dropped and sprawled out like a sack of crushed nuts. Fritz red-carded her and ordered her off the field. She sat cross-legged and arms folded for the remainder of the game. Shirts held out, mainly because nothing could get past Gunter.

After the game finished, they raced to the nearby stream, stripped off all their clothes, and jumped into the icy cold water.

"Any colder, and my willy will fall off," shouted Gunter.

"Rudi, aren't you coming in?" Peter asked. "I better warn you; it'll freeze your balls off."

Too late, she thought. "No. I'm fine."

"Why not?"

"I can't swim."

All the boys stood up in the water, indicating it was only thigh-deep. Blushing, she got up and left the naked boys to their fun. As she walked back to the barn, she knew that she had been lucky so far to keep her true identity hidden. But she also knew that the longer it took them to get to Berlin, the greater the chances of her secret being discovered. She didn't know how the boys would react if they found out she was a girl, and a Gypsy girl at that.

Rosa saw that the loft was ideal as a bed. The straw would make do as a mattress. She went back down the ladder and pulled a large canvas off a farm machine, which she wanted to use to cover the straw. In doing so, she revealed an old light-blue tractor. By this time, the boys had joined her.

"Hans. What do you think?" Rosa asked. "Is it still working?"

"It has to be," said Hans. "The farmer didn't plant this sunflower field by hand."

"Check it out and see if it works."

Once he'd reconnected the battery, the tractor roared into life. The boys cheered. Hans powered up the engine. "The gauge says the tank is full, but we need to see if we can find some more fuel."

Gunter was standing next to a large forty-gallon drum. He twisted the top off and smelled the contents. He screwed his nose. "Sorry, that's not petrol."

"What is it?" asked Hans.

"I don't know, Hans, but it smells awful," Gunter replied. "Like tar."

Hans nudged Gunter over and smelled the contents. "It's synthetic fuel, derived from coal. Used primarily for military vehicles and farm machinery, like tractors."

The boys cheered again. This was turning out to be a great day.

That night, around the campfire, Rosa told them bedtime stories. "And what's the moral of *Little Red Riding Hood*?"

Silence.

"Don't mess with women and children; otherwise, you'll get your head chopped off," said Gunter.

They all laughed.

"We have to go to bed," she said.

"Aww!"

"Just one more story, Rudi," they pleaded.

"Okay," Rosa said. "Just a quick one." Another favourite book of hers was about Greek fables. "This one is from Hesiod, called *The Wolf and the Lamb*. Has anyone heard of it?"

A lone arm was raised.

"I mean, anyone *besides* Fritz?"

They all shook their heads.

"One day, a wolf went to drink from a river when he came across a lamb already drinking there. He couldn't just gobble up the lamb without good reason, so the wolf moved downstream from the lamb and drank from the river. 'By standing upstream from me you have soiled my drinking water,' said the wolf. The lamb apologised and moved back onto dry land. The wolf looked at the lamb and said,

'I remember you now. A year ago, you disparaged both my mother and father'. Since he was only a few weeks old, the lamb reasoned that he wasn't even alive a year ago. The wolf moved closer to the lamb. 'You have the same white wool as the other lamb, the same dark evil eyes as the other lamb, and the same long tail as the other lamb'. Therefore, reasoning all lambs are as evil as each other, the wolf gobbled up the lamb," she said, finishing the story. "What's the moral of the story?"

There was a confused silence as they looked at each other.

Gunter finally ventured a response. "It's better to be the wolf than the lamb?"

"Do you think the lamb had the choice of being a wolf?" asked Fritz.

"I guess not," said Gunter.

"Don't trust a wolf?" said somebody.

"A hungry wolf is not to be trusted," said somebody else.

"A tyrant will always blame the innocent to justify being a tyrant," said an irritated Fritz.

And with his tone, Fritz killed the mood.

They climbed up to the loft, with Charlie next to Rosa. Gunter went to sleep on the other side of her.

"No. Gunter," she said.

"Why not?"

"Because you fart in your sleep."

"I do not?"

"How would you know? You're asleep at the time. You go sleep down at the far end."

Gunter complied.

Peter moved to sleep next to her.

Peter said, "Rudi, guess how old Gunter is?"

"Don't say anything," said Gunter.

"I assumed he's the same as the rest of us. Fifteen?"

"Nope," said Peter. "Tell him, Gunter; otherwise, Rudi won't believe me if I say it."

"I'm twenty," said Gunter.

"Twenty? Impossible. How?"

"My father changed my birth certificate, and when we moved to Berlin, he enrolled me in another school where nobody knew us."

"But you don't look twenty."

"Puberty didn't hit me until I was eighteen. I inherited it from my mother, who didn't hit puberty until she was seventeen. She is a small woman, and she couldn't have any more children after me. At the same time, my father is a giant and was in the army in the first war. He told me some men are natural soldiers, but I wasn't, so he risked everything for me. I owe it to them to find my father and mother."

"Hans. You said your father was a farmer. I don't think the city of Berlin has too many farms."

They laughed.

"We had a beautiful small farm about a hundred kilometres north of Berlin, but one day these officials came along and requisitioned our farm for the war effort. They gave my father a pittance for it and then sent him to Berlin to work in some factory, again for the war effort. But my father couldn't help himself. We lived on the top floor, so he made his little farm on the roof of our building. He grew all these vegetables, which we sold to neighbours to help us get by during the war. My father could grow anything anywhere, as my mother always used to say."

Thinking about their families, they went to sleep.

During the middle of the night, Rosa awoke needing to relieve herself. Peter had wrapped his arms over her. It gave her a chill—the pleasant kind. She gently moved his arm and made her way outside.

She was squatting down peeing when little Charlie stumbled outside to relieve himself. He stopped to see her crouching down. She finished and stood next to him and grabbed Charlie by his arm.

"You can't tell anybody, Charlie."

He shook his head.

She pulled at his arm. "Understand?"

Charlie nodded.

They returned to bed without a word. As soon as she got back, Peter rolled back over and cuddled her. She didn't remove the arm that embraced her.

The following morning, they awoke to a scream. They jumped out of bed in their underwear and raced to the source of the terrifying scream—Gunter was standing at the front of the barn, next to the fence.

"What's wrong?" asked Peter.

"He's gone," said Gunter, pointing to the fence.

"Who's gone?"

"The human scarecrow who was leaning against the post yesterday when we arrived."

"The gruesome golem," said Fritz.

"What happened to him? Did someone take away his body during the night?"

"No," said Fritz. "We would have heard them."

They looked at Rosa for answers. She shrugged.

Wolfgang walked over to the spot and looked down at the soft dirt. "By his footprints, he walked here and then walked away in that direction," he said, pointing to the way that they had arrived at the barn.

"What? How can a dead man walk?" asked Gunter.

"He wasn't dead, Gunter," said Rosa. "He probably stopped for a rest and leaned against the post and fell asleep when we arrived."

"Sleep? But he didn't have a face," said Gunter. "No eyelids. How could he sleep?"

"With great difficulty, I imagine. But we all need to sleep even without eyelids."

"But he would have heard us playing football. Why didn't he come to us for help?"

"Because we're children. What could we do?" she answered. "And he probably didn't want to freak us out any more than we are now." She headed back to the barn. "Come on. We need to go."

After breakfast, they used the barn's pulley, chains and rope to hoist the fuel drum onto the small platform attached to the back of the tractor. They piled on as Hans drove the tractor further into the mountains.

***

They came to an intersection. At one corner, there were signs stipulating that this road was strictly verboten. Rosa could see this dirt road had not been used in a long time. She pointed down the forbidden road, and Hans agreed. The boys looked uneasy, but she knew that they also wanted to find out why this unassuming road in the middle of nowhere was out of bounds.

The tractor puffed and spluttered some hours later and made one final cough before the engine died. They had used up all the fuel in the spare drum.

"That's it," Hans said. "We're out of fuel."

"Where are we?" Gunter asked.

They looked around at the small village nearby It seemed deserted.

"Why would they leave?" Peter asked

"Boys," said Rosa. "Spread out and look for food, fuel or another way out of here and find out exactly where *here* is."

The boys wandered through the ghost town and found a store of food in some of the open shops. They raced back to tell Rosa. She told them to keep searching for anything useful.

Rosa and Charlie entered a store. In the corner an assortment of toys. There was a little toy bear. She picked it up and gave it to Charlie. "Here's a present for you, Charlie, for being a good boy, for keeping my secret."

Charlie beamed with pride, holding his new prize.

She pulled out her Luger pistol. "Put this in your rucksack. I know you don't like guns but things are only going to get worse from here on in, and you need to be able to protect yourself."

He nodded and put the pistol into his rucksack.

"Charlie, where are your parents?"

He looked around and picked up a toy steel train. He pushed it forward and then tipped it over, crashing it.

"They're both dead? From a train crash?"

He nodded twice.

"You don't have any family?"

He shook his head to signify that he was alone in the world.

She knelt next to him. "Yes, you do. I'm your family now. I'm your big sister, understand?"

His smile showed that he did.

"I know my father will love you, just like I do," she said, smiling. "I'm so sorry for throwing that rock at you back at the bridge. I thought you'd be safer with the boys than with me. I always wished I had a brother or sister, and I couldn't wish for a better one than you. You don't talk back for one thing."

They hugged.

Peter rushed into the store. "Wolfgang's found something."

The boys followed Peter up a path. When they rounded a bend, they came to a large metal frame standing in the centre of a cement circle covered in black soot.

"What's that for?"

"I have no idea, but look," Peter said, pointing to the big cave entrance on the far side of the structure. They caught sight of Wolfgang entering the cave.

Rosa and Peter ran over and followed Wolfgang. Once inside the massive cave, they realised that the floors had been cemented, and lights hung from the ceiling. The cave was natural, but the Germans had built a large complex within it.

By the time the other boys caught up to him, Wolfgang had found a generator and started it, turning on the lights. "I think it's a secret research facility," said Wolfgang. "There are plans and scientific papers everywhere and metal lying about with strange-looking tools."

"What were they researching?" Gunter asked.

They turned to Fritz, who shrugged.

"Is there anybody here?" asked Rosa.

"Not that I can tell," answered Wolfgang. "It looks like they took off in a hurry."

"The question is, where did they go?" Rosa wondered out loud. "Maybe we can follow their way out of here?

"This cave is enormous," said Fritz. "It's a massive labyrinth, with caves leading deeper into the mountain."

"Rudi! Rudi!"

She turned as Hans raced up to her.

"You won't believe what I've found."

"What is it?"

"You'll see," he said.

Rosa, Charlie, Wolfgang, Peter, Gunter and Fritz followed Hans. Another part of the cave opened into a large cavern above them; they stopped and stared at a giant black and white rocket standing there.

"It's a spaceship!" said Gunter excitedly. "It looks just like a spaceship from the pages of a *Flash Gordon* comic."

Wolfgang clipped Gunter under the ear. "That's not a spaceship, you idiot. It's a V2 rocket. One of Hitler's wonder weapons. He fills it with explosives and aims it toward France and England."

"The structure we saw outside must have been a launchpad," Peter added.

"I've seen a V1, but I've never seen a V2 before," said Gunter. "Not in real life; I didn't realise how big they are,"

The other boys were equally awestruck. A research facility inside a mountain was incredible, but the rocket was a man-made marvel.

Rosa heard a noise behind her and saw a pair of eyes hiding in the darkness of a nook in the cave wall. She approached the frightened eyes, and when she got close enough, she flicked on her torch and could see that the eyes belonged to a boy about her age. He was dressed in black-striped white pyjamas. He backed away from her.

"Do you speak German?" she asked.

The boy, who was wearing a matching cap, nodded.

"Are there others like you?"

"Yes."

"If you go outside this cave, you will find a small town full of food."

He backed away as Peter joined them. "Who is he?"

"I think he's a prisoner who must have worked here."

"He's so skinny."

"I know. I told him there's food in town, but I don't think he believes me."

"Why not?"

"Because of our uniforms." She turned to the boy. "Trust me. The Americans have come."

The boy's eyes brightened. "Americans? They are here?"

"They will be soon. That's why this place is empty. And we're trying to leave as well. Can you help us get out of here?"

Rosa understood the boy was too frightened to say no, but clearly, he had no desire to help his jailors. It didn't matter; she had to help the children inside the cave and find food for them in town. She went back to her boys.

"Take off your jackets and rucksacks and hats," she said, unbuttoning her military jacket.

They looked at her.

"We have to get the children out of this cave; otherwise, they will die in here. They're frightened of us. Take off your gear."

"But they will attack us?" said Gunter.

"Take off your gear now!"

The boys removed their webbing, jackets and knapsacks.

"Okay, go into each tunnel and tell them the Americans are here waiting outside for them. Now go!"

The boys ran into each tunnel, yelling that the Americans were here and to go outside. Wolfgang stood next to the pile of clothing and equipment.

"Wolfgang? What are you doing?"

"I'm protecting our equipment; someone has to. They could kill us all."

"What if they did?"

"What?" Wolfgang said, surprised.

"After how we've treated them, would you blame them?" she said.

Wolfgang looked fiercely into her eyes, but then his expression softened. Probably, deep down, he realised that she was right. He removed his webbing and took off his jacket. Together, Wolfgang and Rosa ran down another tunnel, yelling out, "The Americans have come!"

The promise of Americans worked its magic, and soon the tunnels were full of ghostly white skeletons, all wearing striped pyjamas. The city of the dead had mobilised as the boys pointed the way towards the main entrance, herding the bewildered former prisoners towards the brilliant sunlight. But they stopped at the entrance, refusing to leave their underworld.

Gunter looked bewildered. "Why aren't they leaving?"

Rosa ran out into the sunshine and pointed, "Americans! Americans! Americans!"

The striped ghosts left the cavernous underworld saying, "Americans! Americans! Americans!" It was as if they were saying, "Freedom! Freedom! Freedom!" They amassed around the massive rocket launchpad, allowing their eyes to adjust to the bright sunshine.

She spoke to several of the older prisoners. "Follow that path. It leads to a deserted village. There is plenty of food and water there, but don't overeat; otherwise, you will get sick and die. The Americans are coming."

As the pyjama army headed down the path, Rosa ran back into

the tunnel where, to her surprise, the boys stood with their arms raised. The boy she had spoken to earlier was holding a machine pistol.

Tears streamed from his eyes. "For my family," he said. "I will kill you."

She walked up to him. "Kill me if you have to, but let them go. Besides, where are we going to run to? We're trapped in these mountains without a way out."

Her words confused him as he aimed the barrel of his weapon at her belly. "I am a Jew, not a murderer like the people who killed my family," he said, dropping the weapon.

"We don't want to kill anybody. We just want to get home."

"Follow me," said the boy. "I know a way out of these mountains. I watched them leave."

They followed their bare-footed guide. They eventually came to a platform next to train tracks. There were train wagons but no locomotive.

The guide pointed at the tracks away from the platform. "Berlin."

"Thank you," she said, pausing. "What is your name?"

"My name is Solomon."

"Thank you, Solomon. You were very kind to bring us here."

Solomon looked as if he was about to cry.

"I know it probably means nothing, but I'm sorry for what's happened to you," she said. "The war is almost over. Trust me. Solomon, we have to go. We have a long walk back to Berlin."

Solomon's eyes lit up. He raced over to the end of the platform and pointed. They joined him and looked down at what he was pointing at.

"Thank you so very much," said Rosa as she waved goodbye to Solomon.

\*\*\*

The three handcars sailed along the train tracks. The gradual declining slope towards Berlin meant that all they had to do was keep clear of the crank handles, which were see-sawing up and down at a rapid rate. Rosa was on the first car with Charlie and Peter. Wolfgang and Hans were in the next car behind them. Then came Gunter and Fritz on the final rail cart and their restocked supplies. These rail tracks seemed to have no destination other than Berlin since they hadn't passed through a single village or town since leaving the caves. She didn't know how far they'd travelled, but she felt sure that they would be in Berlin in no time.

After several hours of descending eastward towards Berlin, they crested a rise in the tracks and picked up speed as the angle became steeper. In the distance, she saw they were headed towards a bridge, but, as they got closer, she could see that bombs had destroyed it. She stood on the brake pedal, and the cart began to slow down. BANG! She saw metal fly off the side into the dirt.

She yelled out. "The brakes have gone!"

The boys turned to look at the great chasm on the far side of the bridge. Peter grabbed their backpacks and weapons and threw them to the side of the train tracks. She looked behind them. Wolfgang's cart was already slowing down.

"We have to jump off before we get to the bridge!" Peter yelled to all on board.

Peter jumped. Rosa looked at Charlie, who was staring at the tracks ahead. He was too terrified to jump, and he didn't seem to hear her. She couldn't get to him because the hand-pumps were going up and down so wildly that they could have done her actual harm. She kept shouting at Charlie, and Charlie kept ignoring her. In no time, the handcart was across the bridge and sailed off the edge. She watched Charlie jump clear the same time she did. She, Charlie and the rail car splashed simultaneously into the water.

She held her breath, swimming back up to the jagged light above her. Something hit her head. She was dazed. She inhaled, but all she did was breathe in water. A hand reached out and grabbed hers.

Darkness.

Some hands were pulling her out.

Darkness.

The same hands fumbled at her mouth, and the air was being forced into her by another mouth. Peter's mouth.

Darkness.

Peter's hands fumbled at her shirt.

Darkness.

She could hear a voice in the distance—Gunter's voice. "Rudi has breasts!"

Darkness.

\*\*\*

Rosa stormed down the road, dripping wet, heading away from the destroyed bridge, holding Charlie's hand. She looked down at him. "Are they still following us?"

Charlie looked behind them and nodded, his little feet working twice as fast as hers.

Once they came to the intersection at the end of the long road, she stopped and turned to the squad of boys who were hurrying to keep up with her and Charlie.

"Why are you following me?" she yelled. "I told you all to go to hell!"

"We're all headed to Berlin, just like you," said Peter.

"Take that road," she said, indicating the major road going to the left. "Me and Charlie will find our own way down this one," she added, pointing to the one going right.

She turned and kept walking.

Rosa and Charlie had stormed another hundred yards past the intersection when the previous scene played out again.

"Why are you still following me? I told you, follow that road behind you."

Peter stepped forward. "Because you're still our leader, and we all want to get to Berlin alive."

"What about him?" she said, pointing at Wolfgang. "He's been a thorn in my side the whole way."

Wolfgang moved beside Peter. "I just knew there was something wrong with you. No one in the Hitler Youth could know so little as you. But I still don't understand, even the League of German Girls get taught military procedures."

"Girl or not, you have gotten us this far," Peter said.

"If I didn't have you along to slow me down, I'd be in Berlin already. I kept telling myself that you'd become useful once we got to Berlin. But I now know that was a delusion. You will continue to drag me down."

"We promise to keep up, Rudi," said Fritz.

"Rosa," she said, correcting him. "My name is Rosa. And to answer Wolfgang's question, I'm not a German League Girl—"

"—The League of German Girls," Fritz corrected her.

"Whatever!" Rosa said. "I'm saying that I'm not just any girl. I'm a Romani."

Gunter raised his arm. "What's a Romani?"

"That means I'm a Gypsy!"

"Oh," replied Gunter, dropping his hand.

"We don't care," said Peter.

"Your parents seemed to care because they locked us Gypsies up because we were so dangerous."

Her words struck a chord deep within, and she was overcome with emotion about her parents. Rosa loved her father and missed her mother, regretting how badly she had treated Martha.

She turned around and went another hundred yards, spun and shouted at them.

"I'm sick of you slowing me down. Anyone who drops behind me, I will leave behind. Do you understand?"

Gunter was slow catching up to her, as per usual, hauling his cart with its annoying creaking wheel.

"Gunter! You've got to fix that goddamn creaky wheel, as I've already told you to do a thousand times."

"Yes, Rudi! I mean Rosa!"

# Chapter 15

## 2 April 1945 (Monday)

*Outside the western outskirts of Berlin*

S everal weeks after leaving Prague, they finally arrived in Berlin, wishing they hadn't. Walking through the pulverised city, it felt as if they were walking among Roman ruins rather than their nation's capital. It was a skeleton of a once-grand city: broken-boned buildings jutting out from the rubble, bled of all its lifeblood, covered with cement-grey dust. The German capital had received its capital punishment, the death penalty by bombing, for committing crimes against humanity. Once the jewel of Prussia, Berlin, with the insides of its buildings spewing out onto the streets, was no more.

"This is metrocide," said Fritz.

The squad looked at their England-educated comrade.

"The murder of a city," Fritz explained.

"What do you expect?" said Rosa. "Hitler started it against all the cities of Europe. This city is where it has to end."

The squad walked along in a horrified silence in the city of their birthplace. Rosa had learned that these boys, whose parents knew that they were useless at war, had bribed the local Hitler Youth commander to keep them out of the war for as long as possible. Berlin had seen the very occasional air raid at the beginning of the war, but it wasn't until January of '43 that the Allied air force started attacking the German capital in earnest. It wasn't long after this when their parents arranged for their sons to serve in a quiet, safer part of the Third Reich, where they finally ended up serving under Director Riefenstahl as armed guards. But they hadn't been back here for over two years, and now it was as if they were strangers in their hometown.

Since arriving in Berlin, Rosa had seen several streets littered with large cement blocks. "What are they?" she asked, pointing to them as they walked by a small side street.

"They are called Dragon's Teeth," said Gunter.

"They're for blocking tanks and funnelling troops into lines of heavy machine-gun fire," Fritz explained.

"Those Dragon's Teeth won't stop a tank," said Rosa.

"It'll slow them down, or force them to manoeuvre slowly around them" said Wolfgang, "Enough to get in close to launch a Panzerfaust or tank-killer."

"That's not all," said Gunter. "They'll have tank mines that will blow up a tank from its weakest side, its underbelly."

"German 88mm artillery pieces are also great at taking out tanks at up to one or two km, as well," Fritz added.

"You know all this, yet how come you can't tell us where we are?" she asked them.

"It's not the Berlin any of us remember," Peter said. "It looks familiar, like an aunt or uncle you haven't seen in years, but this is not the Berlin that we once called home."

Peter was right. Even though the boys were in their hometown, they were clueless. Without street signs or major suburban landmarks, navigation was all but impossible. While some signs had been destroyed, clearly several others had been deliberately painted over or removed by the Germans to disorientate their attackers. Gunter had been able to identify the patch of earth where his father's restaurant and their home on the floor above had been. Not only was it gone, but it was evident, by the way the area had been cleared away, that it had been gone for quite some time. And Gunter's missing home wasn't the only one.

Rosa felt sorry for them all, especially Fritz and Gunter. In another time and place, she knew Gunter would have been a world-class chef. And Fritz could have been a professor or a scientist.

Rosa and the squad crossed over one of Berlin's many canal bridges with debris strewn everywhere. They waited on the other side of the bridge for Gunter, who struggled to pull their modified handcart full of supplies. He tried pushing it up to the crest of the bridge. Fritz and Hans ran back to help Gunter with the handcart as it seemed to be caught on a wire strung across the bridge. With a heave from the three boys on the bridge, the wire snapped, and Rosa saw the wire pull a latch attached to the bridge railing.

BANG!

The air was sucked from their lungs. Lying down, covered in cement dust and with ringing in their ears, Rosa and the three remaining boys tried to stand. They slowly oriented themselves. The ringing in Rosa's ears dissipated. In front of them was a bridge cut in two. She looked into the water: nothing. Fritz, Hans and Gunter were all gone as if they'd been vapourised.

As the ringing subsided and the enormity of what had just happened hit her, Rosa yelled out. "It's all my fault! I've led all of you into this death trap just so you boys could help find my father. My mother was right, I'm so selfish. I never think of others."

"Rosa, it's not your fault," said Peter walking over to her, standing her up to check her for any injuries.

Rosa pushed Peter away from her. "Get away from me. I'll get you killed too. And I can't have that on my conscience too."

Peter came back and grabbed her arm. "If it wasn't for you, we all would have been killed in Budapest months ago. We all said that we'd rather die here along with our friends and family rather than a place we've never been to like Fortress Budapest. This is war where death lurks around every corner with every step we take. This is not like one of your fairy tales where we can magically be spirited away to a safe place. Where is it safe? Prague? Budapest? Dresden? There is nowhere safe. We are in the middle of a war, and we need you now more than ever."

With those final words, she knew he was right. She could feel sorry for herself later, and only if she lived. It'd taken months to get to Berlin. And now she was here she couldn't give up on finding her father. Little Red Riding Hood would never give up on saving her grandmother from wolves. And wasn't Berlin just another wolf to defeat, perhaps the biggest? Her father had always said that death was a natural part of life, and she had seen so much death, especially since the war began that she'd become numb to it or at least she thought she had.

Besides, Peter was right, where was she going to go?

She looked at her remaining squad: Peter, Charlie and Wolfgang, who were still in shock. "We're on our own now. Do you know where we are?" she said, trying to get them moving before someone came to investigate the cause of the explosion.

Wolfgang and Peter nodded. They led the way, with Rosa and Charlie following.

Soon enough, they came to a building where the front had just slid off into the street, exposing the interior, so it looked like it was a massive dollhouse with furniture and paintings all perfectly in place. Peter and Wolfgang seemed to recognise the items on display.

"I knew it!" shouted an angry Wolfgang. "I told you it was a waste of time coming back here," he said, shoving Peter onto the ground.

"And going to Budapest was a better option?" Peter said, getting up and retaliating in kind.

Wolfgang punched Peter. Peter launched himself onto Wolfgang as they rolled in the dust and dirt. Rosa and Charlie tried to break them up.

"Hands up!" ordered a voice from behind.

They all stopped, turning to the source of the order. It was a small group of teenaged Hitler Youth. She recognised the leader instantly. It was Klaus, the boy who attacked her in the barn, or had tried to. He was wearing a cap, but she could tell who it was by his murderous eyes, which didn't seem to recognise her. She kept her face down just in case.

"Klaus?" said Wolfgang.

"Wolfgang?"

"Yes."

"Wolfgang, how did you get here?"

"It's a long story. But we just arrived."

"You're lucky," said Klaus. "I've heard that we're only a week, perhaps days, from being encircled by the Soviets."

"What day is today?" asked Peter.

"Monday," replied Klaus.

"What's the date? We've been on the road for so many weeks now we've lost track of time," Peter said, answering Klaus' questioning look.

"It's the second of April," said Klaus.

"April?"

"The Soviets just entered Austria a few days ago," said one of Klaus' boys.

"Shut up," said Klaus to his friend. "Stop listening to enemy propaganda. It's all lies." He looked at Wolfgang. "How did you get in? The Führer has declared Berlin a fortress, and that was back in February."

Wolfgang gave a sideways glance at Rosa. "It wasn't easy: tunnels, sewers, ditches, and the cover of night. But, in the end, it wasn't that hard sneaking past old men and children."

Klaus looked disgusted. "You're right," he said. "Old men hobbled together from other countries, failed countries, the countries we invaded. Why don't you come with us?" He indicated his cohort.

"Who?"

"We call ourselves Werewolves. We are the real defenders of Berlin. And we will never surrender. Never. Wolfgang, come with us, and we'll avenge your family."

Wolfgang grabbed his stuff and said, "Why not, especially since I no longer have a family."

"What about your friends? We can use all the manpower we can get," asked Klaus.

Wolfgang looked at Rosa, Peter and Charlie and laughed. "Leave them be. Together they don't even make half a man."

Klaus shrugged indifferently at the three of them, as Wolfgang was clearly a Klaus-prized asset. Their former strongman and Mr Fixit walked away with his newly adopted squad of Werewolves.

Rosa couldn't believe it was April already. It had taken them more than three months to get here from Prague when she naively thought it would only take a few weeks at most. Was she already too late to rescue her father?

\*\*\*

Night had come, and they still hadn't found a safe hideout. All basements and enclosures had been occupied by the resident Berliners, who had taken on a mole-like existence, living in holes, hiding their entrances, building escape holes, fending off other hole-stealing-moles to the death, forcing the three of them closer to the frontlines. The frontlines seemed to move like the ocean's tides, which ebbed and flowed with Stalin's attacking and retreating soldiers, testing for weak points in the Berlin fortress.

The Russian tide had just gone back out again with the German counterattack. They could still smell the cordite-fuelled gunfire lingering in the air. They stumbled into a room of a dead family; the Soviets had executed the elderly grandparents, attacking their teenage granddaughter, who had been raped. She lay naked with her middle covered in her own blood.

One of the girl's eyes was gouged out, and although swollen, the remaining eye opened slightly. "Please, kill me," she begged.

They jumped. She was still alive?

Rosa looked at the stricken girl, who was close to death and shook her head. Back at Salzburg, Rosa feared Berliners as wolf-like monsters, beasts that walked on their hindquarters. But here she was now, staring at a Berliner, one whose face looked precisely like Rosa's—a girl of fifteen or sixteen. Rosa had forgotten that she was a Berliner herself, but it was a fact that was not lost on her at this very moment.

"Please," said the girl, looking at Rosa's leather holster.

Rosa pulled the pistol out, stepping over to the girl who was beyond any medical care, especially in a demolished city, which was in the midst of dying itself. Rosa cocked the luger, flicked off the safety catch, and placed the weapon in the girl's hand.

The girl cried a bloody tear. "Thank you," she whispered.

Rosa stood, wheeled around and went to join Peter and Charlie, but before she had walked thirty paces, a shot rang out behind her.

Peter looked at Rosa and her empty holster. "You know we don't have a weapon between us now?"

"It hasn't gone anywhere. You can go in there and take it from her."

But no one wanted to leave the dead girl defenceless, not again.

\*\*\*

The next morning, in the early rising sun, the trio went out and tried to find a map or at least try to establish where they were. But, more importantly, they needed to find some food, as they had lost nearly all their rations and supplies when the cart blew up on the bridge along with the boys.

Their luck held as the only problem they encountered was a couple of large dogs, which had turned wild, and were eating the corpse of someone who had just died from artillery shellfire. A short distance from the body was an old-style rifle with a spike-shaped, foot-long bayonet attached. Peter oiled and cleaned the WWI weapon with his gun cleaning kit, but they didn't test-fire the rifle as it only had a handful of bullets in the magazine.

The three children, wearing the uniforms of men, walked among acres and acres of pitiful desolation and pathetic barrenness. There was the occasional structure collapsing behind them like that of an old, rotted tree falling in the middle of a forest that'd been ravaged by fire. Rosa remembered the day in Cologne when Germany invaded Poland. The Germans celebrated in the streets as if they'd already won the war, but where were those people now?

As they searched fruitlessly for food, Rosa missed her squad, such as Gunter, who, alongside being a fantastic cook, had the uncanny knack of being able to sniff out food like a human bloodhound. Rosa also missed Fritz, who helped her in making informed decisions because of his encyclopaedic knowledge of everything, with nothing too trivial to escape his notice. Hans the farmer with his spooky ability to forecast the weather, was also skilled at hunting and butchering. Wolfgang was the muscle and the protector of the squad. Peter was not only the natural-born leader but also the heart of the squad, while little Charlie was her unquestioning and loyal companion, who, when Rosa was struggling, was always there with his silent emotional support.

Although she'd always thought it would have been quicker and easier to get to Berlin by herself, she now realised how wrong she had been. But the thing that she missed most about her squad was at night-time when sitting around a fire where she had a sense of belonging, a family of sorts.

As they walked around a corner, they turned into a large private garden, where one of the walls had caved into the garden leading to a gaping hole onto the street, but standing in the centre of the yard was a big bull elephant.

"What?" Rosa said.

"It must have escaped from the Berlin Zoo," Peter said.

The large grey animal walked towards them. Peter raised his weapon, But Rosa pushed it away. It didn't look threatening. The animal came over and nudged Rosa, who patted its flanks. It then raised its trunk and opened its mouth.

"I think he's thirsty," said Rosa, pulling out her water bottle from her webbing.

"We can't waste our water," said Peter.

Rosa ignored him and poured all her water onto the grateful tongue. "Whose asking you to waste your water on this beautiful animal? Charlie, give me your water bottle."

Charlie obliged. Peter then handed over his water bottle to

Rosa.

"That's it, boy. It's all we have. I'm sorry we don't have more."

The elephant trumpeted its thank you and then went out the hole in the wall and waddled down the deserted street.

During the day, sometimes it was dead quiet, and sometimes they could hear a battle raging somewhere, presumably on the outskirts of the city. And sometimes, they would have to rush inside to escape from artillery, mortar or aircraft bombs raining down on them, as if it were a passing shower. And once the shell storm passed, they would continue their quest.

But continue onto where? They felt as though they had covered a great distance, but as they still couldn't work out where they were, it was like sprinting in the woods at night. You would always run or bump into something that could harm you. Rosa thought of the great irony as they travelled to Berlin, where there were signposts everywhere stating where and how far away Berlin was, but no one had thought to find a map of the city of Berlin along the way. They were now in the middle of a maze of destroyed multi-storied buildings that were being swallowed up by concrete rock and rubble.

"It's getting late," Rosa said, looking at the setting sun. "We need to find a place to stay for the night."

"But we haven't found any food," Peter pointed out.

"So, we'll sleep another night on an empty stomach, which I've done a thousand times before," she said.

Peter looked at Charlie but didn't say anything.

They heard a woman cry out as they stumbled along mounds of city debris. "Get away from me, you hounds of hell!"

Then they heard barking from several dogs. Rosa ran towards the cry for help. She reached a ridge of rubble and saw a woman at the bottom of a large bomb crater, who was waist-deep in water. And bubbling from the water was gas that had caught fire and was in full blaze, allowing Rosa to see the old woman surrounded by a pack of large wild dogs. To Rosa's eyes, they looked like German Shepherds that had been left to fend for themselves. Some of them were black and long-haired, and, with their hungry eyes and ferocious snapping teeth, they looked very much like a pack of wolves. She knew wolves were always hungry, and they had found their next meal as the old lady swung a heavy metal pipe to keep the ravenous dogs at bay. But Rosa could tell that the woman must have been trapped there for some time as her strength was fading as she breathed heavily between shouting at the dogs.

Peter and Charlie joined her and took in what Rosa was witnessing. "Poor woman," said Peter. "Of all the ways to die in a war, I never thought of being eaten alive by a pack of hungry dogs."

"No-one is getting eaten alive," Rosa said. "Not if I can help."

"How? We have one rifle with only a few bullets," Peter said. "We're not sure it even works."

"I'm guessing they are ex-military dogs whose compound was destroyed, or their handlers killed."

"So what?"

"If I'm right, they'll see our uniforms, their training will kick in, and we can command them to go away."

"Even if you're right those dogs are driven mad with hunger. They can't hear you over the screaming noise of their empty bellies."

"I've been there, but one thing always kicks in."

"What's that?" Peter asked.

"Their survival instinct," she said, grabbing the rifle from Peter. "Their need to survive through fear. Anyway, we haven't found any food or a map of the city, so what's better than a human map that might have some food?"

"Is this stupid idea from one of your stupid fairy tales?" Peter asked, fear rising in his voice.

"It's from the Bible, where Daniel is thrown into a lion's den but defeats and subdues the lions. But you are right; Daniel did it by himself, so you two stay here."

She scrambled down and made her way to the rim of the bomb crater. She cocked the bolt of her rifle. The dogs all turned away from their prey and towards Rosa. She stepped into the massive bomb crater.

"Are you crazy, girl?" yelled the old lady. "Get out of here!"

Rosa instinctively reached for her cap, but it wasn't there. It must have fallen off as she raced down to the trapped old woman. Using her steel-capped boots, she kicked rocks towards the dogs and yelled at them, bearing her teeth as she advanced on the dogs.

She had learned as a young girl that if she didn't move, she would become frozen with fear, but so long as she was moving and doing something, it was as if her fear couldn't keep pace with her body. The further she descended into the eerie light of the gas-fed flames, the more she could feel the tremendous heat and notice how the noise she made echoed inside the cavernous crater.

With the image of the thirsty elephant still in her mind, she didn't want to kill any of the dogs if she could help it. Besides, as anyone who lived inside a concentration camp would know, she thoroughly understood hunger. She truly believed that, once confronted, the dogs would simply run away. She was wrong. They weren't leaving. Instead, their focus was now on Rosa.

The leader of the pack approached her with a low growl and raised hair along the ridge of its back and a stiff tail, followed by the other dogs. It was about to attack. Rosa aimed her rifle at him. He baulked. He knew what a gun could do. Rosa was right about one thing at least. Her uniform and demeanour had kept these ex-military dogs at bay.

The leader feigned attacks at her. When she pointed her steel-bayoneted rifle at him, he would back off, but then the other dogs would lunge at her. They would approach and, when confronted with the bayonet on the end of the barrel of her gun, would back away. But there were so many of them, and already she was feeling tired. Swinging a heavy rifle from side-to-side and sweating from the fire's heat and having no food or water for days didn't help.

From behind, she heard a loud bang. And saw Peter holding her cap in one hand and a smoking Luger pistol in his other hand. And lying at her feet was a dead dog. It must have flanked behind her while the main pack distracted her. The other dogs scampered away.

"Where'd you get that pistol?" she asked.

"Charlie had it. I didn't know he had a gun, but he pulled it out of his rucksack once you left."

"I gave it to him ages ago," Rosa said. "But I forgot all about it."

Charlie nodded vigorously, meaning he'd also completely forgotten about the Luger.

"Can you two stop talking and help an old lady before she boils to death in some kind of grisly dog stew."

Rosa gave the rifle to Peter as she entered the water and grabbed a hold of the old woman.

"Easy, young lady, I've twisted my ankle."

Rosa helped the lady out of the water and then out of the bomb crater. As they crested the top of the mound from where they had first seen her, they looked back to see the pack of dogs eat their fallen comrade.

"That explains why they weren't chasing us," said Peter.

"That could have been me. Thank you for saving an old lady's life."

This was the first time that Rosa could take a good look at the woman whom she just saved. She was an ugly old hag with a mop of grey hair, wiry like a bird's nest, and grotesque teeth protruding from her mouth.

"My name is Aunty Jo, and I've been watching you kids wander around all day. Do you know you have been walking in circles? I think I can trust you. I have no choice with my ankle as it is. I'll need your help to get me home."

Peter and Rosa got under each of the old woman's arms as she directed them where to go, while Charlie followed with the old lady's full pail of water in hand.

"I heard a massive explosion last night," said Aunty Jo. "And when I went out to investigate this morning, I found that crater full of fresh water. The bomb must have burst gas and water mains. So,

I've been ferrying pails of water home all day when the dogs must have sniffed out the water and their next meal."

They eventually entered a half-torn, exposed basement apartment with pictures hanging on the wall and furniture trapped by fallen rubble from the ceiling.

Aunty Jo opened a large cupboard and motioned for the three of them to enter. Once inside, they could see the back of the closet opened out into another room. They kept going until they were in the other apartment. They had entered an enchanting world of classic refinement and respectability, so different from the outside world. Just like *Alice in Wonderland,* thought Rosa. It was as if they'd come through the other side of the rabbit hole. The children were stunned into silence as they surveyed their elegant surroundings. The two boys looked perplexed, but Rosa had worked it out. The other side of the door, the cupboard side, was actually a hallway and not a room. Aunty Jo had disguised the hallway as a half-destroyed apartment so that any unsuspecting passer-by would move on. Clever. Very clever indeed, thought Rosa.

Rosa turned to see Aunty Jo disrobing, firstly removing her scarf and wig, then her ugly false teeth, revealing perfectly enamelled white teeth. She took off her ugly grey overcoat to reveal the pillows tied to her body, and then, standing before them, was a grand old lady of unmistakable refinement.

"I'm sorry for the falsehood, but it pays to be careful, especially now. Plus, I come from a theatrical family. And you are?"

"I'm Peter, and his name is Charlie."

"And I'm Rosa."

"Well, Rosa, wearing a boy's uniform is a smart move, but, from what I heard about Soviet soldiers, they aren't fussy over gender," she said, rubbing Charlie's blonde hair. "If you know what I mean?"

Unfortunately, Rosa did.

"You kids must be starving," she said bringing out some stale bread and going to a pot that was simmering in the fireplace, dishing out stew for all four of them.

"Aunty Jo, we saw an elephant today," Peter said like an excited kid who had just returned from a family day out at the zoo.

"Really?" Aunty Jo said, sounding suitably impressed. "Well, I guess the Berlin Zoo isn't that far away from here, in elephant miles."

"But wouldn't they get rid of the animals to a safer place?" Rosa asked.

"You would think so, but when Hitler declared that Berlin was a fortress and no one was allowed to leave, I guess that applied to the zoo animals as well. But they had to guard them with orders that anybody who tries to eat them will be summarily shot on sight."

"From what I can tell, everyone is starving here, how do you feed and water an elephant?"

"With great difficultly, child, and with a great deal of help from humans, which shows that we're not all bad, at least. And I'm sure the zoo staff would have sent out a search party to find him."

After they'd finished, Aunty Jo looked at Rosa's long blonde hair that had been tied into a ponytail. "How do you hide your hair?"

"I usually cut it, but we broke our last pair of scissors some time ago," Rosa replied. "I've just been tucking my braided hair underneath my military cap."

"Well, you're in luck I have a pair of scissors that are very sharp," Aunty Jo said, pushing Rosa down on a chair that she had just placed in the middle of the room. She produced a set of scissors. Rosa stood to protest but was pushed back down again. "Don't worry; all mothers know how to cut their children's hair. I raised two daughters who were both very particular about their hair, especially when they were about your age. What am I saying? They're even worse now, I imagine."

Rosa sat in compliance when she heard about Aunty Jo's daughters. "Where are they now?" she asked.

"Oh, I don't know exactly, but they're not here, thank God," she said, cutting large clumps of Rosa's hair. "I'm going to give you these scissors, but you can't cut your own hair. Peter, come over here, and I'll show you what to do."

Peter went to protest, but a stern look from Aunty Jo silenced him. He stood directly behind Rosa. Aunty Jo handed him the pair of scissors, holding up some hair and showed Peter what to do.

Rosa sat there quietly. When Aunty Jo cut her hair, it was nothing, but when Peter stroked her hair and gently snipped away at her hair, she felt a tingle run along the back of her neck and across her shoulders, giving her goosebumps. "Peter doesn't need to do this, I prefer to do things by myself," she said as she attempted to stand.

Aunty Jo grabbed a hold of Rosa's shoulder and said, "Don't move Rosa, these scissors are so sharp it will cut your ears off. I'm sure you can do lots of things by yourself, but no-one can cut their own hair properly. However, I have a feeling that you don't like asking for help."

Peter seemed earnest in his new occupation as hairdresser as Rosa looked into the reflection of the large mirror that Aunty Jo had placed the chair in front of. He would gently grab a hold of some of her hair until he got a nod from Aunty Jo when he would cut her hair. Rosa felt a weird mix of enjoying him cutting her hair so carefully and tenderly but feeling bad about her enjoyment. Maybe her discomfort was due to her thinking more and more about him, to such a point that she was dreaming about him and his angel-like eyes. Even when she told stories to the boys, such as *Siegfried and the Dragon,* she started imagining Peter as Siegfried. Previously, she always imagined Siegfried as having brown hair and brown eyes.

"My sore ankle is killing me," Aunty Jo said as she sat on the sofa next to Charlie. "Now tell me about yourselves."

"We've just arrived," Rosa said.

"We had to sneak into Berlin," said Peter.

"Why did you sneak into Berlin?"

"We came to find our families," said Peter.

"And have you?"

"No. My place no longer exists, but maybe they live somewhere else."

"Maybe," Aunty Jo said, sounding unconvinced. "And you girl, why did you come here?"

"My father was imprisoned at the Sachsenhausen Concentration Camp north of Berlin."

Aunty Jo's face twisted. "Your father is a Gypsy? I don't understand. Your German is perfect, and surely, with your blonde hair, you are German or Austrian?" Aunty Jo leaned forward to hear Rosa's reply.

Rosa wasn't sure why, perhaps she felt as if she were betraying her parents, but she felt embarrassed now. She remained silent.

Peter spoke up for her. "She was born in Berlin, but her mother died during the depression, and this group of Gypsies took her in."

"And yet here she is now in a German military uniform no less. The world is full of irony."

"We do what we have to do in order to survive," Rosa said in her defence.

"Yes, you are right, Rosa. But I think the Roma camp you mentioned is in Russian territory now."

"I don't care. I have to find him or die trying."

"Well, I think the Gypsy camp may have closed down before the Russians got there anyway. You must have seen those three Flak towers that we now have on top of what looks like medieval fortresses?"

They nodded.

"Well," she went on, "That took tens of thousands of labourers, which they gathered from all over the place. They even built one of those at the Berlin Zoo. Once the flak towers were built, the labourers were put to work building the outer and inner defensive rings at Seelow Heights. If your father is still alive, most likely, he will be somewhere on the outskirts of the city, working on defences."

"Well, then, Russians or no Russians, I'm not leaving Berlin, not until I've found him."

"Child, don't you know there's a war on? He could be dead for all you know."

"I know he's alive; I feel it, just like one of grandma's gut feelings that she used to have, which were always right."

"It's true, Aunty Jo," Peter said. "Many times, Rosa's gut feelings have saved us, and her guts saved you just now."

Little Charlie nodded, agreeing with Peter.

"Just as I knew I'd make it to Berlin, I have no doubt that I will find my father still alive," Rosa affirmed. "Besides, my father promised me he'd stay alive. He's the one who taught me that when a person makes a promise, you have to keep it. But I have no time to lose. I need to find him before the Russians take over the city."

## Chapter 16

10 April 1945 (Tuesday)

*Berlin*

Early in the mornings, Rosa, Peter and Charlie went out foraging for food and water and would return to Aunty Jo's. And, each day, they ranged further and further into unfamiliar territory. The three of them sneaked along the insides of buildings where there was less chance of being spotted. Little Charlie scouted ahead of them. Once he got to the end of a large hallway, he gave the "all clear" signal—thumbs up. Rosa and Peter got up and moved quickly to join him. They opened two large red doors and entered an empty barroom. Looters had taken all the alcohol, but they found a treasure trove of hidden spots where canned food and goodies were tucked away. Filling their rucksacks, they were walking back the way they came when Peter smashed through some weakened floorboards with an awesomely loud crash.

"Help me," he said, stuck up to his waist and squirming helplessly.

Rosa and Charlie removed Peter's rucksack and put it to one side; however, Peter was still stuck. Rosa took the bottom of the large, heavy curtain hanging over the windows and gave it to Peter, which he used to haul himself out. Peter, half-sticking out of the floor, had been a funny sight.

"Stuck in a trap like a little rabbit," laughed Rosa.

Suddenly, several armed German soldiers crashed through the door. "Who are you, and where is your unit?" the leader demanded.

"We don't have a unit," said Rosa.

"Deserters!"

"No," said Peter. "Our unit was destroyed, and we've only just arrived in Berlin."

"Impossible. What do you mean you just arrived?"

"We entered from the west along the train tracks."

"Liar," said one of the other soldiers whose helmet shrouded his face. "The Russians have completely surrounded the city. There is no way out or in."

"No," said Peter. "Not completely. Not yet. Anyway, we aren't escaping. We've come home."

"Well, I hope you've come home ready to fight because this war isn't over yet," said the leader.

"And we're supposed to kill all deserters," said the shrouded soldier.

"Even kids?" said another soldier.

"We'll let the Swede handle the matter," said the shrouded soldier.

The soldiers, who all looked to be in their sixties or seventies, escorted their prisoners back to their HQ, which was a bombed-out railway station. The commander turned out to be an old Norwegian, "the Swede". Berlin was rife with foreigners from other nations wearing patchwork German uniforms.

"Who are these kids?" asked the Swede.

"We found them rummaging for food in a bar."

"You know the rules. Deserters are to be shot on the spot. Why did you bring them back here?"

"Sir, they claim to have snuck into Berlin, so they may not be deserters."

"Impossible, the city is surrounded," said the Swede.

"They *say* it's not."

The Swede glared at the children. "You actually entered Berlin? Are you kids crazy?"

"No, sir," said Peter. "We are Berliners. We've simply come home."

"Well, then," said the Swede. "We need more fighters—or at least someone with a fighting spirit. Perhaps you have come just in the nick of time. We have a situation here, and if you die anyway, at least you've saved the Third Reich a bullet or three. As for the Russians, it appears that one of their tanks has broken through another sector and is harassing us from behind."

The Swede took them outside to another group of boys. The oldest couldn't have been more than twelve.

"Okay, listen up," said the Swede. "We've been ordered to take out that tank. These three newcomers have tank-fighting experience, and they will lead you."

"Me?" said Peter.

"No, not you," said the Swede. "That one," he said, pointing at Rosa. "That one doesn't talk much, but he has the look of a leader. What's your name, lad?"

"Rudi," said Rosa.

"Okay, Rudi. You're in charge. Go take out that tank. And don't come back until it's done. Understand?"

"Yes, sir. But I have one question."

"Yes?"

"How?"

"Flanking manoeuvres work best."

And so, the group followed Rudi, Peter and Charlie down the quiet battle-strewn street.

"Does anybody know what a flanking manoeuvre is exactly?" Rosa asked.

They all shrugged.

The boys had been armed with guns, and a single Panzerfaust grenade launcher—Panzerfaust or Tank Fist was explicitly designed to take out tanks at extremely close range. Being light and nimble, children were perfect for the task—or so the unit commander wanted them to believe. In truth, the children were burdened by wearing a uniform that was often too big for them, cumbersome boots and oversized helmets that wobbled on their heads. Plus, they had to operate weaponry such as the Panzerfaust while navigating around the armed tank while the enemy tried to kill them. It wasn't just foolhardy; it was suicide.

When the boys turned a corner, a shell burst at the edge of the building that they were cornering. The blast knocked them down, and a Russian machine gunner opened fire. The bullets hit the concrete steel bunker in front of them.

"Stay down!" Rosa yelled.

Rosa saw that the bunker had an attached flak-gun, also called an Ack-Ack gun, from the sound it made when shooting down aircraft. Rosa assumed that the flak-gun had been placed at the top of the building to be used against the Allied and Russian bombers. However, it was evident that the gun and its emplacements had toppled from the rooftops into the street when the building had partially collapsed.

Behind her, the boys lay frozen with fear, holding their hands over their ears with tears running down their dusty-white cheeks.

The firing stopped.

Rosa took charge. "Come to me," she whispered as loudly as she dared. All but one, who was still crying, obeyed.

She crawled over to him and shook his leg. "What's your name?"

Startled at first, he managed to answer her, "Benjamin, Benny."

"Well, Benny, I have an important mission for you."

His eyes popped open.

"Do you think you can find your way back to HQ?"

Benny nodded.

"Well, Benny, I want you to go back and tell them we've found the tank, but we need help. Do you think you can do that?"

He nodded again. "I was the fastest kid in my school."

"Okay, see that ditch there?" she said, pointing to a ditch that ran back towards the building, just large enough for a scrawny child like Benny.

"Uh-huh," he said.

"Well, I want you to crawl in it until you get behind the building, and then run as fast as you can for help. Understand?"

He smiled and nodded then scrambled away. Once Benny was in the clear, she had a look at the tank.

The turret was pointed away from them. Lying on the back of the tank was a soldier with a machine gun. Next to him lay a Russian rocket launcher called an RPG, which had been reloaded. Rosa guessed the Russian must have fired the RPG before switching to his machine gun. The Russian soldier was protecting the rear of the stationary tank. The tank's left track had come off and so it could only pivot left or right.

Then she spotted another unit of Hitler Youth approaching the tank. However, unlike Rosa's group who were invisible to the tank, they'd stumbled in front of it. She wanted to shout out a warning, but they were too far away. Then she remembered her stick grenade, armed it and threw it towards the tank, watching it land. The Russian machine gunner was distracted by the second squad of Hitler Youth and didn't see the grenade. She watched the grenade. Watched. Watched. The smoke emanating from it fizzled out. Nothing. The grenade was a dud.

The other squad, perhaps lulled into a false sense of security as the Russian tank hadn't fired on them, closed in on the front of the disabled tank. These Hitler Youth seemed much older than her lot: fifteen or sixteen at least and therefore much braver or more determined to take this tank out. The teenage boys stalked their way toward the tank in leaps and bounds. Then, all of a sudden, Rosa felt the blast of heat as the tank spewed liquid fire at the squad. The flame-throwing tank was able to pivot on the spot about ninety degrees, and the single stream of hissing death had a devastating effect on the boys. The ones who didn't immediately succumb to the fiery bath scattered. Their screams were unbearable to listen to but impossible for Rosa and her boys to look away from. The man on the rear of the tank had a field phone that must have communicated to the men inside the tank. Whatever he'd said, the machine gun ceased to fire as the boys rolled onto the ground burning to death, until finally, there was no longer any movement.

The entire squad had been incinerated.

While this was happening, Rosa shouted out, "Run into the building, now!"

Once inside, Rosa and the others clambered up steps that gave them a better view.

"What the hell is that, Peter?" Rosa said, pointing at the tank.

"I've heard of them, but I've never seen one," said Peter. "But it must be a flame-throwing tank, which is designed for blasting out hidey-holes, especially in big cities, which are full of basements and sewers that are perfect for setting up explosives or ambushes."

Rosa noticed that the Russian tank turret was fixed and could not rotate like a German Panzer. And the only way they had of manoeuvring was by pivoting with their tank tracks.

She grabbed Charlie's hand and looked at the boys. "Stay here, while I scout around."

She and Charlie continued up the stairs until they were above the Russian tank. As she and Charlie walked along the hallways and searched the upper floors, she realised the building was hundreds of years old and was more of a square shape than the surrounding rectangular buildings that were still standing. She also noticed that the entire building had, until recently, been surrounded by scaffolding, obviously meant for major renovations or upgrades. Still, the repair work had long since been abandoned.

On the far corner of the building, Rosa came to an opening out onto the scaffolding. Rosa and Charlie walked outside. The scaffolding on that corner of the building had collapsed in both directions. One side had angled down at a 45-degrees to the Russian tank while the other was angled away from the tank towards safety.

The collapsed scaffolding looked like an industrial-sized slippery slide in Rosa's mind. She looked around and found one of many old-metal-wheeled bins that must have been used to remove debris and unwanted materials from the outside of a building. Inside was a large open toolbox that had hammers, screwdrivers, chisels and such. She heaved it out and placed it to the side.

She moved the bin to the scaffolding and noticed that it had little train tracks on it, presumably for the small wheelie-bins, so they wouldn't go over the edge, hurting a labourer working below. She positioned the front of the wheels into the tracks on the scaffolding that led away from the tank.

"Okay, Charlie, get in," she said.

He looked up at her with a quizzical look.

"Once you're in, I'll push off and jump in with you, and we'll land down on the street, and we can take off and go back to Aunty Jo's."

Charlie turned to look back at the boys they'd left behind.

"We can't do anything for them. You saw what those Russians did to that other squad of boys. And they were properly trained Hitler Youth, known for their tank-killing skills, and they didn't last five seconds. What chance does a bunch of virtually unarmed boys stand? Now get in, or I'm leaving without you," she said, reaching her hand out to Charlie. "Quickly! Think of it as a giant slippery slide. We can slide down and escape, and no one will notice."

Charlie looked behind him again.

"They can't come. This is a one-way ride. You know what Peter's like. He won't leave the others behind. But you and I can make it."

She reached out to him once again. He stepped back towards the hallway and shook his head.

"If we stay here, we'll die."

But then they both heard shots being fired from the tank—single shots, not from a machine gun as before. Charlie took off down the hallway to the other stairwell, running toward where they left the other boys.

"You little fool," she said, stepping into the small rusty bin. "Does everybody here have a death wish?"

She sat in the bin holding a large metal pole to help push her off on her descent through the scaffolding. The rear wheels were getting caught at the lip. She pushed harder when she heard more shots ring out.

"Damn it!" She stood up, got out of the bin, and walked back down the stairs to re-join Charlie, Peter, and the other boys. Charlie beamed when he saw her stride up to them.

The Russian gunner had spied the boys and was taking pot shots at them with his pistol.

"What are we going to do, Rudi?" one boy asked her.

"We have to kill it ourselves."

"Kill it?"

"Yes. Imagine the tank is a fire-breathing green dragon, and we are the Teutonic Knights of Germany come to rescue the village of Berlin."

"How do we kill the dragon, Rudi?"

"The tank has broken one of its wings, so it can't escape."

"It not only breathes fire but there is still a sting in its tail," Peter pointed out, referring to the Russian machine gunner positioned on the rear of the tank.

"Yes, but while the dragon can't fly, we can."

The boys looked confused, including Peter.

"How old are you?" she asked the smallest boy.

"Eight."

"He is not," said another. "He's seven."

"Okay, Seven, you are a dead ringer for Charlie. You two look so alike you could be twins."

Peter laughed at this comment.

Rosa ignored him. "Boys. I have a plan, and if we all work together, we can slay that Russian dragon."

\*\*\*

"Okay, boys," said Rosa, "let them have it."

And, with that, a boy on the stairwell put up his thumb to say, "Go". Then the boy at the top of the stairs signalled to someone down the same hallway that Rosa and Charlie had surveyed earlier.

Rosa could hear the roar of the wheelie bin as it raced outside of the building down towards the tank. She watched below as the machine gunner manning the gun on the rear of the tank looked towards the source of the noise. He jumped off, armed only with his pistol.

Suddenly, the wheelie bin, loaded with bricks and concrete to give it weight and momentum, came into view. The bottom of the scaffolding was bent slightly upwards, which Rosa hoped would launch the bin at the tank. It did.

The Russian dived to the side as the bin slammed into the side of the tank with a tremendous crash.

Rosa signalled again, and again the boys released another loaded wheelie bin at the top of the scaffolding ramp. There was another thunderous noise. The Russian gunner advanced to where he saw the bin emerging, trying to figure out exactly what was going on. He ducked as the second bin sailed by, smashing into the side of the tank.

The gunner was about to look up the scaffolding when Rosa wolf-whistled loudly.

A little blonde boy stood up at the end of the street and ran away at that very instant.

The gunner raised his pistol at the boy but stopped when he saw the boy was naked.

The naked boy dropped behind a Dragon's Tooth. The gunner aimed his pistol and fired at the reinforced concrete.

Just at that very moment, another naked, blonde-haired boy appeared from behind a Dragon's Tooth, only to run and hide behind another.

The gunner re-aimed and fired a single shot at this boy.

Then the first boy reappeared to hide behind another of the Dragon's Teeth strewn over the street.

The Russian swivelled his pistol between the last two places the boys had been when a third naked boy appeared to the far right and jumped behind another of the Dragon's Teeth.

Just as the gunner was about to fire again, he heard a third wheelie bin race down the scaffolding, so he ducked as it flew over him.

He stood with a big grin. "You missed me again. You boys have to wake up pretty early to catch Ivan out," he said in halting German.

"Hey, Ivan!" shouted Rosa from directly overhead.

As the Russian gunner looked skywards, a toolbox full of tools smashed onto his head.

Rosa looked down to see the gunner lying flat-out on the ground.

"Bullseye," said Peter, who had been holding onto Rosa's belt as she leaned out over the edge. He pulled her back in.

The other boys cheered and joined her and Peter.

He paused. "How did you know that would work?"

"Well, a naked anyone would put anybody off," Rosa said. "We're not used to seeing a naked person, especially in the middle of battle. But when I realised that Seven, Helmut and Charlie looked almost identical, who would expect three naked people during a battle? And that's all we needed. A moment of confusion. I wanted him so absorbed with what was in front of him that he forgot all about his exposed flanks."

"And in this case, his exposed flank was directly above him," said Peter.

"Exactly."

The boys were jubilant. But just then, the tank exhaled another breath of fire.

"The men are still inside, and they can still kill more people," said Peter.

"I heard them banging on the inside. I think our little wheelie bins are wedged underneath the tank, blocking their escape hatch at the bottom, and it appears their top hatch has been twisted shut from a previous encounter."

"So, they are trapped inside?" said Peter.

"So, it would seem."

"What do we do, Rudi?"

The boys walked down the stairs and stopped at the downed Flak gun.

"Stay here, boys; I'll deal with them," said Rosa.

She walked over to the tank, and she saw the receiver that the Russian gunner had spoken into. She picked it up. "Hello?"

Silence.

"Hello? Hello?"

"Hello?" finally came the response on the other end.

Rosa knew some Russian; however, she didn't know the Russian word for surrender, and she wasn't sure that the Ivans trapped inside the tank knew the German word. She tried her poor English instead, "Surrender! You!"

"What did you say, Rudi?" said Peter.

She turned to see Peter and a now dressed Charlie had left the others and were approaching her.

"I asked them to surrender."

"What did they say?"

There was another blast of fire from the tank and, because they were so near, they shielded themselves from the wave of fiery heat.

"They say, No!" said Rosa.

"How do we kill the dragon?" asked a boy.

"How did Siegfried kill his dragon?" she shouted.

"He stabbed it in the belly!" the boys shouted.

"I'm going to punch this dragon in the nose!" she said, remembering the dud grenade she had thrown earlier. She went over and picked it up, very carefully, in case it decided to blow.

"Careful," said Peter, "they can still go off."

"Thanks, Captain Obvious.", she said. "Peter, I want you to speak to them on that tank phone."

"I don't know any Russian," Peter protested.

"It doesn't matter what you say, so long as you say it loud. I need them to be focused on the phone. But only talk once I'm ready."

"Ready for what?"

"You'll know what I mean when you see it."

She climbed back on top of the tank and stepped quietly onto the gun turret. Then she balanced herself as she walked along the tank's gun barrel.

Peter realised that this was what she had meant, and he burst into action and spoke into the phone. "Russland ist Kaput!"

They could hear the Russians inside fight over the phone to hurl insults back at Peter.

Rosa got to the end of the tank barrel without being seen. If they'd seen her, no doubt they would have blasted another wave of fire. She sat down, and with the barrel between her legs, she pushed the stick-like grenade into the tank barrel before swinging down and racing away from the tank to join Charlie.

Once she was safe, Peter stopped raving over the phone and joined them.

The Russians fired the flamethrower. The grenade lodged in the turret went off, and the tank barrel burst into flames. Then the inside of the tank caught alight.

Rosa, Peter and Charlie ran towards the other boys when the tank exploded, the blast knocking the three of them off their feet.

The boys rushed from behind the safety of the barricade of the fallen Flak gun and helped the three of them to their feet.

Rosa dusted herself off as she stood up.

"We won, Rudi. We actually killed the dragon!" the boys shouted.

"Boys, you have two choices," said Rosa. "You can either go back to your unit and fight to the death—your death—or you can run away and hide."

"Hide? We're not traitors."

"No, but you're not soldiers either. When children fight, the war is over, understand?"

Silence. They simply stared at her.

"Go!"

They fled in several directions.

Peter, Charlie and Rosa walked up the road that the other squad had come from.

Out of nowhere emerged two Wehrmacht Military Policemen pointing their weapons at the three of them. "Halt. We saw everything." The German MPs pointed their guns in the direction they wanted them to go.

Rosa, Peter and Charlie had no choice but to go with them.

# Chapter 17

## An hour later

*The Reich Chancellery, the Führer's Bunker*

The MPs, known as 'chain dogs', led them through the warren of ruins, debris and bombed-out buildings. The German Military Police were so-called 'chain dogs' because they wore a stainless steel, half-moon plate with attached chains around their necks. Although the chains made them look more menacing, they weren't practical for a soldier as they made such a jingle as they walked. The enemy could hear them a mile away in the echoes of the concrete remnants of the inner sanctum of Berlin.

Rosa couldn't understand why the MPs were taking the trouble of walking her, Peter and Charlie through this maze. Why hadn't they been shot on the spot? Perhaps there was a firing squad assigned to this gruesome task. They finally came out into a clearing.

As a Berliner, Peter recognised it immediately. "This is the garden of the Reich Chancellery," he whispered to Rosa and Charlie.

"The Reich Chancellery?" Rosa asked. "Isn't this where the Führer lives?"

"It is."

It was a garden in name only. The trees—the ones still standing— were devoid of leaves, as Russian bombs had continuously pruned the trees and tilled over the garden beds. The German MPs grabbed the Panzerfaust launcher, which Peter was still holding on to, and threw it into a pile of weapons that lay to one side of the garden. Other than to disarm them of their carrying weapons, the MPs didn't do a full body search or pat down as Rosa feared, nor did they see fit to remove the Hitler Youth knives that hung in scabbards on each of their belts.

The MP waved his sub-machine gun. "Now, line up with the others."

The three children were pushed around a corner to see about thirty Hitler Youth from the ages of twelve to fifteen standing in a single row, lined up against a wall.

So, this was it. They were to be executed to fertilise Hitler's garden, she thought.

Rosa, Peter and Charlie were pushed in at the end of the row of Hitler Youth. Several members of the German High Command wearing red insignia were watching. Rosa then noticed two camera crews were in operation: one was stationary on a tripod, while the other was handheld as the cameraman walked along the row of boys, filming.

An officer burst into action, standing to attention, yelling an order to the assembled German youths. "Attention!"

They snapped their boots together, including the generals, who were standing on the fringes of the parade. Rosa slapped her boots together, imitating the others. Then she saw something that was impossible to fathom.

The Führer and Goebbels, and their attendants, appeared as if from nowhere. Peter and Charlie's eyes shot open, looking at Rosa. Her heart raced. This was the man truly responsible for the fate of her family and all the Romani.

The parade commander thrust his right arm so hard it sounded like he'd snapped his shoulder blade in the process. "Heil Hitler!"

The Führer, in stark contrast, barely raised his own arm. It was little more than a pathetic half-wave in comparison. The parade commander read from a notebook and introduced the Führer to each member of the Hitler Youth and their act of bravery. It seemed some of the boys had taken out Russian tanks at Seelow Heights and others in Berlin. The Führer handed out an Iron Cross to each of them: a medal for their gallant bravery. Germany was fighting to their last—to their last breath—to their last child.

Each of the uniformed children was stunned: stunned to be receiving Germany's most prized medal; stunned that the Führer was giving it to them personally; stunned to see that the Führer had become little more than a small, shaky old man playing dress-ups in his military uniform, which he'd famously said that he would never remove until this war was won. They smiled meekly at the cameras. None of the children might come out of this war alive, and this film footage was confirmation, at least, they were once heroes. Their lives mattered.

Eventually, the Führer came closer to the end of their row. As he neared, Rosa reached for the handle of her Hitler Youth blade. She was faster than they could aim and fire.

"Rosa, please."

Rosa looked over at Peter and Charlie, who were both staring at her in disbelief, their wide eyes pleading with her not to do this.

The parade commander spoke up. "And these three heroes single-handedly took out a lone Russian tanker that had managed to break through the front lines. The tank was destroyed only a few blocks from here."

"How old are you, child?" the Führer asked Charlie.

Charlie looked at Peter.

"My Führer, apologies, he can't talk. But we think he is ten."

"Ten. And you've already taken out a Russian tank. I wish my generals had your backbone. Well, they will get what they deserve. They all will. Why, if only they had done what I'd said." He put his shaky hand out. Peter shook it and collected his medal and Charlie did likewise with an added boyish salute. The Führer held his trembling hand in front of Rosa. She looked at it and then at Peter and Charlie. It wasn't worth killing Peter and Charlie for. Not this close to the end. Rosa released the grip on her knife, shook his hand, and took the proffered medal.

Like a son caring for his elderly frail father, Goebbels smiled ghoulishly as the proceedings unfolded, seeming to relish this pathetic medal ceremony. Goebbels escorted the Führer to the front of the parade and spoke for him. "The Führer wants you all to know that he is proud of you: Germany's future. And not to give up. Victory is at hand. Heil Hitler!"

The Führer and Goebbels' entourage disappeared back under the ground from where they'd come.

The parade commander about-faced and dismissed the assembled children. Before Peter or Rosa could say a word, a woman approached them. "You three, I need some help."

The voice struck Rosa like a backhanded slap. She looked up to see it was Director Riefenstahl. Rosa looked down again so as not to be recognised. The same MP that had escorted them to the medal ceremony was behind Director Riefenstahl. His MP40 machine pistol was still slung across his front at the ready.

As directed, the three of them grabbed some film equipment and walked down to the main street. The Wehrmacht was hurriedly trying to remove the large pieces of rubble from the major Berlin road. Once the film equipment was neatly stacked, Rosa and her two friends made to leave.

"Where do you three think you're going?" said Director Riefenstahl.

"Our unit will wonder where we are," said Peter. "Besides, there is nothing else to do, is there?"

"Yes, there is. You can wait with me."

The three of them sat down next to her and watched as the chain-dog MP barked orders at the soldiers clearing the cluttered war-strewn street.

Director Riefenstahl sat in between Peter and Rosa. "Hello, Rosa."

The three children all looked up at her.

"You thought I wouldn't know who you are? Costumes and make-up are my bread and butter."

Rosa looked at the MP sergeant, still shouting orders.

"Don't worry, Rosa, your secret is safe with me," she said as if she could read Rosa's mind. "I had to come back to get some of my reels and equipment, including my precious Litax Machine so that I can finish *Tiefland*."

Peter and Charlie looked at her. She laughed as she took out a cigarette and lit it.

"What's a Litax Machine? Don't worry; it's not one of Hitler's so-called wonder weapons. It's a device that allows you to edit a film wherever you are. Plus, I had my film reels that I shot in Spain stored at the Babelsberg Studios in Potsdam, which is not far from here, so I had to come back."

A small recon plane with Luftwaffe markings on the wings burst from the clouds. As soon as it became visible, Russian gunfire and artillery opened, trying to hit it.

Director Riefenstahl stood. "Finally. It's a Storch light plane perfect for reconnaissance and landing in tricky places like this."

"Who would be crazy enough to land in the middle of a battle?" Peter asked.

"Only Germany's greatest aviator," answered Director Riefenstahl.

The aircraft was light and nimble, and in no time, it landed on the street near the Brandenburg Gate and drove along the bitumen, pulling up at their feet.

"Hurry. Load the film equipment into the plane."

The three Hitler Youth helped Director Riefenstahl load the plane behind the two front seats while the pilot jumped out, removing her helmet to reveal long, wavy hair.

Director Riefenstahl yelled over the noise made by the single front-propeller engine. "Rosa, this is Hanna Reitsch."

Hanna spoke, "No time to refuel. We'll have to see how far we can get without it."

Director Riefenstahl looked at Rosa. "I can't save your friends, but I can take you with me."

Rosa looked at Peter and Charlie. "I'm sorry, Director Riefenstahl, but I'm not leaving them behind. They need me," she said, turning when she felt a sudden pain to the back of her head.

Darkness.

\*\*\*

Rosa woke up to the sound of the engine of a small plane. Pain. She rubbed the back of her head. She put her hands down to steady herself and felt the cold steel reel cans. She focused on the Litax Machine.

"You're awake," said Director Riefenstahl, who was sitting in the passenger seat as the pilot navigated through the black clouds. "Good."

"You knocked me out just so that I would come with you? Why?"

"I didn't do it. It was that tall boy who was with you."

"Peter?"

Riefenstahl nodded. "He loaded you into the plane and kissed you. He called you his Sleeping Beauty. Very touching. I only wish I had a camera to film it. Maybe I'll use it in my next film about an aviatrix like Hanna here."

"I'll kiss the sleeping prince if you don't mind," said the pilot.

Both women in the front seats laughed.

"Peter told me to tell you that he knows how stubborn you can get. But he had no choice. He had to save your life. He owed you."

"I don't understand. He didn't owe me anything. I didn't save his life."

"According to him, you did."

Rosa looked out of the window only to see thousands and thousands of Soviet troops, trucks and tanks. But they flew just above tree-top height so no-one on the ground had a clear shot at them.

The plane lurched down several feet. The pilot struggled with the stick until finally, the plane levelled out. "I told you, Leni, the plane is too heavy. We need to lighten; otherwise, we won't gain any altitude. And if we don't lighten the aircraft, we will run out of fuel long before we get to Austria."

"What are you saying?"

"I'm saying we need to throw your equipment overboard."

Director Riefenstahl looked at her Litax Machine and shiny-canned reels labelled *Tiefland*. She looked at Rosa.

The ultra-light aircraft landed on the middle of the deserted autobahn, somewhere outside Berlin, where there were no soldiers. Rosa jumped out.

Director Riefenstahl removed a camera and a tripod and threw them onto the bitumen. "I won't be needing them, but I need my reels and editing machine. I think we're a long way south of Berlin. Just head west, away from the Russians."

Rosa stared at Director Riefenstahl, who paused to stare back at the girl.

"I knew it the day I picked you to work for me," said Director Riefenstahl.

"Knew what?"

"We don't need anybody. Look at me, Rosa. I am your future. I saw it in your eyes. You are a survivor just like me. You and I are one and the same. And you and I live in the real world, not like these other people surrounding us: the sheep of the world. They deserve to be slaughtered, but you and I are wolves. The wolves of destiny, who get to decide our own fate."

"I am nothing like you."

"Yes, you are. But I have to go. However, when you do find the Americans, I want you to do one thing for me."

"What?"

"Tell them how I saved your life and the lives of the others," she said. "I must hurry."

The passenger door had no sooner closed shut when the engine spat and coughed into life as the Storch light plane moved away from Rosa. The aircraft rolled along, gathering enough speed, springing vertically, only to disappear behind the thick low-lying rain clouds.

Rosa spotted a sign that read BERLIN 100 KM, and then looked westward. She thought of Peter, Charlie, and her father, but, at the same time, she knew the impossibility of her somehow getting through all those Russians they'd flown over, who were already at the door of Hitler's bunker.

Time had run out.

From the air, Rosa had seen a large river to the west of her. She had no choice. She followed the deserted road southwards, hoping to find a bridge that crossed over to the west—sooner rather than later.

## Chapter 18

### 11 April 1945 (Wednesday)

*The Spree River (100 km south of Berlin)*

S tanding on a hill overlooking the destroyed Spree River bridge, Rosa stared at the twisted metal that spiralled and snaked from the German-controlled side of the river, where she was standing, to the opposite side, which was controlled by the Americans. Rosa wasn't the only one trying to cross this mangled, metal wreckage of a bridge. Although impassable to vehicles, thousands of German military men streamed along the tangled girders to the US side of the Spree River. The German sailors, soldiers and airmen were fleeing the vengeful Russian hordes.

But it was a very controlled and orderly flight. They dropped their weapons onto a growing pile in front of German MPs on the German-military-controlled side and, once over the destroyed bridge, they surrendered to the GI MPs on the other side, all without a single shot being fired. Despite this orderly surrender, Rosa could hear German artillery being fired from a nearby hill behind her. The Russians were firing back but, being outgunned by the superior and easily-recognisable German 88mm, the Russian artillery was dropping well short of the Spree River bridge. Meanwhile, the American artillery, lined up on a hill directly opposite, didn't fire a single shot at the Germans, who were firing on their allies—the Russians.

It was clear to Rosa that the German artillery was sacrificing themselves to buy time for their comrades-in-arms to cross over to the safety of the Americans. This bizarre exodus was witnessed by thousands of American soldiers sitting on the side of the hill directly in front of their silent guns.

Rosa had heard many horrific tales from the numerous refugees she'd encountered on the road. The Russian atrocities committed against the German population, both military and civilian, were legendary, especially regarding what the Russians were doing to women and young girls. Regardless of your age, if you were a female, you wore a big target on your back. It didn't seem to matter if the women were Germans or not because Polish women, Hungarian women, and Czechoslovakian women—all women—suffered the same brutality from the bloodlust of the Russian soldiers.

Because of these reports, thousands of German women rushed to this bridge to escape the invading Russians. Rosa saw civilian women crying and begging to be let over to the safety of the Americans. The German soldiers didn't listen and formed a human barrier to prevent the panic-stricken women from crossing over.

Rosa lined up in the mainline that led directly onto the bridge. As she got closer, she could see why it had taken so long. German soldiers were removing everyone's hats and helmets. A German MP removed a helmet, and long blonde hair fell over her uniformed shoulders.

"Another one!" yelled the German MP corporal.

"Please, I work for the Wehrmacht," the woman pleaded.

"Well, for one thing, you're not even wearing a Wehrmacht uniform," the corporal responded. "Where are your ID tags or identity papers?"

"I lost them. There's a war on, you know."

"No civilian women allowed. Go," the corporal said, pointing to the other civilians. The woman was in tears as she walked solemnly toward the massive group of distraught women. As she passed the point where the German soldiers were dropping off their weapons, she rushed over, grabbed a Lugar handgun, cocked it before placing it to her temple, and fired, dropping dead.

Still dressed in her Hitler Youth uniform, Rosa took this moment of drama to slide past the German soldiers blocking the path to the bridge. Using her hands and feet, she slowly made her way over the treacherous bridge. Below her lay the bodies of dead Germans who had lost their footing and landed fatally on the debris below. As she got to the end of the bridge, she saw a gaping hole. She watched as German soldiers took a running jump to land on the soil of the riverbank, where they were being led away by armed Americans.

Rosa took a run-up, leapt over and landed on the river bank. As she rolled to get up, her cap fell off, revealing her shoulder-length blonde hair.

"Another one," said a GI rushing in to grab her.

A GI corporal yelled out, "Take her to the truck with the others, be quick. They're just about to leave."

The GI pointed his rifle at Rosa and indicated a truck full of women in uniform. Rosa had nowhere to run as she was surrounded by thousands of American and German soldiers. She trudged up to the side of the road where the lorry was idling.

"Here's one more before you go," said the GI as he unhooked the rear of the truck and lifted Rosa into the outstretched arms of the waiting German women, who helped her up.

"Where are they taking us?" Rosa asked one of the German women.

"My English is very good," said another woman. "They are taking us back to another bridge further south from here and will hand us over to the Russians."

"What?" Rosa asked. "Why would they do that? Don't they know what will happen to us?"

"Rape us to death. The Americans know that."

Just as the truck was about to drive away, a jeep pulled up and stopped in front of the truck, preventing it from leaving. A blonde-haired woman got out of the passenger seat and climbed onto the bonnet of the jeep.

"My God, that's Marlene Dietrich," said one woman.

"Marlene Dietrich," said the others in amazement.

"What's so special about Marlene Dietrich?" asked Rosa. "She's just an actress."

They all stopped and stared at her.

"Marlene Dietrich is not just anybody; she is the most famous actress."

"Not just in Germany, but in the entire world," said another. "It was said that before the war, she was the highest-paid actor in all of Hollywood."

"A German actress, who has betrayed her country," said an older woman, who didn't seem to be as impressed as the others. "She's here performing and entertaining for our enemy."

Rosa looked at Miss Dietrich, knowing exactly who it was before anybody mentioned her name. Rosa immediately recognised the image of the woman from the poster of *The Blue Angel*, which hung in Director Riefenstahl's office—a reminder of the person who stole the director's starring role in the classic German film.

Marlene Dietrich finally spoke after a crowd of GIs had circled her. "Driver, where do you intend taking these women?"

"Back to the Russians."

"You know what will happen to them once the Russians have them. They won't last five minutes."

"Miss Dietrich, I'm only a soldier. Orders are orders."

"That's what the Germans always say."

The blocked truck was holding up traffic. Drivers in other military vehicles behind started pressing their horns, trying to beep the traffic jam away. Over the noise, the German woman who spoke English translated the conversation.

An American MP in his white helmet raced up to the truck driver, signalling him to cut the engine, which the truck driver did. "What's the hold-up? Move it, Buster."

"I can't. Miss Dietrich refuses to get out of the way," said the truck driver, pointing.

The MP turned to face the woman as if seeing her for the first time. "Miss Dietrich?" he asked. "What is going on here?"

"Do you know what they are going to do with these women? They are going to hand them over to the Russians."

"That's correct," the MP replied. "I'm sorry, Miss Dietrich. We can accept the surrender of military members only, and all civilians are to be handed over to the Russians for processing."

"Processing? Do you know what the Russians will do to these women? Some of them are just teenagers, for Christ's sake. And we all know that there won't be any *processing* going on. We can't do it. It's inhumane."

"I'm sorry, Miss Dietrich, but this is strict orders from up high. We've made a deal with the Russians about the processing of civilian prisoners."

Rosa could see that while Marlene Dietrich was distraught, the MP was unmoved.

The driver of Miss Dietrich's jeep cut his engine before speaking. "Corporal, do you know why Miss Dietrich is here in Germany?"

This question caught the MP off guard, but he answered nonetheless. "Who are you, Buster?"

The driver stood up on his driver's seat so that Rosa had a good view of him. She could see that he had a black patch over his left eye and a hook where his left hand should have been. He reminded Rosa of a pirate dressed in a GI uniform. As Rosa looked at his hook, she instantly thought of her mother's missing finger.

"Corporal, it's *Sergeant* Mayflower to you," he said with a stern look from his steel-grey right eye.

"Sorry, Sergeant," the MP said in a distinctly softer tone.

"I'm Sgt. Mayflower, and I'm Miss Dietrich's personal escort while she's entertaining us Americans on the front lines. And I'll ask again, do you know why Miss Dietrich is here in Germany?"

"To entertain the troops."

"Yes. But everyone here, including the top brass, knows she's really here to rescue her family, including her sister and her mother. And Miss Dietrich has just identified her sister."

"She has?"

"Yes. And do you want to be known as the person who handed Marlene Dietrich's sister over to Ivan the Terrible?"

"Of course not, Sarge."

The MP looked at Miss Dietrich. "Which one is she?"

"There, that one there, she's my sister," she said, pointing to one of the women.

The corporal nodded to his fellow MP, who jumped into the back of the truck and helped the identified woman down.

Once the nominated woman was off the truck, Marlene pointed to another woman. "She is also my sister."

The MP standing in the back of the truck looked at the Corporal, who was now standing next to Sgt. Mayflower, who said, "She has more than one sister. How many sisters do you have, corporal?"

"Three." The Corporal nodded, allowing the second woman off the back of the truck.

Once the MP removed the second woman, Marlene pointed to yet another woman. "She's also *Meine Schwester*, I mean, my sister."

Marlene's slip back into her mother tongue gave the German women enough information to work out exactly what was happening. They all screamed at Marlene, "*Schwester! Schwester! Schwester!*"

Marlene pointed at the other women. "She's my sister! And she's my sister!" Marlene rushed to the back of the truck. "Help me, boys. These girls are all my sisters!"

The assembled GIs rushed forward and helped all the German women alight from the back of the truck.

The corporal MP glared at Sgt. Mayflower.

"What can I say?" Sgt. Mayflower shrugged. "She comes from a big family."

***

The driver had been ordered to take the truckload of Miss Dietrich's *sisters* to wherever Miss Dietrich stipulated. Miss Dietrich's jeep, driven by her hook-handed and black-eye-patched GI sergeant, lead the way from the bridge.

According to the driver, the truck stopped at a German town

about 50-miles away from the bridge. US military vehicles were quartered in the town, and personnel were moving about the town as if they owned it. This seemed a very welcome sight to all the women alighting from the truck with the help of passing GIs.

Miss Dietrich came up and spoke to the assembled girls, handing each of them bundles of American money. "You should be safe here for now, but, remember, frontlines move every day, and the Americans could move out tomorrow to be replaced by the Russians, so act wisely and quickly."

The drive through American-held territory had given Rosa plenty of time to think things over. Rosa's plan of finding and rescuing her father in Berlin was gone the moment Leni *rescued* Rosa from Berlin. There was no way she could break through Russian lines to get back into Berlin, which would fall any day now. No, she had only one thing left to do, and that was to avenge her family.

Director Riefenstahl, in her drug-addled state, had laid the blame squarely on one Miss Marlene Dietrich. Over the years, Rosa had come to believe that Leni Riefenstahl was in Cologne that day on the orders of the Führer to have a meeting with Miss Dietrich. Rosa didn't know what the meeting was about, but she did know one thing for certain. Marlene Dietrich was at the centre of it, and, if it hadn't been for Miss Dietrich, then her family would have made it to France and then Spain, and they would have been free. Rosa hadn't been able to kill Leni Riefenstahl in her office or Adolf Hitler in the garden above the Führer Bunker. But she could kill Marlene Dietrich.

And here she was now, standing only a few feet from Marlene Dietrich. It was fate. How many forks in the roads did she take, how many miles had she travelled, and how many bridges had she crossed to get to this very moment for the two of them to each meet their shared destiny? She felt the hilt of her Hitler Youth knife still in its scabbard: no one had removed it from her. Maybe it was because she was *only* a girl.

As each woman received the money, they thanked Miss Dietrich before leaving, even the older lady that called Miss Dietrich a traitor took the offered money. Rosa waited until she was last in line. She grabbed the hilt of her blade, tightening her grip. Then Rosa was left alone with Miss Dietrich with money in hand. Rosa took a step back.

"No, it's for you," said Miss Dietrich with a bundle of money in hand, advancing on Rosa. "Take it."

Rosa suddenly sprang at Marlene Dietrich, knife in hand.

Rosa was catlike, but Sgt. Mayflower was an ambushing tiger. He rifle-butted her in the head, knocking her out.

\*\*\*

Rosa slowly came to. She was on a chair. She went to move but couldn't. She looked at her hands, and they had been tied to the arms of the chair by a white cord. She tried moving her feet but couldn't; she could feel the rope tied to the front legs of her chair.

Rosa looked around and recognised she was inside the building where they had pulled up. It seemed to be the local post office, which the GIs were now using. One of the soldiers who was sorting several letters looked up at Rosa.

"Go tell Miss Dietrich the prisoner is awake," he said to another soldier, who disappeared into another room.

Miss Dietrich and her one-eyed GI entered the room and stood immediately in front of Rosa. Rosa stared intensely at Marlene Dietrich. Rosa saw for the first time that Miss Dietrich was very tall—six-foot-plus. Her face pale with high cheekbones and the widest of eyes; her long, dark eyelashes highlighted her sultry eyes, and her face was quite rigid—almost mask-like. Miss Dietrich spoke in German to Rosa. "What is your name?"

Silence.

"If you don't answer my questions, I will have you returned to the other side of the river."

Rosa's eyes opened in response because it looked like the woman meant it.

"Yes. The Americans are returning all civilians back across the river. So, I suggest, if you don't want to be handed over to the Russians, you need to start talking."

"Rosa."

"What?"

"I said my name is Rosa."

"And why are you wearing that Hitler Youth uniform?"

"I had to so that I could find my father in Berlin."

"Berlin? Have you been to Berlin?"

"Berlin is destroyed. It is nothing but rubble and ruin. The jewel of Germany is nothing more than a ghetto now."

Marlene looked distressed by this news. She sat down in her chair. "My God, I'm too late," she said in English. "My mother is surely dead." She looked at the girl and spoke in German again. "Did you find your father?"

"My father's camp has been destroyed. He's either dead or been moved to another camp somewhere. Either way, I'll never see him again."

"Camp? Was your father a political prisoner?"

"Romani."

"So, you are saying that you're a Gypsy girl wearing a Hitler Youth uniform?"

"Yes," said Rosa.

Marlene moved her chair closer to the bound teenager.

"Why did you do that?" said Miss Dietrich holding Rosa's knife. "Is it because you think I am a traitor to the German Fatherland?"

"What? I don't care about the Fatherland. I care only about my father, and it is your fault that he's probably dead!"

"What? How could I possibly—"

"—The church."

"The church?"

"The church at Cologne. You were there. It's all your fault. Director Leni Riefenstahl told me everything."

Miss Dietrich's face registered in understanding.

"What church in Cologne?" Sgt. Mayflower asked. "What on earth is the child babbling on about?"

"She's talking about the Cologne Cathedral. Half a decade ago, on the eve of war, I was supposed to secretly return to Germany to get my family out before it was too late. We were meant to meet in Switzerland. But my family said it was impossible to leave Germany and instructed me to get a boat and pick them up on the Rhine in the city of Cologne. I had a very good friend, French actor Jean Gabin who, when he wasn't filming a movie, was helping rescue Jews from Germany." She laughed, "You should have seen his face when I asked him to smuggle a German back into Germany..."

*** 

## Flashback...

Early morning, 1 September 1939 (Friday)

*On the Rhine River, somewhere north of Cologne...*

Marlene Dietrich stood next to Jean Gabin as he steered the motorboat down the Rhine River. He stared through the front window up at the incandescent full moon. Normally, this would allow him to navigate these treacherous waters, but it was useless in the fog that now blanketed the river, so now he was steering more from memory and desperation than anything else. Marlene could hear the other river vessels in the cloudy whiteness—horns blaring, bells ringing, and engines chugging. She understood his caution, but her stomach was churning now that she was this close to Germany and her family. She hadn't been back here in years. Back in 1933, when Adolf Hitler first became the Chancellor of Germany, she had tried to convince her family to move to America with her. They refused. But with the war now imminent, they saw the light and contacted her.

The water vessel turned around a bend and faced a strong breeze, which helped to thin out the fog. The dawning sun then burnt off the remainder of the mist hanging over the river, allowing Gabin to see lights emanating from the other watercraft and familiar landmarks. After another three sweeping bends in the river, they both saw the distinctive mediaeval towers and arches of Cologne.

Gabin fumbled for the lamp near the wheel and turned it on. Squinting as his eyes adjusted, he looked at the large brass compass, colourful maps and a wall-mounted barometer. His instruments told him that today would be ideal autumn weather, a sign that their luck was holding.

Above the headboard was an engraved wooden sign: *The Seagull*. Marlene thought that this was an apt name for this small white vessel whose engine's high-pitched squawk matched that of a flock of hungry seagulls. Her eyes focused on a flyer lying on a table against the back wall of the cabin:

## THE BERLIN PEACE RALLY

### Dr Joseph Goebbels presents

## THE ARMIES OF THE THIRD REICH

### Berlin

### 01 September 1939

Gabin smiled at her. "My plan is perfect. All of Germany's Wehrmacht will converge on Berlin, on Germany's eastern border with Poland, for this Nazi propaganda parade—and no one loves parades more than the Nazis. My friends have reported that, as a result, Germany will have only fat, lazy border guards protecting the western points of entry; there would be none of the feared SS or Gestapo. We will sneak in through the back door from the west via Holland. Pick them up at a Cologne jetty next to the distinct Hohenzollern Bridge. And then keep on moving up the river to France so that you can go to Paris and catch your ride back to America on the ocean liner the *SS Normandie* with your family in tow. Perfect!"

Their cover was that of a French husband and wife exporting wines to and from Holland. The vessel's cargo consisted of spirits and wines—ideal for bribes. Border guards around the world were the easiest to bypass—as long as they felt they were getting something for nothing, they were always happy.

Gabin turned and looked into his reflection in the glass, combing his naturally lush hair, now dyed grey. His nose matched his strong jaw, which ended in his trademark dimpled chin. He stuck on a matching moustache and beard. He added an eye patch for good measure.

"Maybe my next movie should be as a sea captain," he said, smiling.

Marlene smiled back at him. "You know Jean, the American press has already labelled you as France's version of their acting great, Humphrey Bogart."

"Humphrey Bogart? I don't mind that. However, my English is perfect, and if only Hollywood would give me some work, then America could have the real thing: Jean Gabin."

She put on a short-haired brunette wig and scarf using the same mirror her friend had just used. Then she donned a large pair of sunglasses.

"*Voilá!* What do you think?"

"*C'est magnifique*," he said, kissing the tips of his fingers, imitating a chef.

Jean pulled at the *Seagull*'s wheel. The boat rounded the final bend, and there was the centre of the river-split city of Cologne. They came alongside one of the city's many unremarkable jetties not far from the distinguished Hohenzollern Bridge—named after German and Prussian emperors.

Marlene leapt off the deck and landed lightly on the wooden landing.

"What are you doing?" Gabin called out in a loud whisper, alarmed. "We are supposed to wait here for them!"

"I'm sorry, Jean, but they aren't here. They couldn't possibly know which jetty would be empty. I have to go and meet them. You can wait here for me if you wish. I won't be long."

He cut the engine, and the boat's screeching died. Other than the sound of fast river water flowing under them, all was silent. He checked his watch. "Marlene, where exactly are they?"

"They said that they were going to wait inside the Cologne Cathedral." Her eyes were riveted on their surroundings. "I can't believe it. I am back in Germany!" She inhaled. "Germany smells so different to America. Perhaps it is the smell of home." She paused and looked about. "But it's so odd…"

"What?"

"There is nobody around. No fishermen, no port authorities, no passers-by on their way to work. Nothing. It looks like a ghost town, like in an American western."

"Maybe it's a trap? Perhaps we should—" He stopped talking as she hurried away. "Come back! It isn't safe!"

She halted and turned. "Don't be such a worry-wart. My family is waiting for me at the Cologne Cathedral. It's not far from here." And off she went.

Jean jumped onto the wharf and secured the boat to the moorings before chasing after her. They walked up the stairs onto the street and looked around—still absolutely no one walking around. Germany's fourth-largest city was deserted.

"I have to stay with the boat. If the authorities come and no one is here, they could seize it."

She looked up and spied the towers of the cathedral and ran towards them.

Jean waited on the jetty.

\*\*\*

Marlene slowed as she walked towards the grand old building; she was transfixed by the vast 700-year-old masterpiece. At an intimidating 157-metres high, it was not only Cologne's tallest landmark but also a monument to Germanic architecture.

Halfway up the tall building, flying buttresses propelled upwards into the clear blue sky. The cathedral's dominant two dark-brown spires, which felt entirely Germanic to her, guarded either side of the main entrance where she now stood, engulfing her in its morning shadow.

She stood in the shadow of the cathedral and looked around the empty market square in front of the cathedral, which was only a couple of hundred metres from the Hohenzollern Bridge, one of the many that crisscrossed the Rhine to join west Cologne to east Cologne. This bridge was by far the largest and most modern; the upper level was for pedestrian and automotive traffic, while the lower level was for trains and trams. But today was different. Although the bridge and the market square should have been teeming with early-morning traffic by now, it was deathly quiet. Neither person nor vehicle was seen to be moving about this great Teutonic city.

Once inside the cathedral, she saw the twelve-foot stone statue of St. Christopher, the patron saint of travellers. She instinctively reached for her St. Christopher pendant hanging around her neck, which she wore whenever she travelled—for protection and good luck. Marlene took her sunglasses off. Her eyes adjusted to the gloomy interior, which was still dark despite the early morning light. The sound of the door closing echoed loudly behind her inside the reverberating building. Hundreds of candles, the major source of light, lined the cathedral walls and flickered with the gust of fresh air that she brought in with her.

The Cologne Cathedral had the usual Gothic cruciform plan— in the shape of the Lord's cross—with its typically high ceilings. She'd heard this church was the home of such treasures as the Shrine of the Three Holy Kings, reputedly a golden sarcophagus studded with jewels containing the bones of the Three Wise Men from the Bible, and the Gero Cross—the oldest surviving crucifix in Northern Europe. She imagined the holy relics hidden somewhere in the catacombs below this great church. She felt the whole place reeked of Catholicism and Christianity. It wasn't just old; it was so archaic that Marlene felt as though she was breathing the same air as her medieval ancestors.

As her eyes adjusted to the dim, smoky light, she could see some figures seated towards the front of the cathedral. She walked down the aisle to the people sitting on the front-row pews. As Marlene drew nearer to them, she could see the group consisted of a youngish couple and an elderly woman.

The young woman was Marlene's sister (Elizabeth, or Liesel as she preferred to be called). Liesel had none of Marlene's looks, talent or sense of adventure; nonetheless, she had inherited all of their mother's haughty Prussian mannerisms. Although Liesel was a year younger than Marlene, she would always try to order Marlene around—without much success.

The man seated next to Liesel was her husband, Georg, a cinema fanatic who had run several playhouses, theatres and cinemas over the years but wasn't very good at it. Just like his wife, Georg was devoid of any creative or business talent. Marlene was also convinced that he'd only married the plain-looking woman because of her famous sister. Marlene loathed her brother-in-law.

The regal, older woman was Marlene's mother, Frau Dietrich von Losch. The Dietrich matriarch remained seated and stared ahead the whole time. She had inherited that proud aristocratic arrogance for which the Prussians were famed.

The younger woman and man rose to greet Marlene. In a place like this, a whisper travelled to all corners of the cathedral, as the original architects would have intended—not only could the congregation hear the priest's sermon and the choir's singing, but it also encouraged the congregation's quiet contemplation of God and not to whisper to one another.

"Liesel, how are you, sister dearest?" Marlene kissed her sister on the cheek.

"Marie Magdalene—sorry, I forgot, it's Marlene now." Liesel politely kissed Marlene on the cheek in return.

"It's been *Marlene* for quite some time now," Marlene said with a forced smile.

"And Georg," Liesel said, indicating her husband.

Georg went to kiss Marlene's cheek, but before he could do that, she raised her hand. Georg, flustered for a second, clumsily reached for her hand and kissed it instead.

"My dear brother-in-law, how I missed you," Marlene said in an even tone.

Georg smiled, seemingly oblivious to the insult.

Marlene knelt down next to the elderly lady. "Mother. You don't know how good it is to see you again." Marlene kissed her mother tenderly on her pale, wrinkled cheek.

"Marie," her mother said coldly without looking into her daughter's eyes.

Marlene stood and looked around. "Where are your suitcases? Where are the children? We must leave straight away. Our boat is waiting for you."

"We are not going," said her mother flatly.

"What? I thought you said you had changed your mind!"

"Your German must be getting rusty, big sister," Liesel said. "We meant that we wanted to change *your* mind."

"Change my mind?"

"About coming back to Germany. Sister, the Fatherland needs you now more than ever."

"You mean my fatherless land. This country has already taken away both my fathers in fruitless wars. And, sister, if you don't want to make your children fatherless as well, you'll come with me now."

Georg looked uneasy at the implication.

"Georg is safe," Liesel said in a raised voice. "*He* has nothing to fear. *He's* not a traitor to Germany like you are. You don't know the pain you have caused this family. Oh, the shame you bring to the *Dietrich* name!"

"What shame? I'm an international movie star. The whole world now knows the *Dietrich* name because of me."

"All your films have been banned in Germany," Georg said in an effort to break the awkward silence. "By the Führer himself!"

"A hypocrite, nothing more," Marlene quipped. "I've heard he has copies of all my movies, including my Hollywood movies."

"You think this a joke?" her mother said, snapping. "We are giving you a chance to restore the family honour—or does that mean nothing to you, Marie?" Frau Dietrich von Losch implored her daughter, looking directly into Marlene's eyes for the first time.

Marlene broke the gaze and looked down.

"How? By becoming a Nazi?"

"By being a loyal German citizen! It's the Prussian way."

"Look, I have a big, empty mansion in Hollywood, the biggest in a big street," Marlene said. "Big enough for all of us not to see each other for days at a time if that's what you all wish. But we have to get out of this country right now. War could break out at any—"

The cathedral doors suddenly swung open, followed by the sounds of a goose-stepping march.

*** 

Marlene turned to see Leni Riefenstahl dressed all in white stride down the aisle of the cathedral flanked by two armed SS Storm Troopers. The nailed heels of the armed, helmeted men echoed on the marbled floor; they marched in time with the clicking of Leni's high heels. When they reached the hub of the cathedral, she snapped her fingers. The two men abruptly halted in unison.

Leni sauntered over to Marlene, drawing out the moment, stopping next to her and pausing to unbutton her white greatcoat.

None of the Dietrich family said a word.

"What a marvellous example of German engineering, don't you think?" Leni asked Marlene in English. She knew that, as no one around them spoke English, they could have their public conversation in private. "The nice little clergyman, the caretaker here," Leni continued, "told me that they started building this cathedral in 1248. Do you know how old it is? I do. I had plenty of time to figure it out while I was waiting for you to arrive. In 1948, this old girl will be 700 years old. And when it was finally completed in 1880, the Cologne Cathedral was the tallest building in the world." She looked at the vacant seat next to Marlene. "May I?"

Marlene nodded.

Leni sat down. "And do you know what that means, Marlene?"

Marlene shook her head.

"It means not only do the German people build things to last, but also they are a patient people. And the Führer has been very patient with you." She took off her white satin gloves and pulled out a rose-gold cigarette case, offering a cigarette to Marlene.

"No thanks, Leni," Marlene said. "In case you haven't noticed, this is a church."

After taking one herself, Leni snapped shut the cigarette case. "Oh, come now. You and I were never church-goers—or has the land of the Puritans changed you?"

"It must have. In Los Angeles, as of June this year, I became an American citizen. Citizenship Certificate number 4656928. Americans are as fond of numbers as Germans are. You must have read about it. It was in all the papers."

"Quite. Please, let us, sisters of cinema, not argue. We have come a long way from our hungry actress days, have we not?"

"Please. We're neither sisters nor friends. And as I remember, Leni, you were never hungry for long."

"We do what we have to do to survive," Leni said, lighting her cigarette and inhaling deeply. She exhaled, watching the smoke caught in a beam of light shining down on them like a spotlight on the two German actresses. "Besides, I don't remember you being so virginal." Leni then pointed to the large wooden cross with its life-sized Jesus Christ hanging before them. "Maybe you should be up there on the cross instead." Leni exhaled again, smoke hovering about her head like a halo. "And I'm sure you didn't become *the* Marlene Dietrich by being an angel, indeed, the *Blue Angel* if I'm not mistaken," she said. "You know better than any of us that in this man's world one does what is necessary to get ahead in this business."

"Is locking up Jews *business*?"

"Hardly what I was talking about, but it's for their own protection."

"And who protects them from their protectors?"

"You think we don't know about your traitorous activities?" Leni said. "We could arrest you for illegally smuggling German Jews to America!" She composed herself by straightening her hair.

"I am an American now. You wouldn't dare."

"Being an American is immaterial to us. We do as we see fit."

"Leni, I'm sure you aren't here to reminisce. What was the point of all this?"

"Quite. I have a plane waiting, so I'll get to the point." Leni threw her cigarette on the floor, crushing it with her heel. "I was sent here to ask you to serve the Fatherland. The Führer wants you to head the UFA studios in Berlin. You can film any movie you want, for any budget you want, for any salary you want."

"A blank cheque?"

"A disgusting American term. Call it whatever you like."

"What about the Minister for Enlightenment and Propaganda?" Marlene asked. "I seem to recall a certain Dr Goebbels always hanging around backstage, smarming around young aspiring actresses, promising them the world if they played with his clubbed foot."

"You don't need to be concerned about him. You will answer directly to the Führer."

"Like you?"

Leni didn't answer the question. "So, what is your answer?"

"Never. I will never serve Hitler."

Leni stared into Marlene's eyes.

"What will you do with me now, Leni?"

"I'm sure the German authorities will know what to do with you. You are not my problem now."

Leni got up and took a few steps towards the door of the church.

"So, this is how you want to go down in history?" Marlene called out after her.

Leni wheeled around and walked up to Marlene until they were inches away from each other. "What do you mean?"

Marlene smiled. "If you do this, from now on, regardless of what you have done or what you do in the future, you will always be remembered as the person who sent Marlene Dietrich to the gallows. You won't be famous; you'll be infamous. And what do you think your American friends will think of you then? Artists are supposed to be above politics, and they certainly don't murder other artists. Unless you are trying to tell the world that you are jealous of me and my success?"

"Enough!" Leni turned away from Marlene. "I knew this would be a waste of time. But luckily for you, the Führer has more pressing concerns."

"What will happen to my family?" Marlene asked.

Leni looked at Marlene's family, still sitting silently in the pews. "Your family are loyal Germans. In fact, I have seen to it that your brother-in-law will be promoted."

Georg and Liesel's tense faces broke into a smile upon hearing this news.

Marlene looked at Georg. "I should have known it was you who betrayed me."

"If you will excuse me," Leni said, walking away.

"Going to Nuremberg to film another Nazi rally, I suppose?"

Leni stopped and turned around. "I'm going to Berlin to hear the Führer's address before I head off to Poland."

"Poland?"

"Haven't you heard? Germany invaded Poland this morning."

This shocked Marlene.

"Did you not wonder where the people of Cologne are? Like all Germans throughout the country, they are inside their houses listening to the radio as the announcers describe in detail what is happening in Poland, bullet by bullet. Germany's greatest triumph is at hand, and the Führer wants me to shoot it."

Outside the cathedral, the city had come to life. The streets were full of boisterous cheering and smiling faces. The citizens of Cologne waved their little Nazi flags. Germany had indeed invaded Poland.

***

## 11 April 1945 (Wednesday)

"I don't remember seeing you," said Marlene Dietrich. "But I do remember seeing a Gypsy wagon burning in the street outside the cathedral. Yours?"

Rosa nodded.

"I don't understand. None of this explains why this girl just tried to kill you," said the GI sergeant.

"I'm guessing this girl came across Leni Riefenstahl and she has somehow blamed me for whatever happened to her family. Is that right, Rosa?"

Rosa nodded again.

"What did Director Riefenstahl say exactly?"

"Director Riefenstahl said my family's arrest at Cologne Cathedral was *your* doing."

Miss Dietrich laughed. "I suppose, in a way, *Director Riefenstahl* is technically correct. If I didn't meet my family at the Cologne Cathedral on that particular day, then you and your family would never have been arrested."

Rosa knew Miss Marlene was right. "I can't explain it," said Rosa. "I knew deep down it was a lie, yet at the same time, I was convinced she was right, even though I knew Director Riefenstahl was incapable of speaking the truth."

"Don't feel guilty. If you get told a lie often enough and loud enough, the lie soon becomes your reality. The entire German nation fell for exactly the same trick with Adolf Hitler. Eventually, they believed they never lost the First World War. And, somehow, it was the fault of the Jews." After a contemplative pause, she asked, "How long were you with Leni?"

"Three years."

Rosa sunk into her chair.

"Rosa, the reason why I'm here serving on the frontlines with the USO is to find my family. I don't know where they are but my fear is that they are all in Berlin where the Nazis can keep an eye on them. That's why I was so interested when I learned you just came from Berlin. But from what you've just said I may be too late."

Rosa lit up when she realised that Miss Dietrich was planning on going to Berlin. Maybe Miss Dietrich would be there once Germany was defeated. Rosa could still find her father.

"Okay, Sgt. Mayflower, you can untie her now. I think we're all safe from this girl."

"A girl who almost killed you," Sgt. Mayflower said, cutting the cords using Rosa's knife, which he handed back to Miss Dietrich.

"Please, Miss Dietrich, let me stay with you. I can help. I don't know what the USO is but I can learn. If I can learn about films, I can learn about the USO," Rosa said, pleading.

Miss Dietrich stared into Rosa's eyes for what felt like an age before speaking. "Okay. I'll give you one chance. I'm in the middle of a war, surrounded by men. I mean, I love them, but they are all next to useless when it comes to working backstage, especially when I'm almost naked all the time. I need a girl to help me backstage, especially as I change costumes, etcetera, etcetera. I have a performance tonight. And if you pass, then you're hired. How does that sound?"

"Fine, thank you," said Rosa, her head swimming.

"No way," said Sgt. Mayflower. "I forbid it."

"Well, that's settled. If a man forbids me, then I absolutely *have* to help this poor Gypsy girl. Anyway, what's the chance of lightning striking twice," said Miss Dietrich, handing Rosa's knife back to her.

"What? We can't! You can't trust her!"

"Why not?"

"Apart from trying to stab you, since when are Gypsies blonde?"

"Gypsies adopted an abandoned girl from the streets of Berlin," Rosa said, "but I'm a Romani, and we always honour our word. I will never try something like that again."

"You're a Berlin-born girl like me?" asked Miss Dietrich. "Sounds good enough for me. Let's go. I'm starving."

She led the way out of the building, jumped into her jeep and beeped the horn for them both to hurry.

"You'd better get used to the sound of that beep," said Sgt. Mayflower. "She's always in a hurry. But, girl, know this. I may have only one eye, but if I see you looking at her in the wrong way, I will kill you. And give me that thing." He snatched the Hitler Youth blade and his one steely-grey eye stared at hers. "I don't want you even using a spoon around Miss Dietrich."

## Chapter 19

12 April 1945 (Thursday)

*Somewhere inside US-controlled Nazi Germany*

A man in uniform and spectacles walked out onto the brightly lit stage, which had been hastily erected in the middle of a paddock. "Here she is, the lovely Miss Dietrich."

He left the raised stadium that overlooked the thousands of grinning GIs sitting on the grass crossed-legged. The stage was empty. Tension increased the longer the stage remained empty. The GIs started to boo and shouted for Miss Dietrich to come out.

The compere came back to the stage and looked awkwardly to either side. It seemed someone off stage was prompting him towards the microphone. "I'm sorry, fellas, but it appears that once the officers learned that Miss Dietrich was in town, they seconded her to the local Officers' Club for a *debriefing*."

Sgt. Mayflower, who was sitting next to Rosa backstage, jumped to his feet. "What? Why wasn't I informed?"

This shock announcement rallied the boys to stand up and throw things at the stage as they hollered and hooted in protest.

Then, from the rear of the grassed area, Marlene Dietrich appeared as if from nowhere. She was wearing an officer's uniform with the rank of colonel. As she marched towards the stage, the men parted as they applauded. Rosa had never heard anything like it. The applause and screaming were deafening. Miss Dietrich walked up the stage stairs and over to the vacated microphone.

Silence.

"Hello, boys."

They cheered again.

"It's true. The officers tried to commandeer me for the war

effort, so they said," she said with a wink.

The men booed at this notion of officers keeping her just for themselves.

"But, as some of you may or may not know, the US Army has given us entertainers the imaginary rank, I mean, the honorary rank of captain."

The boys laughed at the "imaginary rank" reference. She knew what it was like to be a soldier mixed up in an officer's toy-soldier war. They loved her for that.

"Only captain? But I've done my tours in North Africa and Italy, I say, so I demanded a promotion. So, they made me a major. What do you think of that, boys?"

One of the GIs yelled out, "I'd serve under you any day, Major Dietrich!"

The boys around him gave him a playful shove as the other GIs erupted with laughter.

Once she had stopped laughing, she spoke again. "However, the officers still refused to let Major Dietrich go to the frontlines and serve with her troops." She let the boos die down. "So, I promoted myself to colonel and ordered them to release me, and so here I am."

They whooped and cheered again.

She looked down at her military garb and then feigned a look of surprise. "Oh, no. It looks like I'm out of uniform." Before any of the audience had a chance to make another innuendo, she ripped off her uniform to howls of delight. Her new uniform was a beige skin-coloured figure-hugging dress, which she referred to as her "naked" dress because from a distance, it did appear as if she was indeed naked.

She started to sing "Falling in Love Again" from her international movie hit *The Blue Angel*.

The boys fell silent as the haunting melody echoed over the fields of sad, smiling, faces as they remembered their sweethearts back home. But once she finished that song, she roused the boys with her *Destry Rides Again* hit, as she sang to her crowd: "See What the Boys in the Back Room Will Have".

Once this number was finished, she quickly did a costume change with Rosa from her naked suit to a full-length white dress, before returning to the stage. She wiped her forehead. "I'm pooped. I think I need to sit down."

A military stagehand raced out with a seat. The body-length dress split open, revealing her world-famous million-dollar legs. Rosa had learned many things about Marlene over the years of being in the employ of Director Riefenstahl, including that a Hollywood studio had insured her legs for the princely sum of one million dollars each, and every man who saw her legs on stage tonight thought they were worth every penny.

"I think I need something long between my legs. What do you think, boys?"

The men screamed their lungs out.

She turned, and the stagehand brought out a bladeless saw and violin bow. She placed the wooden handle of the large saw on the stage floor and, with her left hand, bent the top of the saw blade over. "And now I'm going to play 'Pagan Love Song' for you boys." She used the large bow on the flat side of the saw, and although she was playing it like a cello, the sound that emanated from between her legs was more akin to a harp—a wobbly-sounding harp, it had to be said. And she was a hit.

As she climbed down off the stage, the GIs were yelling their approval. Miss Dietrich handed Sgt. Mayflower her bow and said, "To quote Julius Caesar: 'I came, I saw, I conquered.'"

While Rosa helped Marlene change costumes, she looked over at Sgt. Mayflower, still holding the saw and bow, before he stormed off. Rosa learned from Miss Dietrich that he was a career soldier and had enlisted years before the war began. He finally saw battle when he fought in north Africa against General Rommel's war-hardened Africa Korps, who defeated the inexperienced Americans in their very first battle against the Germans back in early 1943, where he lost his left hand and left eye.

In place of his left hand, he had two stainless-steel hooks splayed at the bottom and merging upwards to within an inch of each other, where he could pick things up. He'd specially designed his twin hook so that he could twist the splayed hook around so that the wider part of the hook could snuggly hold the stock of a US M1 carbine rifle. But despite all this, the US Army refused to send him back to the frontlines to rejoin his troops.

But his relentless campaign to return to the war in Europe was finally rewarded when he was offered the job of escorting Marlene Dietrich, which he seemed to resent. Here he was back on the frontlines, but not as a fighter as he'd wished for but rather as a lowly escort to an entertainer. In Rosa's eyes, he didn't seem to appreciate that he was only on the frontlines solely because of Miss Dietrich, who, unlike the other USO entertainers, thought the frontline troops were in the most need of her entertainment rather than performing back in Paris or London.

Rosa was surprised when she learned that Sgt. Mayflower was also born in Berlin and moved to America when he was ten. His family changed their name to Mayflower because their German family name was related to flowers, and the Mayflower was one of the first English ships to arrive in America.

Miss Dietrich was in full swing, performing the second half of her show when an officer entered the stage mid-act. The music stopped. The hooting and hollering ceased. The colonel whispered something into her ear and handed her a piece of paper. Her smiling face dropped, replaced with a stunned expression. She stepped up to the microphone stand that had been quickly moved into place.

"Boys, I'm afraid I have some bad news for us all."

Silence.

"Today, in the early hours of the morning, President Franklin Delano Roosevelt, our president for the last twelve years, died in his sleep," she said solemnly.

A stunned silence. Some of the younger men cried.

She continued speaking. "As of this afternoon, Vice-President Harry S. Truman has been sworn in."

Silence again.

Marlene Dietrich sang 'The Star-Spangled Banner'. "Oh, say can you see, By the dawn's early light..." The assembled men rose as one. All the on-duty guards and officials removed their headdress and joined the soldiers and officers in singing with her.

"What so proudly we hailed / At the twilight's last gleaming...."

# Chapter 20

## 18 April (Wednesday)

*Somewhere inside US-controlled Nazi Germany*

According to Miss Dietrich, Rosa was the perfect German POW, and everybody should have one. Initially, Marlene had tried to get Rosa into a dress, but being surrounded by tens of thousands of military men would draw too much attention. Within a few hours of joining Miss Dietrich's USO, Rosa was wearing a GI outfit, and with her blonde, shoulder-length hair, she was Marlene Dietrich's twin in miniature.

Rosa's English improved noticeably in only a matter of days as she was the most consummate of imitators. Once she heard an English phrase, she would use it almost immediately. One morning, while Miss Dietrich was seated in her white bathrobe and matching slippers reading the American military newspaper *Stars and Stripes*, Rosa brought in Miss Dietrich's breakfast and sat it on the dressing table.

"Miss Dietrich?"

"Yes?"

"Thank you for helping my English and telling me about the United Service Organizations and all things American."

"English is not that hard, but I have to admit the day I set foot in Germany, I think and dream in German. Isn't that strange?"

"And thank you for helping me and not sending me back over the bridge."

"Darling, I would never have done that. That was simply Sergeant Mayflower bullying a frightened little girl."

"A little girl who tried to kill you."

"You're not the only one. The German army almost killed me."

"Really?"

"Yes. In the Ardennes. They call it the Battle of the Bulge, but I call it my 1944 Christmas Hell. We were caught behind enemy lines. But Sergeant Mayflower did his duty, as my escort and looked after me until General George Patton and his 3rd Army came to rescue me from the Third Reich. George, a close personal friend, even gave me one of his famous pearl-handled revolvers as a present."

"What is that necklace you wear?" Rosa asked, pointing at Miss Dietrich's silver pendant that she wore along with her dog tags that she was required to wear whenever on the frontlines, as all soldiers were required to do.

"Oh, that's my St. Christopher, patron saint for travellers and wanderers, which I always wear whenever I'm on the road," she said removing her necklace and handing it to Rosa. "I have spare ones, so I'll give you this one. I know this one works," she added with a wink.

"Thank you," said Rosa, taking the offered necklace. "You've been so good to me." She rose to leave but wanted to compliment Miss Dietrich before she left. "Miss Dietrich, you have great gams."

"Really? Where did you hear that word?" asked Miss Dietrich with a grin.

"I hear the men say it all the time, especially when you are up on stage smiling."

"*Gams* doesn't mean smile or teeth," Miss Dietrich laughed. "It's American slang for a woman's legs."

Rosa looked down at Miss Dietrich's exposed crossed legs. "Miss Dietrich, you still have great gams," she said as she left.

Rosa had soon become accustomed to Marlene's daily shows, which Miss Dietrich performed at various locations, sometimes three, four, five or six times a day. What Rosa also instantly recognised about Marlene Dietrich, which nobody else seemed to acknowledge, was that she was a little German dictator herself. There was no job too small for her and no detail too trivial that she wouldn't dismiss. She worked with what she had, but she still demanded professionalism from everybody around her.

## Chapter 21

20 April (Friday)

*Somewhere over Cologne, US-controlled Germany*

For the third time, Rosa found herself in a plane, much to her discontent. She didn't peer outside to look down at the Earth rolling by as everyone else did. The uneasiness in the pit of her belly upset her; the plane seemed to be at the mercy of the winds as it was buffeted from side to side or bucked up and down. Moreover, they had to keep out of the way of any roving Luftwaffe planes looking for an easy target.

Rosa sat directly across from Miss Dietrich and Sgt. Mayflower, whose one good eye always seemed to be glued on Rosa.

Miss Dietrich had told Rosa that Sgt. Mayflower had lost his eye and arm at the Battle of Kasserine Pass in Tunisia, North Africa. And Sgt. Mayflower's only way back into the war was as Marlene Dietrich's escort. Miss Dietrich said they'd been together for so long now that she and Sgt. Mayflower argued like an old married couple.

Miss Dietrich also explained that she was expressly ordered never to speak German, especially once they'd entered Germany. But knowing that she probably would, the US government made sure her personal escort was not only fluent in German but also a man who wouldn't fall for Miss Dietrich's charms. And, from what Rosa had seen of Sgt. Mayflower with Miss Dietrich, they had chosen well.

The aging C-54 transport plane landed at Cologne airport. The noisome bloated aircraft taxied in and cut the propellers. As men wearing overalls placed the steps outside the craft, Marlene Dietrich adjusted her outfit: a fashionable olive gabardine suit with a beige scarf. As she exited the aircraft and walked down the steps, war correspondents and representatives from the press swarmed around her. They fired questions at her, never allowing her to respond to any of them.

Bang! Bang!

Two gunshots suddenly rang out in the air.

All ducked instinctively and then looked over to see Sgt. Mayflower holding his smoking 9mm above his head. He didn't say anything—he didn't have to. He re-holstered his side arm.

"Okay, boys, ignoring my escort's cowboy antics, one question at a time," said Miss Dietrich.

"Are you over here in Germany because your movie career is over back in Hollywood?" asked one.

"You haven't had a hit since *Destry Rides Again*, and that was back in '39," pointed out another reporter.

"I am through with Hollywood. Besides, anyone who has played for soldiers overseas will never be satisfied with another kind of audience for a long time. The boys are full of generosity and never gloomy. Not while I'm around, anyway."

"Are you saying that you prefer performing live in front of troops rather than acting on screen?"

"There's something about an American soldier that is just so gratifying. They're so grateful, so heartbreakingly grateful, for anything, even a film actress who originates from Germany."

"It sounds like you have a special affinity for the American GI."

"Of all the soldiers I meet, the GIs are the bravest."

"What about the British and the French? Aren't they brave, too?"

"Bravery is simple when you are defending your own country, and I'm sure in the weeks and months to come, we will see many brave Germans defending their Fatherland, but these GIs are special. Lonely men fighting in strange lands on foreign soil simply because it was the right thing to do. To have their eyes shot out and their brains scrambled, their bodies torn, and their flesh burnt in some faraway country takes great courage. And the GIs fought and fell as if they were defending their own soil because, for the GI, the very soil they were standing, fighting and dying on was indeed 'the land of the free and the home of the brave'."

Someone asked her whether it was right and proper to kiss so many men.

"I kiss them because, unfortunately for many of them, it will be both their first and last kiss ever. I have kissed more men than any woman in history, and I'm sure any woman in the future, and I've only just begun. I'm sure I would hold the Guinness World Record if there were such a category. And it suits me just fine. No woman can please one man, but this way, one woman can please many men through a simple act of generosity and kindness."

Another reporter asked her about the fate of Germany.

"The Germany I once knew as a little girl is no longer, I'm afraid. I don't think of it. I suppose if I did, I could never do these tours, especially here in Germany."

"It's Adolf Hitler's 56th birthday today. Is there anything you would like to say?"

"We'll be in Berlin very soon to help him blow out his candles," she said with a smile.

*** 

Rosa sat next to Sgt. Mayflower in the theatre aisle seat, looking up at the stage. Miss Dietrich was rehearsing for tonight's show. Rosa usually assisted with costume changes, but Miss Dietrich wore only one dress during dress rehearsals. Marlene was wearing an elegant long-sleeved, flesh-coloured net gown with gold sequins. She was talking to one of the military band members, and they were both standing next to an upright piano in the centre of the stage.

The musician soldier sat on the piano stool, and Miss Dietrich went behind the piano as she continued smoking her cigarette.

"All right, nice and easy," she said.

She began singing, 'You're the Cream in My Coffee'.

The piano player got overly excited as he pounded at the piano keys and drowned out her voice.

She stopped singing.

The piano player stopped playing.

She glared. "It is music, remember?" she said, gently flicking her cigarette ash at him.

They started over.

The scene was repeated, but this time the piano player was so nervous that he was pumping at the keyboard so fast that Miss Dietrich couldn't possibly keep up.

She stopped again. "Call that piano playing? How can I sing to that rubbish? You're not playing a washboard! Jerk!" She puffed furiously at her cigarette, smoke billowing out her flared nostrils. "Again!"

Sgt. Mayflower didn't appear to like the way she was treating the piano player. He stood and slowly walked down the centre aisle toward the stage. Rosa could sense another fight was coming.

Marlene started singing again; on her face was a bright, endearing smile as she tucked her hands underneath her chin. Her icy glare from only moments earlier had wholly evaporated.

She sang while she stared at Sgt. Mayflower. She always needed an audience, even if it were only one person. "*Who's going to shed tears if we go our separate ways, when just around the corner the next guy is waiting? You say goodbye, while you're thinking secretly, 'Well, I'm rid of another one finally,' when just around the corner waits your next true love. You say goodbye. Finally, I'm free!*"

The piano player slowed down, but as the song went along, he went faster and louder, just as he'd done before.

She smashed her fist on the piano.

"Christ almighty!"

She moved around and bent down until she was only an inch from his downcast face.

"This is impossible," she said, poking him in his forehead. "You don't get it! What do you have for brains?"

196

She walked behind the shaking pianist, placing her mouth right against his ear.

"And I have to sing this crap. It's all you play."

She climbed onto the piano, sinking her heels into the keyboard in the process, and sat cross-legged on top of the upright. "Don't screw up again, or I'll kick you," she said while adjusting her stockings.

Sgt. Mayflower walked up the centre steps of the stage to join them. "Leave the poor fellow alone," he said. "Don't be such a bitch."

"Oh, I see, when you rouse on the men, it's for discipline, but when a woman does it, she's a bitch."

"It's clear that you, the *famous Marlene Dietrich*, intimidate him."

"And you think the men don't find you intimidating?"

"I'm a sergeant; they're *supposed* to find me intimidating."

"I don't mean your stripes. Look at you with your eye patch and hook. Not only do you look like a pirate in uniform, but you also remind them."

"Remind them of what?"

"Remind them that war is not always fatal. Sometimes it is grotesque, leaving you half a man, and I can tell that really scares the shit out of them."

He looked at the piano player, who was staring at them both. "Come on, soldier, we don't need this crap."

Sgt. Mayflower headed for the side door. He stopped and turned. The musician soldier remained seated at the piano, looking up at Miss Dietrich.

"How about it, soldier? Do you want to go with him and fight millions of krauts or stay in here with me and fight with just one? And I promise I don't bite, not unless you want me to," she said, laughing playfully.

The soldier finally spoke. "Sergeant, I'm going to stay here with Miss Dietrich and try to play better if you don't mind?"

"See that? The bitch won." Miss Dietrich looked back at the musician. "I mean it; every time you make a mistake, I will kick you. Got it!"

"Yes, ma'am."

"*Sehr gut.*"

Sgt. Mayflower stormed out of the building, slamming the door shut behind him.

Rosa compared Miss Dietrich to Director Riefenstahl. In the end, there was no comparison. They were both headstrong, tough-minded women, but for Miss Dietrich, it was all about the audience and winning the war; whereas, for Director Riefenstahl, it was all about her and nothing else.

After the evening performance, they finally arrived back at their hotel, which had been requisitioned for the war effort. Rosa and Sgt. Mayflower were exhausted. While he collapsed onto his bed, Rosa used the water bowl for a quick wash before going to bed. Miss Dietrich went to use the showers, which were shared by everyone on the same floor. She came back to Sgt. Mayflower's room, holding a toilet brush.

He looked at it. "What's that for?"

"It's for cleaning toilets."

"I know what it is. I mean, why are you holding it?"

"The toilets here are disgusting. They haven't been cleaned in weeks."

"So?"

"So, it's unhygienic and spreads disease."

"So, get one of the soldiers to clean it up for you, Colonel Dietrich," he said, smiling as he stretched out on his bed.

"They're too busy fighting a war."

"What do you think I'm doing?"

"Well, you're not at the front lines, and I don't ever see you up there on stage with me."

"I'm doing my job, which is to guard and protect you."

"Really? You weren't at rehearsals today, *protecting* me."

"Well, rehearsals aren't that important. It's only rehearsals anyway. Nothing's going to happen to you there."

"Really. Do the Germans suddenly take a break from trying to kill me because I'm rehearsing?"

"I didn't mean it like that."

"What do you mean?"

Silence.

"And what do you do all day when I am rehearsing? You're getting drunk, feeling sorry for yourself, that's what. Well, I'm putting a stop to it. Idle hands make a Sad Sack soldier, so get to work and help me clean the toilets."

He jumped from his bed and glared at her. "I'm a goddamn sergeant; I'm not cleaning any goddamned stinking toilet! Understand!"

"I understand that I need a new escort."

"What? You wouldn't."

"What is the military-career expectancy of a one-eyed, one-handed escort who won't do as he's told? You couldn't re-enter the war any other way than by being my escort because you are fluent in German and can eavesdrop on me and report back to Allied High Command."

Sgt. Mayflower looked astonished.

"I know your game. I know why they chose you to protect me, but I have friends in higher places, and if you want to stay in this war, you better get off your ass and help me." She held up the toilet brush.

He stared at her with his gun-metal-grey eye.

She glared back with both her blue eyes as Rosa watched on.

He snatched the brush away from her hand.

She snatched it back again. "This is my brush. Find your own." She answered his quizzical expression. "My mother, Wilhelmina Josephine Felsing Dietrich von Losch, was tougher than any general I've ever met, and she always said that if you want to do a job properly, then do it yourself." She spun on her heels and headed down the hallway towards the communal toilets.

He rolled up his sleeves and followed her.

Rosa couldn't believe what she had just witnessed. She had always resented that she wasn't a boy because they could do whatever they wanted while she and the other girls could not. But Marlene Dietrich had just shown her what it meant to be a woman. Marlene had been showing her all along. Rosa stopped washing herself, picked up a scrubbing brush, and followed the two of them down the hallway.

***

The next morning, Rosa sat in the back of the jeep with Miss Dietrich as Sgt. Mayflower drove along a wet and muddy road.

"Where are we going, Miss Dietrich?" Rosa asked.

Miss Dietrich said nothing.

Sgt. Mayflower answered for her. "It's a mobile military hospital."

"I don't understand; how can a hospital be mobile?" asked Rosa.

"It's a hospital made out of tents, and it follows wherever the battles are being fought."

"Oh," said Rosa, still not understanding properly. This was Rosa's first hospital visit, but clearly, Miss Dietrich had done this before—many times. Rosa noticed that Marlene had been pensive on the drive out there. She was not her usual, outgoing self.

The jeep pulled up outside the city of green tents.

"Oh, they are huge. They are as big as circus tents."

"Except the only show inside is that of young boys dying," said Marlene grimly.

All three of them got out. The sergeant escorted Miss Dietrich towards the large tents.

"I hate these visits, but these GIs need me most of all," Miss Dietrich said, more to herself than to Sgt. Mayflower.

Sgt. Mayflower stood next to the flap of the tent. She put her hand up so that he would give her a moment to compose herself. He seemed to know the routine. She took a few deep breaths and then pinched her cheeks to give her face some colour.

"How's my smile?" Miss Dietrich asked Rosa.

"Your smile outshines the morning sunshine," replied Rosa.

Miss Dietrich looked at Sgt. Mayflower. "Remember, once I enter..."

"Hold the tent flap open so that the morning sun will give you that halo effect," he said. "I know. I know. The key to Miss Dietrich is lighting."

"You see, Rosa, men *can* learn. You just need to be patient and give them plenty of encouragement."

Rosa smiled.

Miss Dietrich nodded, and Sgt. Mayflower opened the flap for her as she made her entrance. The men lying on the hospital beds held up their hands to stop the morning sun from assaulting their eyes.

"Hello, boys."

"It's Marlene Dietrich!" yelled one patient.

The others talked excitedly.

"It's okay, boys, don't get up," she said.

The injured, bandaged and legless men laughed.

Sgt. Mayflower entered and dropped the flap behind him and Rosa. They followed Miss Dietrich as she walked around, introducing herself to the men on the beds. The ones who could talk told her their names and where they were from. One man had all four limbs missing and was bandaged entirely except for his mouth, which was smiling brightly at the sound of her soft and sultry voice. She asked him how he was.

"I'm fine, Miss Dietrich. You should see the other guy."

She kissed him on his lips. "Is there anything I can do for you?"

"My ears work fine—how about a song?" he croaked.

"For you, how about three?"

Miss Dietrich walked over to Rosa, who was carrying an army duffel bag. Rosa opened the bag and pulled out Miss Dietrich's musical saw. Marlene grabbed it, sat down on a chair provided for her, and sang three songs: 'Swanee River', 'Oh Susanna', and 'My Darling Clementine'.

Before she sang the last chorus of the last song, the limbless, smiling man died.

Marlene was taken to a makeshift part of the hospital where some men were laid out on stretchers while a tent was being erected for them. Some were wearing German uniforms.

"Who are they?" Rosa asked Sgt. Mayflower.

"They're POWs. Prisoners of War. Germans."

The German POWs all stared at Miss Dietrich, wearing her American GI uniform. They spoke to her in German.

"Is it really you? Is it Marlene Dietrich?"

She replied in German. "Yes, it is me."

"Why are you fighting against us, your Fatherland?" asked another German soldier.

"America is my homeland now. Germany took away both my fathers in pointless wars before I had even turned sixteen. Germany is my Fatherless-land."

"You were born in Berlin; therefore, you are a traitor to Germany."

"Don't worry about him, Miss Dietrich," said the first soldier. "He ordered us to attack because he wanted an Iron Cross, and then he fell into an American foxhole and was knocked out. By the time he woke up, he was a prisoner without his beloved Iron Cross."

The other Germans laughed at him.

The petulant German corporal kept quiet after that.

"I know you are no longer German," said the blonde-haired, blue-eyed youth, "but would you mind singing *Lili Marlene* to us?"

The other Germans urged her to sing.

"Okay. Okay."

By the time she'd finished singing in German, there wasn't a dry-eyed German to be seen, including Marlene.

Once the hospital visit was over, Miss Dietrich walked over to the latrines but kept walking past them. Sgt. Mayflower and Rosa followed at a respectful distance. Miss Dietrich stopped next to a pile of chopped firewood. Once she was certain no one was around, she dropped to her knees and wept uncontrollably.

Sgt. Mayflower finally spoke to Rosa. "She hates these hospital visits, but she'll be back here, or another one just like it, next week. Let's go back to the jeep. It looks like she will be a while."

Rosa thought about her boys and wondered if Peter and Charlie were okay. Her life had been a blur since she'd left Berlin and she'd been too exhausted to think of them until now.

No.

No crying. No tears. No self-pity.

Rosa turned and headed back.

"Rosa, where are you going?" he asked.

"I'm going to tell Miss Dietrich a children's story in German."

"She's a woman, not a child."

"We are all children at heart, especially when we are crying and all we want is for our mothers to hug us and kiss us and tell us no matter how dark things get, everything will be okay."

"What story are you going to tell?" Sgt. Mayflower asked.

"The best story ever told: *Little Red Riding Hood.*"

"Do you mind if I come?" he asked. "I mean, I haven't heard that story told in German, not since..."

"Since you were a boy."

He didn't reply.

"Come on, Sergeant."

***

After the hospital visit, Sgt. Mayflower drove his jeep through the deserted ghost town of the once-great medieval city of Cologne. The few streets of untouched buildings soon gave way to suburbs of decayed ruins, all white-washed in ghoulish dust. Although it was near lunchtime, it felt much later, with the dark clouds blanketing the sky. Lightening flashed across it, and a low rumbling could be heard deep in the belly of the beast above them. Although the city was now declared safe to travel to, it had an eerie feel about it. With the inclement weather and the possibility of snipers, Mayflower had argued against this trip over the Rhine but, as usual, Marlene Dietrich batted her eyelashes at some general, and here they were.

The streets were full of rubble, but the citizens of Cologne had conveniently cleared the roads and placed all the rocks and debris by the roadside, allowing the US troops to move freely about. Despite the ruins and the devastated terrain, his passenger directed him as if they were driving in downtown New York City. She knew exactly where she was going.

"Where are we going? There's nothing here. Cologne has been wiped off the face of the German map."

Without looking at him, she smiled. "A miracle."

"We're going to a miracle?" asked Rosa.

"Yes, my sweet. I overheard the boys talking about it, and as soon as I heard, I had to come to see for myself."

"A miracle in this godforsaken country?" said Sgt. Mayflower.

"I don't think God abandoned Germany; it was more the other way around."

"They found a new god with a tiny little moustache," Sgt. Mayflower remarked.

Marlene stood and pointed to somewhere ahead. "There it is!"

Rosa's and Sgt. Mayflower's gaze followed her finger. They could see a black castle in the distance. But as they got nearer, they could see it looked more like a dark tower.

"What is it?" Sgt. Mayflower asked.

"It's hope," Miss Dietrich beamed.

The jeep slowed and pulled up in front of the grotesque building. It was a cathedral of some sort, an ancient cathedral. A couple of GIs were sitting in the market square, taking pot-shots at it with their rifles. One of them recognised the famous passenger seated in the jeep.

"Look, guys, it's Marlene Dietrich!"

They dropped their weapons and helmets and surrounded the jeep. "Can I have your autograph," said one.

"To hell with an autograph, grab Jimmy's camera," said another.

"It's out of film."

"Out of film? Jimmy, you're an idiot."

"You know there's a war on? It's not like there are any stores around here."

Marlene raised her arms and flashed her big toothy-white smile. "Easy boys, I don't want to start a war."

They laughed with her.

"Miss Dietrich, what are you doing here?" asked a baby-faced soldier.

"Well, boys, I heard about this miracle, and I had to come to see it for myself."

"Miracle? I beg your pardon, Miss Dietrich, but this place has been bombed to smithereens. There ain't nothing much left."

"That's right, Miss Dietrich," piped another. "This place is fresh out of miracles."

"But Cologne Cathedral is still here," she said, pointing in front of them. "They started building it in the thirteenth century and, after a million bombs, she still stands. I call that a miracle."

One of the GIs looked at her.

"But Miss Dietrich, I heard that the US Army flyboys deliberately didn't blow this landmark up so that they could navigate their way around Germany."

"I didn't say how the miracle happened, but destroyed or not, I had to come here and see it for myself."

"Why's that?" the boys asked, hanging on her every word.

"Well, this is where my mother and father were married and where I was married as well. I even buried my second father here. Anyway, boys, I just want to thank you for keeping an eye on this place for me. I want to go in there and give my thanks to God, and when I come back, I'll sign all the autographs you want and give each one of you a big wet kiss."

Their beaming faces showed their collective approval.

Sgt. Mayflower followed Marlene into the dim dark building. They could still hear the clouds rumbling above, which sounded like cannon fire in the distance.

"I'm sorry for the boys shooting at this building, especially considering this is where you got married."

"Oh, I didn't get married here," she said nonchalantly.

"What about your parents and your dead second father?"

"Yes, we all got married, and I did bury my fathers, but not here."

"Do you lie naturally, or does it come easy for you Germans?"

"And I suppose you never lie?" she returned fire.

"Never."

She marched down the aisle, leaving him alone.

He followed her. "So why did you lie to those young boys outside?"

"I got them to stop shooting at this ancient marvel, didn't I?"

"Only by telling them a lie."

"I didn't lie to them. I just reminded them, that's all."

"Reminded them of what?"

"That they are the *good* guys in this war. What would their parents, girlfriends and wives think if they knew their loved ones were over here shooting at old churches?"

"These aren't American churches; they're Nazi monstrosities."

"What are you saying? That, 700 years ago when our forefathers built this monument to God, they were Nazis?"

"No, I didn't say that."

"What are you saying, then? Those good boys out there can be God-fearing souls in America, but, in another country, they can do whatever they feel like?"

"No, I'm not saying that either."

"Well, Sergeant, for a guy who's not saying anything, you sure do talk a lot."

Her grimace turned into a beacon of joy once again. "Don't you see? If this building can survive the war, so too can my family."

Walking around the cathedral, Rosa recalled how, six years earlier, she was a ten-year-old girl who knew nothing about the real world and what her parents had been protecting her from. Her selfishness had landed her entire family in trouble.

As Rosa stood at the entrance to the cathedral, she stared across the street, and it was as if she could see her family wagon burning, with her promising her father to look after her mother. He gave her the necklace as a reminder. Rosa pulled out the leather strap that attached to her family amulet that she'd managed to keep hidden all these years. If she had lost it or it was taken away from her, then she would have known he was dead. Somehow, she felt that the amulet was telling her that her father was still alive.

Another jeep in the distance honked, startling Rosa out of her daydreaming, and the honking became louder until the jeep finally pulled up at the front of the cathedral.

The GI driver yelled, "Miss Dietrich! Miss Dietrich! I've been dispatched from headquarters, and I've been looking everywhere for you. HQ thought you should know immediately." He held up a piece of paper as he got out and handed it to Sgt. Mayflower. "We've found her! We've found her!"

"Whom have you found?" asked Miss Dietrich.

"Your sister," said Sgt. Mayflower.

"We've found your sister, Miss Dietrich," echoed the driver. The GI's face turned serious. "In Bergen-Belsen."

"Bergen-Belsen?"

"It's a women's and children's concentration camp."

"My sister is a prisoner in a concentration camp?"

"Not exactly a prisoner."

# Chapter 22

2 May 1945 (Wednesday)

*Bergen-Belsen Concentration Camp (300 km west of Berlin)*

Sgt. Mayflower drove the jeep through the small German town of Belsen while Miss Dietrich and Rosa sat in the back.

He stopped the jeep next to a group of passing GIs. "Hey, buddy, where's the Bergen-Belsen Concentration Camp?"

The GI pointed. "Just follow your nose to stink central." The GI's eyes opened wide when he recognised the famous back-seat passenger. "Hey, isn't that Marlene Dietrich?"

"Yes, it is," said Sgt. Mayflower before grinding the vehicle into gear and speeding off.

Miss Dietrich was in no mood to sign autographs, smile for Boxed-Brownie camera photographs, or kiss any GIs. In fact, since learning the precise nature of her sister's predicament, Marlene Dietrich had been silent.

Rosa had initially wondered what Elizabeth, or Liesel, as Miss Dietrich called her sister, was doing in a concentration camp in the first place. Had the Germans imprisoned Miss Dietrich's family because of their relationship with her?

They drove along a dirt road with untouched pine forests on one side and a huge barbed-wire fence on the other. They had been debriefed during their flight here. The camp was outside Belsen, about 300 km west of Berlin and 60 km north of Hanover. The British liberated the camp on 15th April. It had 73,000 inmates for a camp designed to hold about a quarter of that number. Thirteen thousand inmates had been left where they died as the war encroached on the camp. Most camp guards had fled, but some of the SS men and women had remained behind, including the camp commandant.

There had been brutal revenge killings in one of the satellite camps, strangely enough not on the SS, who had fled, but on the kapos—prisoners who had helped the guards maintain discipline within the camp. The kapos didn't stand a chance, and 170 of them had been beaten to death. For the worst offenders, they held mock trials followed by real hangings. The British liberators didn't intervene. No one did. Not after the horrors of the camp, they'd just witnessed. But the British did get the local town folk to bury the dead. And that's why Marlene was here. Her sister was a local citizen.

The camp had also started as an 'exchange camp' whereby the Germans would swap Jews for German civilians incarcerated in other countries. Highly influential Jews could be bought and sold to the highest bidder.

"Just like the ransoming of high-ranking prisoners back in the medieval days," Miss Dietrich had whispered to herself.

As the war escalated, the Bergen-Belsen Concentration Camp morphed into a POW camp holding thousands of Soviet prisoners. But by the end of the war, the camp mainly held women and children who had been moved away from the eastern camps, which the Russians had been closing in on fast. The women and children were a mixture of Jews and Gypsies.

When Rosa heard this during the debrief, her ears pricked up. Maybe her extended Romani family were here? Perhaps her mother had been evacuated here?

The jeep pulled up at the front gate, which was manned by several US Army MPs dressed in their typical Military Police white helmets and embellishments. The officer recognised Miss Dietrich immediately and spoke into his field telephone.

"Miss Dietrich, the General will be here presently."

Sgt. Mayflower switched off his jeep. They sat in silence, with the MPs sneaking sideways glances at the famous Hollywood icon.

A jeep soon arrived adorned with silver stars on a red board— Rosa had learned that in wartime, red screamed military power— on both sides of the war.

The man seated in the back jumped out. "Marlene!"

Miss Dietrich jumped out of her jeep. "*Liebchen*. Jimmy, my darling!" They hugged and kissed each other.

"That's General James Gavin of the 82nd Airborne Division," Sgt. Mayflower told Rosa. "One thing she has taught me is wherever Marlene Dietrich is that you can't swing a cat about without hitting a general or three."

"I'm so glad it's you," Miss Dietrich said, letting him go. "I need to get in here."

"I'm afraid that's impossible, Marlene," said the General.

"Not impossible for you? You are a General, are you not?"

"General or not, we have typhus in there. Since their liberation, we have lost 500 people a day due to illness. We've moved the healthy ones to a nearby German military barracks. However, we've sent for flame-throwing Bren carriers and flame-throwing British tanks to destroy this place. It's the only way to kill the disease, I'm afraid."

"I need to get in there."

"No. Believe me, this is the one place you should never enter."

"Why not? General Eisenhower has opened up these camps to everybody, so the outside world can see what these Nazis have done."

"Yes, he has, but you're not an outsider, are you? You were born and raised here, in Germany. If you take a step inside the camp, you will hate yourself, the German part of yourself, forever."

Rosa watched on with increasing anxiety. If Miss Dietrich was refused entry to find her sister, Rosa would have no chance of entering the camp to search for her mother. Miss Dietrich looked at the ground where the gates opened into the camp. She looked at her muddy GI boots as if she were making a decision. The breeze changed direction, and then a fresh wave of stench struck the party with the full force of death. She covered her face with her scarf once again and took a step away from the camp. It was evident to all that she would not enter.

"Besides, we can't risk the life of someone such as yourself getting sick," the General half-joked.

"I know. I know. My death would be bad for the morale of the troops."

"The troops? It would be bad morale for me and several other generals as well. I think General Patton is your biggest fan. He's ordered all your movies to be shown to his troops."

"He has?"

"But one thing is certain: he would court-martial me if something happened to you. Why do you need to get in there? Most of the inmates have been relocated."

"I'm not here to see the victims of the camp. I understand you have several high-ranking city officials and business people in here digging the graves."

The General looked at her awkwardly. "I'm sorry, we didn't know your sister was one of them."

"You're not as sorry as I am." She fished out a black and white photo and passed it to the General. "Her name is Liesel."

Sgt. Mayflower jumped out of the jeep, snatched the photo from the General's hand and marched into the camp.

The General was angered by the sergeant's insubordination, but Miss Dietrich placed a hand on his sleeve. The General then nodded at the MPs blocking Sgt. Mayflower's path, who then moved away to let him through. This was Rosa's chance; she raced after Sgt. Mayflower and walked by his side. No one said anything or attempted to stop her.

They walked past military men in chemical suits and masks who were burning bedding, clothes, and anything that might contain typhus. With Rosa close behind, Sgt. Mayflower entered the barracks buildings, where rows of sick and starving people were being cared for by the Allied medical orderlies—those too sick or fragile to be moved. They passed through the barracks in silence. On the other side of the buildings were large mounds of what looked like white sandbags. The two of them got closer, then froze in horror. The sandbag mounds were in fact mountains of dead-white bodies. And it looked as if they had all starved to death.

"I wonder if the Americans would have been so helpful to the Germans on the Spree River had they witnessed this camp," Sgt. Mayflower said. "I'd heard rumours. Even when General Eisenhower opened up the camp to the world's reporters and cameras, I still thought it was more anti-German propaganda," Sgt. Mayflower said more to himself than to Rosa, who was silent. "I mean, words and horror stories are one thing, but to see it and smell it first hand, breathing in the foul air of inhumanity, is something else entirely. They were right to stop Marlene at the gates of hell. She's suffered so much since entering Germany, and it rocked her steely resolve to see Cologne as a wasteland. But to see this place would have killed her German soul."

In the days and weeks she had come to know Marlene Dietrich, Rosa knew he spoke the absolute truth.

Ahead of them, they observed a group of civilians digging large square holes, placing the dead bodies into wheelbarrows, and wheeling them over to the pits. Bulldozers and other plant equipment were sitting idly nearby; the Allies must have decided not to use them, letting the German citizens bury the mountains of the dead by hand instead. Armed GIs smoked on cigarettes and talked as the German citizens carried out their grim task diligently and without complaint. As they approached the large work party, they saw a woman slump next to the wheelbarrow and cry. Her straw hat fell off to reveal her face.

Sgt. Mayflower looked at the photo in his hand, and recognised her. "Liesel?"

She looked up at him. "*Ja*," she said, and when she realised it was an American speaking to her, she corrected herself in English. "Yes. I'm Liesel."

"Are you Marlene Dietrich's sister?"

The blonde woman bounced back to her feet. "Is my sister coming? My sister has rescued me?" She rushed over and hugged the sergeant. "Thank God. Thank God. I am saved from this hellhole."

Rosa looked at Liesel and thought that she didn't look like Miss Dietrich in any way.

Liesel raced off and addressed a large German man, who returned with her. "This is my husband, Georg Will. He comes too?"

The four of them left the mass graves and returned to the front gate.

Liesel rushed up to Miss Dietrich and hugged her. "Oh, dear sister, sister. *Danke. Danke.*"

The General stepped forward. "I have to make this official, Marlene. Is this woman your sister?"

Without looking at the General or Liesel, Marlene answered. "This is Elizabeth and her husband Georg Will, but I have no sister."

The husband and wife looked forlornly at the ground. Sgt. Mayflower opened the jeep's door, and their guests squeezed into the back of the open-top jeep. The sergeant started the engine and drove to the nearby Panzer army camp. The Americans and British called this place a "Displaced Persons" camp, but in Rosa's eyes, all camps looked pretty much the same: barbed-wire fences and guards in uniform—only their names, uniform colour and language differed.

Once they pulled up at the new camp, Rosa jumped out of the jeep.

"Do you want us to wait for you?" Miss Dietrich asked Rosa. Rosa shook her head. "Once you are done here, just hitch a ride into town, and HQ will tell you where they've billeted us."

Just then, an army chaplain walked over to the jeep, taking off his cap and squeezing it tightly. Rosa had never seen chaplains in the German military, but she had seen several in the US military since meeting Miss Dietrich. At first, it seemed wrong to Rosa to have a priest wearing a military uniform, but after a while, it made sense. Who wouldn't want God on your side? And as Miss Dietrich had pointed out, the Germans didn't need God—they had the Führer.

"What is it, Father?" Miss Dietrich asked the army chaplain.

"I'm sorry to ask this of you; I've heard about your sister. But what these boys have witnessed, and had to work with, has been hell on earth, and morale is at an all-time low. I was just wondering…"

"If I would perform?" she clarified.

"Yes."

"When?"

"Tonight. I've arranged to use the small paddock just outside town. I'm sorry this is such short notice, but—"

"—But nothing. There's a war on don't you know, and if the boys can't take a break from this war, then I can't take a break from performing either. I'll see you there after chow time." Miss Dietrich looked at Rosa. "Rosa, will you be there? You do the work of ten men, and I think I'm going to need your ten-men-help tonight."

"Yes, of course, Miss Dietrich. I'll be there."

"Okay, Sergeant, we have a show to get ready for. Move it!"

The jeep took off back towards the town of Bergen.

Rosa turned and entered the Displaced Persons Camp in search of her mother. She was given a surgical facemask to protect the camp inmates from outside infection. As she walked along, she talked to the various survivors, questioning them. She learned piecemeal that when the Russians advanced on Auschwitz back in January, about 80,000 inmates were marched through the worst European winter in decades to Bergen-Belsen, where only 20,000 had survived the death march. She asked about her mother, but no one could help her. She asked them about the Romani—again, no luck.

She sat on a bench in despair, when she heard a familiar voice singing.

She raced around a corner of a wooden hut, and there he was. He was as bald as ever, but he was half the size compared to the last time she'd seen him, but he was noticeably bigger than the inmates she encountered while searching this place. And he was wearing neat civilians instead of prison-issued striped pyjamas.

"Pat! Pat!" she said, racing up and giving him a bear hug. "You're alive! You're alive!" He looked horrible, but if he'd survived, it gave her hope that her mother had done so too.

He stared at her GI uniform. "I don't understand. Are you an American soldier now?"

"No. No. Of course not. It's a long story. What happened to you? Is my mother here?"

Pat rested both hands on her shoulders. "Steady, girl. One question at a time."

She took a deep breath. "Did you find my father? How did you get here?"

"After you were taken away from the parade ground, I was sent on the very next cattle train to Berlin."

"What happened to my mother? Did she go with you?"

"No. We heard that when they closed the camp in '43, most, if not all, the prisoners were sent to Auschwitz."

"Auschwitz? Oh no."

"But then we heard a rumour that some women and children were sent here to Bergen-Belsen."

"Then Mama must be here. She has to be." Rosa looked up at Pat's bald head shining in the clear sunshine. "But I don't understand. If the Nazis sent you to Berlin, how did you end up here?"

"Berlin was bombed night and day. They never gave up, the American and Allied bombers. Not even Christmas Day. But luckily for us, the Germans needed repairs done, especially to clear the roads of rubble, so they sent us out every day on work parties. And one day, there was an unexploded bomb stuck in the middle of the road. It was so perfectly upright it looked as though it belonged there, just like it was a city fountain or statue. And while all our guards stood around the bomb, discussing what to do with it, it exploded. It was God's work, I'm certain of it."

"Pat, I didn't think you were religious."

"I'm not, or rather, I wasn't, but that was before. Every day I survived a German concentration camp was a miracle, and then for that bomb to land like that was a gift from the heavens. So, with all our guards dead, we ran and came across some recently killed civilians and swapped their clothes for our rags. We all took off towards the west away from the Russians and towards the American Allies. We used our Romani ways to survive off the land and to sneak past the Germans until the Americans finally rescued us."

"We?"

"Me and your father."

Her eyes popped open. "Papa is here?" she said, standing up straight and looking around.

"He is. When we found out about the liberated camps, we had to sneak back past the Americans and the British. First, we went to Buchenwald. Nothing. And then we heard about this camp, so we came here as quickly as we could."

"And?"

"We only arrived two days ago. We had to sneak into the other camp before they buried any more bodies. But we didn't find your mother or any other Romani from our tribe. So, we came here, and your father has been searching for your mother night and day. I tell him that he must rest, eat and sleep; otherwise, he will die from exhaustion."

"Well, now that I'm here, he will listen to me."

Pat looked away from her.

"Pat? What is it?"

"I told your father everything that happened."

"The finger?"

"Everything. He is my best friend. He knows when I lie. I also told him that it wasn't your fault that they took you away from the camp, but..."

"But?"

"He blames you for breaking your promise. He knows that you are a natural-born survivor, and so long as you were with your mother, then surely she would survive too."

He became serious. "Rosa, did your parents ever tell you how they met?"

"No."

"They met as children when love is at its purest."

"Of course, they did."

"Rosa, have you ever wondered why your mother has no siblings or relations?"

"She never talked about them, so I guess I just assumed she didn't care about them."

"She didn't have a family to talk about. She was an orphan just like you."

"What?"

"Our tribe was staying at some grounds not far from a big building in the middle of nowhere. It was an orphanage. This is where your father, who was only twelve, met your mother, who was ten. They instantly bonded, and he vowed he would come back and rescue her from the orphanage, which he did a few years later. Against everybody's wishes because your mother was an outsider, when they came of age, they married."

"My mother is an orphan just like me?"

"She's a German orphan exactly like you."

"Father kept saying that we were more alike than I knew. Now I know what he meant."

"Guess where the orphanage was?"

Rosa shrugged.

"It was in a small place not far from Berlin."

"Berlin?"

"Your mother was a Berliner, just like you. I guess when we saw you that day in Berlin, sucking on the tit of your dead mother, she saw herself. Then she forced your father to grab you. And you were like a greasy pig, squealing and biting your mother and father the whole time, begging them to take you back to your dead mother."

"I don't understand; they told me I was a baby when they found me."

"They lied about that part to protect you. You were at least three years old when they found you with your dead mother. A street kid run wild. And your mother said that she was now your new mama, and you cried every day for a month, wanting us to take you back home. When you tried to run away, she was always there to catch you. Maybe, deep down, you always saw her as the woman who stole your mother away from you."

"Mama wanted me to fit in just like she had done, but I thought I knew better."

Rosa saw her father walk past them. She raced after him. "Papa. Papa. I've finally found you!"

He didn't say a word. He was thinner than Pat, and skin folds drooped from his face. His hair was shaved, but he now sported a white, bushy beard.

She looked at the small bundle of white sheets he was carrying in both hands. He strode into the woods at the rear of the barracks. Rosa caught up to her father and walked beside him.

"Papa. It's me, Rosa."

Nothing.

"Papa, did you find Mama?"

He grunted, "Yes."

Rosa looked around, wondering where her mother was, when a withered white arm fell out of the sheets. She looked at the hand and saw that it was missing a little finger. She reactively reached for her pocket. "Oh no, Mama."

They entered a clearing, and as her father gently laid down the white sheet, Pat approached holding up two spades. He gave one to her father, and both men got to work digging a hole. Rosa stared at her mother's four-fingered hand and gently placed it back under the sheet.

Once the grave was dug, the two men lowered the body into the chest-deep hole. They shovelled some earth and gently spread a layer of dirt over the sheet-covered body. Then they both jumped out of the pit and filled it in. All without saying a word—two men expert at death. While they had worked, Rosa held onto the amulet hanging around her neck, looking at her father. He had aged considerably since she last saw him outside the Cologne Cathedral six years earlier. But it wasn't just his body; his eyes seemed harder, colder as if a fire hose had doused the life out of them.

The men patted down the earth and held their hats as they silently prayed for Martha. Rosa didn't know what to say. Her father finally turned around, and for the very first time, he looked at her.

She blew him a kiss.

He stormed towards her as Rosa flinched and took a few steps back. He grabbed her by both arms. "Where were you, Rosa? You promised me. You promised that you would look after your mother for me."

"I did. I mean, I tried to."

He pointed back towards the mound.

"You call that trying? Why are you alive and well, wearing that stupid uniform, when your mother is nothing but skin and bones? She only died a couple of days ago."

"I, I, we were separated. I had no choice."

"No choice. We all have choices."

"Children don't."

"Really. Was it your mother's choice to cut off her little finger, or was that your choice?"

"That was a mistake."

"No, the mistake was the day we picked up an orphan girl back in Berlin."

"Papa, you don't mean that," she said, tears streaming down her face. "Papa, you were the only thing I cared about."

"And the only thing I ever cared about lies inside that grave," he said, pointing.

"Papa, I want to stay here and look after you."

"If you want me to live, then bring back my wife. Bring back my Martha." He pushed Rosa out of the way, with Pat following behind.

"Papa. Wait for me. Wait for your daughter."

He walked up to Rosa and slapped her face—hard. And then he pulled at her amulet, snapping the leather string off her neck. He turned and, as he stormed off, speaking over his shoulder. "I no longer have a daughter."

***

Rosa caught a ride and made it back to the empty paddock on the outskirts of Bergen, where the night's impromptu performance was taking place. All the preparations had been done as good as could be expected under the conditions. Rosa assembled the microphone and set it up on the open space in the middle of the grass, encircled by five-thousand US troops.

"We want Marlene! Let's get this show on the road!" the soldiers yelled.

Rosa nodded to the sound man before leaving the area lit up by large military flood lights.

The comedian bounced up to the microphone. "We had a pretty bad flight into Europe. On the way in, I started reading a novel, and on the way out, I'm going to read the second page. I tell you, it was rough. The flight was so rough that I asked the pilot if there were any parachutes on board. And he said, 'Don't be silly, the people with parachutes jumped out an hour ago.' I said to him, 'It's too rough up here. Can't you put this thing on autopilot?' And he said that the autopilot was the first one to jump."

After a sufficient pause to let the laughter die down, he spoke again. "I hope you enjoy our show today, which has several great acts. And I'm sure you'll enjoy the girls. You remember girls?" The olive-drabbed military men laughed. "We only have one girl here today and only one act, but I'm sure none of you will mind. There was only one girl brave enough and foolish enough to be this close to the front lines. Marlene Dietrich!" The applause was deafening. "She won't be joining us because as soon as the officers found her, they whisked her away in an armoured car to the nearest Officer's Club for her own protection."

"Boo!"

Then Marlene walked up to the microphone wearing her GI uniform to the great delight of her keen audience. "Hello, boys," she said. "I just wanted to say that sharing this entertainment with you today is a great honour for me. I wish to express my respect and admiration for you. The people back home know that you are doing an important job that needs to be done, and I'm certain you will deliver us a speedy victory. Good luck, and God bless."

And with that, Marlene Dietrich performed her show as usual and was greeted with the enthusiastic applause of five-thousand pairs of hands clapping loudly and the cheers of five-thousand excited men.

She announced she was taking a break and rushed to the small tent where Sgt. Mayflower was sitting with a pistol.

Miss Dietrich looked at his pistol. "I'm sorry, the only Kraut you're going to find in here is me," she said, rushing to change into a dress.

"Let's just say I've stopped one or two soldiers from taking a souvenir or three," he said.

"Rosa," said Miss Dietrich, "Go ask Father Jones... the army chaplain we spoke to earlier, and ask him if he wants to do a prayer for the camp victims with me?"

Rosa burst out of the small tent and saw the chaplain talking to some men assembled nearby. She raced over to him.

"Slow down," Father Jones said. "You'll injure somebody if you don't slow down."

"Father..." said Rosa, intent on relaying Miss Dietrich's message.

"Please, call me Max," he said.

"What did you say?" asked Rosa.

"You don't have to call me Father. My name is Max."

"Your name is Max?"

Her head started to swirl. It had all happened so suddenly. She had found and lost both her parents in one day. Today. She had kept faith that they were both still alive. And until a day earlier, she had been right. But maybe her father was right. If only she had stayed with her mother, then Rosa would have found a way to keep her mother alive until he found them today. But she had been taken from the camp; she had no choice. But when she escaped from the film, she should have gone looking for her mother instead of her father. But where would she have gone? Rosa wouldn't have known that they had sent her mother to Auschwitz and then onto the Bergen-Belsen camp. And she had been right: her father was in Berlin all this time—until his miraculous escape.

She thought her father was angry with grief, and he would forgive her as he always did. But there was something in his voice today. The way he didn't turn to look at her, as if she was dead to him already. Although he may have given up on her, she couldn't give up on him. She would visit him tomorrow. She would make him see that it wasn't her fault. But what if he didn't forgive her? What if he'd left town? What if, for the second time in her short life, she was once again an orphan?

"What do you want, child?" asked Father Max Jones, snapping her out of her thoughts.

She burst into tears. "I want my father," she said, hugging Father Jones. "I want my father to know it wasn't my fault. I'm so, so sorry, Father. I didn't mean to let you down. I should have looked after Mother. I'm sorry. I'm sorry." And she collapsed.

Big strong arms scooped her up.

"I'm sorry, Father," said Sgt. Mayflower. "She's had a big day, perhaps her biggest."

"I understand," a shaken Father Jones said.

Sgt. Mayflower carried Rosa into the small tent and laid her gently on an unfolded stretcher.

Rosa sobbed until she ran out of tears. Sgt. Mayflower didn't say a word, but he never left her. Eventually, Rosa stopped crying and splashed her face with water. She left the tent to watch Miss Dietrich perform her final song, but the stage lights died when the generator broke down mid-performance.

Miss Dietrich yelled out into the blackness, knowing the thousands of GIs were still seated in front of her. "Sorry, boys, I guess that is that, and the show is over."

Then one GI turned on his flashlight and then another and another. Pretty soon, thousands of handheld flashlights were shining on her makeshift stage.

"Well, I guess the show will go on after all," she yelled. "And if you don't like it, you can simply turn off your flashlights."

They never did. And she finished her entire show, complete with two encores.

## Chapter 23

4 May 1945 (Friday)

*Bergen (Liesel and Georg Will's Flat)*

Rosa walked around the lounge room of her host's home. It was neat and cosy, and the Wills seemed to have all the conveniences of life. It was as if the war in Europe had forgotten this town in Germany. Marlene had barely said a word since arriving here at her sister's place. She just wanted to find her mother.

"Are you sure you have no idea where Mother is?" asked Marlene Dietrich.

Liesel looked up at her. "No. The last we heard she was still in Berlin."

"At the Kaiserallee flat where we grew up?" Marlene asked.

"No. That was bombed by the Allies months ago. Luckily, Mother had moved by then."

"Why is Mother still in Berlin?" asked Marlene. "Why isn't she here with you?"

"We tried, but you know Mother. She missed her beloved Berlin. She's still a proud Prussian at heart."

Rosa looked at Marlene's brother-in-law Georg Will, who was a Special Services Officer for the Wehrmacht. Ironically, like his famous sister-in-law, he was in charge of entertaining the troops of the Third Reich. He ran the camp cinema and canteen at the concentration camp for the camp guards, while he ran another cinema at Fallingbostel for the German troops. Rosa looked at the feature wall in front of the lounges and noticed that it was completely bare except for a void where a small portrait or painting had once hung for years.

"What did you have hanging here?" Rosa asked Liesel in an

attempt to change the topic of missing mothers.

Marlene got up and inspected the vacated area of the wall. "Tell me, my dear sister, how did your husband get such a prestigious job and such a pristine place as this?"

Liesel's husband, Georg, spoke up. "I'd hardly call being a caretaker for the local cinema as prestigious."

"Oh, wouldn't you, my dear brother-in-law? Would you rather be fighting on the eastern front against the Russians or be on the beaches of Fortress Normandy fighting the American and British D-Day Invasion?"

"I didn't mean it like that."

Liesel put down her cup of coffee. "Sister, what are you implying?"

"I'm *stating* that you were both members of the Nazi Party. You must have been to garner such privileges."

Liesel and her husband both jumped to their feet. "How dare you! We despise Nazis. You have no idea what it was like living under Hitler."

"Rosa," Marlene said, "if you went around all of Germany, there would be voids like this everywhere, where Hitler's portrait once took pride of place. And now, I bet you won't even find one Nazi, but they'll all tell you about the Nazis living next door or in the next village. Isn't that right, dear sister?"

Liesel and Georg didn't say a word.

"You both worked at the concentration camp," Marlene said. "How dare you sit here and tell me you didn't know what was going on. On April 4th, Buchenwald was the first concentration camp to be liberated by US troops. And do you know what they found in the camp commandant's house? Beautiful hand-made lampshades. Upon closer inspection, the soldiers saw the lampshades were made from human skin. The camp commandant weeded out one hundred inmates with beautiful tattoos on their bodies. They were given a lethal injection so as not to spoil their tattoos. The camp commandant gave the lampshades to his wife as a Christmas present. So, don't pretend you didn't know."

"Only in the canteen. We had no part in, in—"

"—Making lampshades."

The door burst open with Sgt. Mayflower waving a newspaper above his head. "He's dead. He is dead," he yelled.

"Who is dead?" asked Liesel while Marlene grabbed the *Stars and Stripes* newspaper from the sergeant's hand. On the front page was a photo of Hitler underneath the heading HITLER DEAD, which took up the top half of the front page. The news had been broadcast on both the German and Allied radios on April 30th, but to see it in print on an American military newspaper made it official.

"The war is over!" Liesel shouted.

Marlene read aloud in English: "Führer fell at CP, German radio says; Doenitz at the helm, vows war will continue."

"The Führer is dead," said Liesel. "How can the war continue?"

Sgt. Mayflower looked at her. "The war is Germany's fault, not Hitler's. Even with a dead Führer, you Germans fight on."

Rosa knew Sgt. Mayflower understood German, but this was the first time she had heard him speak it.

Liesel glanced up at him. She looked as if she were going to say something, to argue against him, but her eyes appeared to register the truth of what he was saying. She collapsed on her sofa in defeat. Her husband consoled her. "It's true. It's true. We fight on even when there is no Führer to fight for."

They settled down as Marlene read out the news reports. Afterwards, Liesel went into the kitchen to make lunch.

"Oh, I forgot to ask you, Rosa," said Marlene, "did you find your mother?"

Rosa looked up in surprise. "Yes, but she died the day before I got there."

Marlene and Sgt. Mayflower looked shocked.

"Dead?" Marlene asked. "Why didn't you tell us?"

"We were busy with the shows."

"But still—"

"—But I did find my father."

"You did?"

"Yes. But he died this morning," Rosa said. "That's why I was late getting here today."

Marlene went over and hugged Rosa. "I'm so sorry Rosa. You didn't have to come here, not after…"

"Burying my father? There was nowhere else to go. Miss Dietrich, if you don't mind, I'd like to stay and work for you. Just until I figure out what to do."

"What? Yes. Yes. Of course."

Rosa had returned to the camp that morning and found her father in the camp infirmary. Pat was in tears, holding onto her father's dead hand. According to Pat, her father had collapsed the night he'd buried Martha. It was as if he was just holding onto dear life to find her. But when he found her dead, his heart and soul had given up on life. Pat and Rosa buried her father in the same grave as her mother. After placing her mother's finger in the grave, Rosa took her family amulet from her father and put it back around her neck. That was only an hour ago, but now in this lovely house, it seemed a world away. Rosa wandered around the beautifully decorated room, browsing.

"I have not been inside beautiful apartments such as this," replied Rosa. "I always wondered what people put inside them."

"I guess you have spent your entire life on the road," said Marlene.

"It has lots of pretty things and photos," she said, staring at all the family photos hanging on the wall and lining the tops of shelves and cupboards. She picked up one of the black and white photographs. "Why do you have this photo of Aunty Jo?"

Liesel entered with a food tray just as Rosa spoke, "What did you say, girl?"

Marlene jumped to her feet and stood next to Rosa. "What did you call her?"

"Aunty Jo."

"She goes by the simpler name of Josephine von Losch these days. It didn't pay to be the mother of *Marlene Dietrich*," Liesel explained.

"Josephine von Losch, yes," said Rosa, "but she prefers to be called Aunty Jo."

Marlene hovered over the girl, "Where did you see this Aunty Jo?"

"In Berlin."

"When?" asked Marlene.

"A couple of days before I met you."

"Was she still alive?"

"Aunty Jo was alive and well when I saw her last."

"Where? Where is she? What part of Berlin exactly?" Liesel grabbed a map of Berlin and placed it in front of the girl.

Rosa looked confused. "I don't know maps. But Berlin is rubble. These streets and buildings are all gone."

The two women looked despondently at each other.

Rosa smiled. "I don't know where Aunty Jo is on the map, but I can take you to her."

# Chapter 24

## 16 July 1945 (Monday)

*First day of the Potsdam Conference*

Rosa's olive-green US Army truck and two lead jeeps drove through the ruins of the city that was once the thriving metropolis of Berlin. The Berliners had worked night and day to clear the rubble from the streets to allow the passage of foot and vehicle traffic. They hadn't been ordered to do this, but it was part of the psyche of the average German to live in a neat and orderly world, even if that world meant that they had just lost another world war.

The small US Army convoy passed many lines of hundreds of women, children, and old or disabled men working in the piles of debris, trying to collect any salvageable bricks or materials to help them rebuild their bomb-torn buildings. In the worst parts of the city, there wasn't a building standing, only the remnants of a corner wall or the square shell of a foundation. The brown and red bricks were covered in concrete-grey dust, and the German people were also covered in the chalky dust, looking like the walking dead of a dead city. It was pitiful.

Rosa knew that she probably shouldn't feel pity for the Germans, as they had brought it upon themselves, but she didn't want to think that way. She had spent considerable time with the Americans and had softened somewhat as a result. They were a kind and generous people and loved to joke and play around. Many times, too many to remember, she had witnessed the Americans being kind to the German people, both civilian and military. At the Potsdam Conference being held now, Prime Minister Winston Churchill and President Harry S. Truman discussed rebuilding

Germany. At the same time, all Joseph Stalin wanted to talk about were the spoils of war.

Sgt. Mayflower laid down the law to Rosa. "Okay, Rosa, we are in Berlin, which Ivan controls, and since there are very delicate negotiations going on at the Potsdam Conference, we can't afford an international incident, especially after Miss Dietrich pulled every string possible to get us here. Technically, we aren't here. So, I want you on your best behaviour. Understood?"

Rosa was shocked at this insult. "Sergeant Mayflower, Rosa always good, always," she said in her improving English.

"What about yesterday morning when you gave that young private a bloody nose?"

"That was different. He says I overeat American food, and my ass is getting big. So, I hit him."

"Okay, but promise me, Rosa."

She folded her arms. "I promise." After a moment of reflection, Rosa asked him a question. "Sergeant Mayflower, what is an ass?"

He didn't have time to answer as the small American army convoy pulled up at a Russian checkpoint. Sgt. Mayflower got out from the driver's seat, and Rosa jumped out the passenger side. She was now wearing a GI uniform and an oversized helmet that wobbled so much the Russian soldiers laughed at her.

One of them spoke to his comrades. "Look at these puny Americans, no wonder they needed us to win the war by destroying Berlin for them."

Rosa drew out her 9mm sidearm the sergeant had given her for her personal protection only. She replied in Russian, "How would you like to taste American lead?"

The Soviets aimed their weapons at her, and the American GIs drew their guns in response.

Sgt. Mayflower raised his arms, trying to regain control of the situation. "Rosa, do not shoot the Russians. The war has finished, and I'm not going to die now. I have too much to live for, and so do you."

An image of a smiling Peter flashed in her mind. "A waste of a good American bullet," she said, holstering her weapon.

The Soviets and the Americans lowered their rifles.

Sgt. Mayflower stepped up to the Russian officer. "Rosa, can you interpret for me?"

The Russian smiled. "I speak very good English."

"You do? How?"

"Not all Soviet soldiers are Russian. They take over the country and then enlist its men into their army. Very smart, the Ivans. Why fight when you can force other people from other countries to fight for you? If the Germans had thought of that, instead of putting millions in camps and then killing them, they probably win the war, no?"

"How is it that you speak English?"

"I am a Polish actor, and I went to England to study Shakespeare." He pulled out a skull tucked away in a box, which had a little Adolf Hitler moustache inked over the top of where the mouth would be. The actor struck a pose with the skull held out before him. "Alas, poor Adolf. I knew him. Hitler—a fellow of infinite jest," he said, laughing at his own joke. "Tell me, Hitler, are you laughing now?" He worked the jawbone as he mimicked the voice of Hitler. "Who can laugh in Hell? It's so goddamn hot down here!"

His Russian comrades applauded.

He bowed.

Rosa didn't know what to make of him. He seemed to speak more like a woman than a man. His voice was both higher and softer.

"I have signed papers from Generals Patton and Bradley allowing us entry throughout Berlin," said Sgt. Mayflower. "And we need to enter this part of the city."

The officer's smiling expression turned severe. "I'm afraid I can't let you through here."

"Why not? We have signed papers," he said, holding them up.

"I don't care about papers. It is for your own protection."

"Protection? The war is over, or so I thought," Sgt. Mayflower said, looking at the Russian rifles.

"No, you misunderstand, not protection from us—them," he said, pointing behind him. "For you, the war is over, but not for them."

"Them?" Sgt. Mayflower said, not disguising his frustration. "Who exactly are you talking about?"

"We call it the Werewolf Zone. Werewolves are what they call themselves. They are young boys, mostly ex-Hitler Youth, and they kill Russians and any Germans they think are collaborating with the enemy. And they scalp our dead for souvenirs. And I am certain they would love to add a couple of American GI scalps to their trophy wall."

"Look, we can take care of ourselves, but if what you say is true, then it makes my mission even more important. I must get through to rescue an old lady."

"Old lady? Look around you. The city is full of them. Take one. We call it even."

"This one is special; she is the mother of Marlene Dietrich."

The officer's eyes opened wide, and he let out a cry. "I love Marlene Dietrich. She is the best." But then his face turned serious again. "But still, I refuse entry. They are killers, brainwashed by Hitler, and I am responsible for anything that happens in there."

Rosa pulled out her Hitler Youth knife, showing it to the officer. Everybody knew that soldiers from either side were souvenir hunters, whether to sell later or as gifts to friends or girlfriends. "This is the knife that almost killed Marlene Dietrich."

The cherub-faced Russian officer was fascinated. "It is? Why would anyone want to kill her?"

"Do you want it or not?"

He looked at her eyes. "I give up. You'll just try and sneak in somewhere else. That is what I tell my superiors when they find your rotting carcasses." He motioned for his men to remove the barriers. "Stick to roads and be out of there before night falls."

Rosa gave him the knife.

While the Russian officer showed his prized knife to his men, the US convoy moved into the Werewolf Zone.

***

This part of Berlin was eerily quiet. The few people they did happen to see quickly scurried away. Rubble was piled high, and the shattered buildings made perfect ambushing points. They stuck to the roads as best they could, but this part of town hadn't been cleaned up and cleared away. They would turn around from one dead-end, only to end up in another. Luckily, their tyre tracks in the dust helped to indicate where they'd been. While the sergeant worked at the steering wheel, trying to find a path forward, the other soldiers in the back of the open top truck were ready with weapons pointed outwards and upwards. They stopped in an extensive circular clearing around a still intact and working water fountain.

"This is as far as we can go by truck," said the sergeant. "We'll leave the vehicles here. I'll pick two men, and we'll go ahead on foot."

Rosa and the two soldiers followed the sergeant. He seemed to come alive, almost catlike, as he moved from pillar to post using available cover as he advanced. His injuries didn't impede him here as they seemed to do back at camp. He moved fast, and they struggled to keep up with him.

After following the sergeant through a couple of blocks of bombed-out buildings, Rosa recognised the water pump she had helped Aunty Jo use. "We are here. Stay here, and I will go and find her."

The sergeant's eyes showed he didn't like this idea. He looked at his men. "Okay, guys, we'll hold up here. And don't get itchy fingers; we don't want to shoot the girl when, and if, she returns."

Rosa stumbled over broken bricks while looking upwards. She eventually found the large cupboard that doubled as Aunty

Jo's front door. She listened. Nothing. She opened the doors and entered the cupboard. "Hello?" she whispered.

Nothing.

"Hello?" she said a little louder.

Nothing. She slowly inched her way forward and allowed time for her eyes to adjust to the dimness. Then she stopped to listen.

Nothing.

"Hello, Aunty Jo, it's me, Rosa."

Nothing.

She crawled in behind the fake wall covering the entrance to Aunty Jo's apartment and pushed the front door panel aside.

A hand grasped her wrist and flung her inside. She crash-landed onto the ground. She turned. And from underneath her massive helmet, she saw Peter, Charlie and Aunty Jo, who was holding a shovel to Rosa's throat. Rosa went to remove her helmet.

Aunty Jo shoved the blade of the shovel in Rosa's face. "Don't move, Yankee," she said in English.

"Aunty Jo, it's me."

"How do you know my name?"

With a shovel pressed against her neck, Rosa edged off her GI helmet, revealing her long blonde hair. The recent summer sun had yellowed her hair from a white blonde to a golden colour.

Charlie immediately recognised her. "Rosa!" he said, jumping on her and giving her a big hug.

"You can talk, Charlie?" said Rosa hugging him back.

"He started speaking after you left, and now we can't get him to shut up. We thought you were dead," said Peter.

"Not this one," Aunty Jo said, putting down the shovel. "She's a fighter."

Rosa stood up. They looked at her American uniform in wonder. It was the first time any of them had seen an authentic GI uniform up close.

"Rosa, are you a GI now?" asked Peter.

She smiled. "Yes, I am."

Peter went up to her and hugged her. "I missed you, Rosa."

She hugged him back. She didn't know why, but she felt some warm tears trickle down her dusty cheek. "I missed you, and Charlie of course."

Peter looked confused. "Why are you here? Did you come here just to find us?"

"The Americans have come here for Aunty Jo."

Peter and Charlie were astonished. "Aunty Jo?" Peter asked.

"She is not just anyone, Peter. She is famous."

"She is?"

Aunty Jo collapsed into her soft chair. "I'm not famous, Peter. But I do have a famous American daughter."

"You do?" Peter asked. "Who?"

"Marlene Dietrich," announced Rosa.

Peter's eyes opened wider. "Marlene Dietrich, is your daughter? Wonderful."

"You have come all this way for nothing," said Aunty Jo. "The last time we spoke, I said some harsh words to her. I was wrong, but I couldn't face her. I am too ashamed."

"You must come; she is waiting for you."

"She is here? But she can't be; it is too dangerous—the Werewolves will kill her."

"She's not here. We brought a radio, so you can at least talk to her."

"A radio?"

"Please come and talk to her; she is waiting to speak to you. The Americans wouldn't let her into Berlin, but they have allowed her to speak with you via radio, as long as you both speak in English."

Aunty Jo looked at the two boys. "Boys, I don't know about you, but I'm sick of living like rats."

The boys beamed.

"I don't understand; if this place is so dangerous, why didn't you leave?"

"When the Russians arrived, they weren't exactly friendly," said Aunty Jo. "They were hell-bent on revenge. They raped and killed anybody they could get their hands on, everywhere except here. The Werewolves seem to be able to keep them out of here, and, for some reason, the Werewolves have left us alone. But we still keep on guard, just in case."

"I still don't understand," said Aunty Jo. "Why exactly did you come here, Rosa?"

"I wanted to help Miss Dietrich, who has helped me so much. Besides, I knew where you lived, and in a destroyed city, it's not like I could draw them a map."

"Child, they are cold facts, and from what I've learned about you, you run on hot emotions. By that, I mean you are controlled by your heart and not your head," said Aunty Jo. "I think the *real* reason that you came here was because you love a boy named Peter."

Silence. She couldn't deny it, but with Peter standing directly in front of her she most definitely could not say yes. "I mean there's little Charlie, of course."

Peter moved forward, awkwardly putting his arms around Rosa and tilted his head down and pressed his soft lips against hers. Rosa didn't know how long they were like that, but her legs felt weak.

A wolf whistle rang out.

They split apart and turned.

Charlie and Aunty Jo were standing at the doorway. "Come on, you two lovebirds, there will be plenty of time for that later."

"The Americans are just at the end of the street at the water fountain, so let's get going," said Rosa.

Aunty Jo grabbed a bag of her belongings. And the boys, both in civilian clothing, grabbed their knapsacks. Aunty Jo and Charlie left the room. Peter held Rosa's hand and spun her around. Rosa looked at his smiling blue eyes. She had missed Peter's eyes.

"I like your hair," he said, stroking it. "It suits you."

"I'm sorry for lying to you, Peter."

"You did what you had to. I have had a lot of time to get over my shock."

"So, you forgive me?"

Peter smiled. "Are you kidding? I am so glad my first kiss was with a girl after all and not with some strange boy from Bavaria on a football field."

Rosa blushed as she laughed out loud.

"I was your first kiss?"

"Come on, you two lovebirds," shouted Aunty Jo from outside.

***

Sgt. Mayflower didn't ask about Peter and Charlie; one look at Rosa and Peter holding hands seemed to be enough. The soldiers and their guests moved quickly back to the trucks. The sergeant went to the second covered jeep. He spoke to a radioman working at his radio in the back of the jeep. The American GIs knew that Marlene Dietrich was back in the American-controlled sector of Germany, standing next to General James Gavin, awaiting this radio call. "Have you got base camp yet, soldier?"

"Yes, Sarge. Miss Dietrich is standing by."

Aunty Jo spoke in German over the radio.

"*Mami, you have to speak in English,*" Marlene Dietrich said over the radio.

"Okay, my love. It is so good to hear your voice again."

"*You don't know how happy I am to find you alive.*"

"They all try to kill me, but I am a Dietrich."

"*Yes, you are a Dietrich.*"

They spoke for another few minutes but needed to finish up when Sgt. Mayflower gave the signal to Aunty Jo.

"*Mami, you suffered for my sake. Forgive me.*"

"Yes, my love."

"*Mami, take care of yourself.*"

"Yes. Goodbye."

"*Goodbye, Mami.*"

"Goodbye, my heart. Goodbye."

The radioman ended the transmission to the operator on the other end.

Aunty Jo wiped away her tears.

Sgt. Mayflower barked out his orders. "Okay, boys, time to leave."

Rosa, Peter and Charlie went to get in the lead jeep with Sgt. Mayflower at the wheel. "I'm sorry, Rosa, I'm only authorised to collect Miss Dietrich's mother, not anyone else. The Russians wouldn't like it."

Rosa's eyes turned in an instant. "They not go, I not go."

"Rosa, if it were up to me—"

"Shhh!" Peter shushed them. He turned, looking up at the rooftops. It was as if he could hear or smell something the others couldn't. He suddenly turned and grabbed Rosa and dived to the ground. At the same time, a shot rang out from high above.

The soldiers jumped out of the vehicles and aimed up in every direction as the shot echoed around them. More shots were fired at the Americans. A single shot came from behind them. The soldiers at the rear swung their weapons around. Behind them, kneeling on rubble high above them with a smoking rifle barrel, stood Wolfgang. But his gun was not aimed at the Americans; instead, it was aimed at the topmost floor of the exposed building opposite.

There was a large crash behind the GIs. They turned around to see a body had fallen onto a broken piano below. Several footsteps could be heard running away. Wolfgang had shot and killed the sniper who had been targeting the Americans. Wolfgang spoke to Rosa as he looked at the body stretched before them. "Klaus. He tried to kill you."

She turned and looked at the dead sniper, and she could clearly see Klaus' face. She raised one arm and said to the Americans, who were still pointing their weapons at Wolfgang, "Put down your rifles. He is not here to harm us."

One by one, the soldiers lowered their arms.

Wolfgang threw down his scoped German rifle, raced down the grand mound of rubble and knelt next to Peter. Only then did Rosa look down to see Peter's white shirt covered in bright red blood—

his blood and the red-stained circle was getting bigger. Wolfgang tried to stem the flow as he spoke to Peter. "I told you, brother, to not stick your head out for anyone, but you wouldn't listen to me."

Rosa dropped to her knees. "Brother? You two are brothers?"

Peter smiled and then coughed up bright frothy blood.

Sgt. Mayflower swooped Peter up. "We need to get him to a hospital and quick."

The sergeant drove wildly back to the checkpoint with Wolfgang, Charlie, a bleeding Peter in the back of the jeep, and Aunty Jo in the passenger seat, who sat solemnly quiet and dared not turn her head. Peter's head was cradled in Rosa's lap. Blood bubbled from his mouth, trickling down the side of his cheek. Charlie was crouched down beside him crying, and Wolfgang had Peter's lower legs draped over him.

"Stop the bleeding!" shouted Sgt. Mayflower over his shoulder.

Rosa searched Peter's clothes. She found a reddish-pink rag. Peter stopped her. "Not my lucky scarf," he croaked.

Wolfgang gave her a bandage from his satchel.

"Not Peter's lucky scarf," Wolfgang repeated.

"Lucky scarf?" queried Rosa.

Peter tried to talk but had another coughing fit. "Wolf. Wolfy," Peter begged.

"I don't understand. How can you two be brothers?"

"We are twins," said Wolfgang. "Not identical, but we are brothers. Peter is older than me by fifteen minutes. But we are nothing alike. Peter was so weak, so soft. He wasn't a true German. He wasn't a Nazi, and he would say so. I was too embarrassed to be his brother, but I promised my parents to look after him, so we told everyone that we just had the same family name. I'm so sorry, Petey."

Rosa looked up at Wolfgang, who had tears streaming down his cheeks. His face was much softer now, and for the first time, she could see that they were indeed brothers—not identical, but very similar.

Peter smiled and placed his hand on Wolfgang's arm and said in a weak voice, "Wolfy. Tell her."

Wolfgang started to talk, more a whisper. "That's his lucky scarf. Years ago, the day the war started, Peter led a group of us kids after a caravan of Gypsies. There was some girl, no more than eight or nine at most, who dared to stand up to us. Anyway, she nearly killed Peter. While Peter lay dying from a head injury, he would not let go of this red scarf, which he'd grabbed from the girl." Wolfgang paused. "Despite what the doctors said, Peter didn't die, and the girl's headwear became his lucky scarf. But after this incident, Peter changed. He was always stopping to smell the flowers or sit atop a hill and look down at the daffodils on the meadow below. The doctors told our parents that it was a result of a brain injury. But Peter told me it wasn't. He had almost died, and God had given him a second chance, a chance to live again and undo all his wrongs. I used to be the quiet, soft one, as our father had put it, but after Peter's accident, it was up to me to stand up and honour the family name. So, I did."

The convoy pulled up at the checkpoint they had used to enter the Werewolf Zone.

"What do you have here?" said the same Russian officer. "Your papers were very specific: you had to be out by 1800hrs, and no passengers." The Russian officer looked at the kids. He saw the Werewolf logo on Wolfgang's lapel, a crudely drawn wolf's head. "The mark of the Werewolves!" he cried, as he tried to unbuckle his pistol from its holster.

Sgt. Mayflower planted his foot on the gas, and the jeep sped off. Instinctively the following GI drivers did likewise. The Americans in the back of the truck faced outwards with weapons pointed at the Russian guards, but no one fired a shot.

Sometime during Wolfgang's story, Peter died. He died with a sweet smile on his face, and he was still holding her hands tightly.

Charlie whispered, "Goodbye, Petey," and kissed Peter on the forehead. The silence was broken only by little Charlie's whimpers.

They drove through Berlin and deep into the American-controlled sector on an autobahn heading west. The jeep suddenly lurched to a halt by the side of the road next to a field of sunflowers with the horn blaring.

Sgt. Mayflower's head rested on the steering wheel.

Aunty Jo pulled him off the steering wheel and looked down. "He's been shot in his legs."

"We thought there was only one shot, but the sniper must have shot at both Peter and the sergeant," said Rosa.

"Sniper bullets are powerful weapons," said Aunty Jo. "One bullet can easily hit two people. I'm guessing the sergeant didn't think it was that bad. He thought wrong."

"I'm fine. I've had worse. I have to get you to Marlene," said the wounded sergeant to Aunty Jo. "I promised her." He then looked at the blood streaming from both of his legs. He laughed. "Tell your daughter that she was right. Death is a joke. Here I am dying, and the war's already over." He laughed, and seconds later, he was dead.

Wolfgang got out of the jeep and grabbed his dead brother and a shovel from the jeep's bonnet. He looked at the field of golden sunflowers. "This is the perfect resting place for Peter."

Wolfgang walked into the setting sun carrying his dead brother in his arms. The convoy departed, leaving Wolfgang to his shovelling.

\*\*\*

The convoy pulled into the American base camp deep inside western Germany as the sun hung low in the early morning sky. Marlene Dietrich was waiting expectantly by the side of the road when they pulled up.

Aunty Jo got out and hugged her daughter. "Mother, I was so worried. I was fretting all night. I finally have you safe and sound."

"Marlene, I am so sorry for what I said to you. I was wrong. Can you ever forgive a stupid old lady?"

"I forgave you the moment you said it. You are my mother, and I don't have another one."

Rosa got out of the jeep with Charlie standing by her side.

Marlene looked around. "Where is Sergeant Mayflower? I must thank him."

Aunty Jo and Rosa did not respond. They both looked downcast.

Marlene's smile shifted to concern. "Mother? Rosa? Where is Sergeant Mayflower?"

Just then, the soldiers removed a stretcher from the back of the truck. It was holding a body covered in a green army blanket.

Marlene watched as the stretcher-bearers headed for the hospital tent across the road. "Wait," she called out.

They stopped, and as they halted, the shiny silver double hook dropped to the side of the stretcher. Marlene moved over and tenderly picked up the hook. She saw it had some blood on it and took the white silk scarf from her head. She tried to remove the blood, but it had dried hard.

Aunty Jo came up behind and put a hand on Marlene's shoulder.

"He liked to keep it nice and shiny just like his boots," Marlene explained to her mother.

"I'm sure his American buddies will take care of him."

Marlene stopped rubbing. "You're right."

Aunty Jo grabbed the hook from Marlene and placed it underneath the blanket and the soldiers carried Sgt. Mayflower's body into the military hospital.

Marlene looked at the cemetery with hundreds of white crosses directly across the road from the field hospital. "He came back here to be with his buddies, and now he can be buried with them. It's really where he belongs." Marlene burst into tears and hugged her mother. "Why is it always the good ones who pay for the mistakes of evil people?"

"Because, my child, they are good. It is in the nature of good to stand up to evil, wherever that evil may be."

"I don't understand. The war is over?"

"Sometimes war is never over, especially for the loser."

"But it's not fair, Mother."

"Child, war is never fair, especially to women and children."

Rosa watched as Aunty Jo and Marlene followed Sgt. Mayflower into the hospital.

"Rosa!"

She turned to see Charlie driven away by MPs. "Charlie! Charlie!" she shouted after the jeep as it sped past her. She grabbed one of the GIs. "Where are they taking him?"

"He's a POW now. They're probably taking him to a camp, goodness knows where."

"But he's my brother. I must find him."

"Good luck, Sister."

## Chapter 25

### 11 February 1954 (Thursday)

*Stuttgart, Germany*

Rosa and Charlie stood outside the Stuttgart Cinema, trying to keep warm in the winter snow. They were wearing hats, scarves and heavy coats, but by the way Charlie was moving and rubbing his gloved hands together, this wasn't enough.

"Can't we wait for her inside?" Charlie pleaded.

"You can, but I have to be here the very moment she arrives," Rosa said, looking up at the cinema sign posted above them: "Leni Riefenstahl presents the World Premiere Opening of *Tiefland*." All Rosa could focus on was the name in black capital letters on a white backboard: LENI RIEFENSTAHL.

"Thanks again, Charlie."

"What for?"

"Paying my airfares here. They are so expensive. You even paid for the clothes I'm wearing. You don't have much need for winter clothing when you live in a desert."

"Hey, nothing is too much for my big sister."

"But brand-new clothes? Surely there was a second-hand store here in Stuttgart?"

"Those new clothes will get plenty of use, especially when you come back here to visit your little brother for Christmas."

She looked at him.

"Sis, you promised. If I got you here today for this World Premiere, you would come back to Germany to visit me, at least more often."

"You hardly get holidays working in a kibbutz."

"A deal is a deal. You won't go back on your word now that you have what you wanted?" he asked with his deadly serious eyes.

"No, of course not," she said with a smile. "I'm just saying it won't be as regular as you seem to think it will be."

"Sister, I have to go inside and warm up before I freeze to death. I don't know how your desert blood is coping with this," he said, putting out his cigar and pocketing it.

Rosa had been colder, especially in Nazi concentration camps. Now, just like back then, she ignored the biting cold. Little Charlie had grown up very quickly. He was only twenty years old, but he talked, acted and looked much older because of his premature balding and perhaps from smoking all those cigars. After the war, he had been adopted by a wealthy Berlin couple who had no one to leave their shoe factory to—having lost all five of their sons to the war. They could not have found a better heir, as he took to the shoe business as Marlene Dietrich took to a camera lens.

Despite his brilliant and rapid success, he couldn't stop thinking about his older sister—Rosa. Charlie's parents helped him by putting ads in various papers across Europe and even paid for a private investigator. He could not find a single trace of her; she was presumed dead, which was a safe assumption in post-war Europe.

But they had been looking in the wrong continent. They were looking in Europe when she was living and working in the Middle East. It had been a chance photo in an article about an Egyptian dig led by a German archaeology team that Charlie happened to see in the paper one day. He immediately knew that the woman on the back far left of the black-and-white group photo was his Rosa—no doubt about it. He could recognise his sister anywhere.

Fate had drawn them together in the first place, and Fate, it seemed, wasn't done with them. Charlie eventually tracked Rosa down to where she was living in Israel. They had spoken over the phone, but they hadn't physically met until two days ago when she arrived back in Germany: for the first time in almost a decade. The memories flooded her to the point that she couldn't sleep—her parents, their incarceration, Peter and the boys, including Charlie and Leni Riefenstahl. She could never forget Director Riefenstahl, no matter how busily she worked herself.

She never forgot about Charlie. She had spent weeks and months searching for him. She told Charlie she never found him, but that was a lie. But by the time she did catch up to him at one of the thousands of orphanages that had sprung up at the war's end, it was the very day he was getting adopted by an elderly kind-looking couple. She fought off an overwhelming urge to race up to him and hug him. The new family seemed happy with each other, and Rosa didn't want to get in the way. Besides, she didn't have anything to offer, such as money or a home, as she was like everybody else, living from the food provided by the US and her allies to stop Germany from starving to death. Charlie was better off without her, or so she thought up until the day he contacted his big sister, as he put it. She wasn't sure what shocked her more, his phone call or the fact that she finally had a sibling.

Just then, in the distance, she could see two women wearing matching white fur coats. As they walked closer, Rosa thought the two women looked and talked the same. Finally, Leni Riefenstahl arrived alongside an elderly lady who looked like an older version of Leni, so much so that Rosa felt confident that the older woman had to be Frau Bertha Riefenstahl, Leni's mother. The two women entered the cinema, with Rosa following close behind. Rosa kept within eavesdropping distance as she overheard the two women meeting the owner of the cinema. He'd set up an area just inside where the Riefenstahls could greet the audience as they arrived. But there was hardly anybody around.

"Leni, where are they?" asked Bertha.

"I don't know, Mother, maybe the snow has kept some of them away. Please be patient."

For Rosa's sake, Charlie had kept an eye out for all things related to *Tiefland* and put aside all the newspaper and magazine articles for Rosa to read when she finally arrived in Germany for the premiere. According to numerous articles, Leni Riefenstahl's post-war life had been far from easy. Since the end of the war, Leni had spent much time in the law courts. In the beginning, the authorities tried her four or five times, accusing her of being a Nazi, but she hadn't joined the Nazi Party, as all high-ranking officials were required to do. She never worried about such trifles, and no one had ever asked her to do it. Maybe everyone in the Nazi Party had just assumed she was a Nazi? Was that her fault?

When that failed, the authorities went after her for crimes against humanity. The charge against her was for filming the Nuremberg Rallies, thereby spreading hatred in the world. But she argued, successfully, that Nuremberg was simply an annual party rally—very normal in international politics. The world authorities threw every conceivable book at her, but nothing ever hit home. Her signatures, witnesses, or any evidence, simply could not be found to condemn her. Although she was morally reprehensible, technically and legally, she was no criminal. In the end, nothing was proven, and she was free to go.

Of course, there had been libellous innuendos and slanderous incriminations about her wartime past, which Leni efficiently dealt with by suing each and every one of her accusers. Being the consummate actress, she slew her opponents and made quite a living from her successful lawsuits. In early 1953, she had successfully sued the French government to finally release the prints of *Tiefland*. The world premiere had got off to a rocky start when the distributor started the advertising campaign and the Association of Survivors of Concentration Camps announced a film boycott. Leni Riefenstahl was once more in the papers, and once more not in a good way.

Regardless, the theatre was almost full. But, according to Charlie, when the theatre owner realised there was no one coming, he had called on his friends and family to fill the empty seats. The ushers closed the theatre doors, and the owner of the cinema introduced Leni Riefenstahl.

Leni got up to polite applause and walked over to the lectern as the owner sat down. "Thank you all for coming," Leni said, speaking into the microphone. "Early last year, after years in French courts, the French government finally released *Tiefland* to me. Ever since then, I have been editing and working on it daily as my mother, Bertha, can attest," she said, indicating her mother, who was seated in the front row. Bertha stood momentarily for polite applause. "And not only did I have access to the best editing suites in Munich, my much-loved new home, I even had help from Vienna to help me score my 99-minute soundtrack. And seated by my mother is my co-star, Franz Eichberger, who plays my *Tiefland* hero, Pedro."

Rosa remembered seeing Franz during filming, but she had had little to do with him. He came, did his scenes, and left. And when he wasn't on set, he kept to himself. Franz stood momentarily to receive much bigger applause from the audience. It seemed some fans still remembered him.

"Today, at my World Premiere release of *Tiefland* here in Stuttgart, I'm so glad I can share with you my German masterpiece. It has taken me twenty years to finish my *Tiefland*, apparently a World Guinness Record to complete a film, and I'm sure you will agree with me that it has been well worth the wait."

The lights dimmed, and Leni took her seat between her mother and Franz Eichberger, with Rosa and Charlie seated directly behind. Sitting so close to Leni and Franz brought back memories of being on the film set. But then, with a stab, Rosa remembered her mother's missing finger. Then she remembered trying to find her father and then the boys. Emotions welled up inside Rosa. This had been a mistake. She wanted to leave, but for some reason, she couldn't. Perhaps she felt guilty for Charlie, who had gone to a lot of trouble and expense to get her here for this very moment.

In the dark, as the movie credits rolled by, Rosa finally tore her gaze away from Leni to the screen, only to look up and stare at the Gypsy children's bright smiling faces on the fifty-foot screen. These children on the screen weren't merely extras on a film; they had been her family. She knew all their names. She also knew that every one of them was dead. Rosa wondered how the Stuttgart audience would feel about this so-called German masterpiece if they knew what Rosa knew. Every one of those brown-eyed Romani children, smiling down at the audience, had been sent to Poland to be gassed. Tears streamed down Rosa's cheeks.

Dead.

Dead.

Dead.

They were all dead. And in the worst possible way—away from family, friends and loved ones. No one to care for them or console their frightened tears, except for the hobbled-heels of an SS Camp Guard or the butt of a weapon. No. Rosa needed to be here. She needed to be the voice of those who could no longer speak—the Romani dead.

Ninety-nine minutes later, the longest ninety-nine minutes of Rosa's life, *Tiefland's* closing credits were rolling down the screen as the movie finished. The lights came on, and Leni Riefenstahl stood and turned to face the audience with a professional smile. But it became clear to all that more than half the seats were now vacated. Dozens of people must have slipped away during the movie. Leni Riefenstahl ignored the vacant chairs and accepted the polite but awkwardly long applause.

The theatre manager got up and announced that they had organised refreshments in the foyer where Leni would sign autographs. In the foyer, a small gathering remained behind, but, from what Rosa could see, no one asked for an autograph. The group mainly consisted of elderly people, who were extremely polite about *Tiefland*. Nonetheless, Rosa had still managed to overhear several disparaging remarks.

"Did you see her name all over those credits?" said one.

"It appears she made the entire film all by herself," said the second.

"I know. She should have called it Leni-land," said the third.

"Or Boring-land," said the first as the three young ladies laughed.

A French reviewer spoke to the woman holding his arm. "You know the Germans invented the word *Schadenfreude* where 'pleasure is derived from the misfortune of others' for these exact moments. How fitting for a Nazi film director."

Another film critic said, "*Tiefland* lacks soul."

Most of the remaining people were news reporters for various papers, radio and TV stations, who were busy taking notes in the foyer as they fired questions at her.

"Fraulein Riefenstahl?" one of the newsmen asked.

"Director Riefenstahl," she said through a forced smile.

"Director Riefenstahl," he corrected himself. "Do you believe that you should have been tried at the Nuremberg trials like your close friend, Julius Streicher, the editor and publisher of *Der Stürmer*, whom they ended up executing for his pivotal role in inciting the extermination of the Jews and the Gypsies?"

"Please, I have been asked and answered that question numerous times before."

"Not here in Stuttgart for my readers of their local Stuttgart paper," the journalist quickly countered.

"Julius Streicher was never a friend. An acquaintance at best. Just like I was with the Führer, Goebbels and Albert Speer."

"You were officially cleared as a Nazi, but they did find you as a 'fellow traveller' with the Nazi Party."

"Another word for Gypsy is 'traveller', so after playing a queen of Gypsies, I'll accept that compliment as a badge of honour. All I did was to make movies before, during and since the war."

"But you filmed the greatest propaganda films of all times, the Nuremberg Rallies, which surely was as instrumental in the murder of the European Jews as any edition of *Der Stürmer*?" the young man said, determined to continue his line of questioning.

"You mean my award-winning documentaries, *Triumph of the Will*, which was purely a political rally, and *Olympia*, where I filmed the 1936 Berlin Olympic Games? I was the first director to use cameras on wheeled tracks, and today, all film directors use tracking shots in sports films, which I pioneered as a female film director in a man's world. Are these current film directors today also somehow part of your same conspiracy?"

"Hardly the same thing."

"My point exactly. Anyone else? I mean, anyone else who has a question specifically about *Tiefland*?"

Another reporter put up his hand. "Director Riefenstahl, rumours have been plaguing you since the announcement of the release of *Tiefland* that you had personally been at a concentration camp, which meant that you must have known what was happening inside those death camps."

"That was an outrageous lie, and I successfully sued all those publications that slandered my good name."

"Yes, you won your suit because there weren't any eyewitnesses— not that the authorities could find."

"I'm sure they are all living happily," she said tersely.

"Where are they?"

"Wherever Gypsies live happily. They are travellers, you know."

"Why didn't you ensure the children were safe or saved from the camps?"

"I was told that the children would be cared for."

"And did you make sure they were safe?"

"I didn't do it myself," Director Riefenstahl said, getting angrier.

"Why not?"

"I'm a film director making a film, and besides, don't you know there was a war on? And do you know what? I can't remember anyone being so concerned about the welfare of Gypsies back before the war. Back then, everyone seemed happy to be rid of them. But after the war, Europe suddenly grew a guilty conscience, especially a guilty Gypsy conscience."

The assembled newsmen erupted in an uproar of questions, which only had the effect of ending up as noise. While this 'public interrogation' happened directly before Rosa, she noticed one gentleman sitting in a peacock chair, writing furiously.

When he finished scribbling in his notepad, he pushed his way through the throng of journalists and came up directly to Leni Riefenstahl. "My name is Alfred Polgar, and I'm a freelance art critic," he said, introducing himself without shaking her hand. "This is what I have written so far," he said, reciting his notes, "There is one insignificant detail that one can't help but think about as one watches *Tiefland*: the fact that, shortly after having the pleasure of serving Director Riefenstahl's cinematic art, the extras—including women and children—were shipped off to feed the hungry gas ovens of Auschwitz."

She glared at him. "I'm not scared of you, Mr Polgar. Print that at your own peril."

"The same peril as you exposed those Romani children to—I will." He departed, along with most of the newsmen, who appeared to tire of this charade with a woman who wasn't showing the slightest hint of guilt, regret or remorse.

The remaining newsmen asked a few more questions, seemingly out of politeness rather than a genuine interest in *Tiefland*. The assembly in front of Leni Riefenstahl soon dispersed.

Rosa could no longer remain still as she felt anger rising from deep within her stomach—years of suppressed rage rose to the surface of her emotions. With teeth clenched, she stormed up to Leni Riefenstahl. "Director Riefenstahl, this is my young brother Charlie, and my name is Rosa. Do you remember me?"

Leni looked at the serious young woman in front of her. "You look familiar, but I'm sorry I don't remember you. I once had a school friend named Rosa."

"I know; you told me that once already. You said she was a plain-looking girl just like me."

"I did? When?"

"When you purchased me at the Maxglan Concentration Camp for your film. I was your 'Little Rosie'."

Leni appeared to recognise her now. "I did not *buy* you."

"What do you call it?"

"I hired you."

"Hired? I don't remember being paid."

"Well, I didn't pay you. I paid your..."

"You paid my owners. My concentration camp owners."

"No. It was nothing like that," said Leni. "It was just a business transaction. Ultimately, all wars are mostly business, aren't they?"

"I came here tonight to see if it was all worth it. All those years, all those people."

"And?"

"It wasn't. It was wasted years and lives wasted."

"It seems everyone's a critic tonight," Leni said, turning away.

Rosa stopped Leni from leaving. "What you did in Germany was not create a great work of art; rather, it was to commit a great wrong. Instead of trying to be a great artist, you should have tried at being a half-decent human being."

With that said, Rosa and Charlie turned and walked away.

"No one understands the plight of the Gypsies better than me!" Leni shouted after them. "I played not just any Gypsy, but Martha, the queen of all Gypsies!"

Rosa was impressed with how restrained she'd been. She had come a fair way since she was an angry young girl, always getting into fights. But the moment she heard Leni shout the name, Martha, something snapped. She turned and strode back to Leni.

"My mother's name was Martha, and she died because of you." Rosa slapped Leni's face once, and then again. "And that one was for my father's death; his name was Max. You are responsible for both of their deaths." Then Rosa spun around and left.

"Who was that?" Leni's mother asked as Rosa and Charlie exited the theatre.

"Them? Nobodies. Just extras annoyed that they didn't get a film credit. I tell you, Mother, there is no pleasing some people."

Rosa walked outside the theatre, where the bitter cold air soothed her fiery temper. She turned to face her little brother. "Thanks, Charlie. I needed you here with me tonight."

"You're my big sister; of course, I would be here for you. And I'm only standing here right now because you kept a stupid kid alive."

"Charlie, you were never stupid. Just quiet. A rare quality I love in people."

They both laughed.

"Excuse me, are you Rosa?"

Charlie and Rosa looked up to see a man standing in front of them.

Rosa's legs buckled. "Peter?"

The man's mouth opened wide in surprise. "What? No, I'm not Peter. I'm Peter's brother, Wolfgang, but all my friends call me Wolfy."

"Wolfgang?" she said, remembering the tough time Peter's brother had given her all those years ago. She'd always thought that if he'd had the chance, he would have reported her to the authorities or, worse, killed her. "What do you want?"

Wolfgang looked awkwardly to Charlie and back to her again. "I've kept in touch with little Charlie here, and when he told me you were coming, I thought that I had to come and talk to you."

"Talk to me? About what?"

"I don't know exactly. Peter? We both loved him, so we have that in common, at least. Everyone else who knew and loved Peter is dead."

She looked at Charlie, annoyed with him for not telling her about Wolfgang; she hated surprises. "I don't know; it's getting late."

"Go on, Sis," said Charlie. "There's a café just across the street."

"Okay. I guess if you came out and waited in the cold just to talk to me, I can at least have a cup of coffee with you. For Peter's sake, if nothing else." She looked at Wolfgang directly. "But I'm telling you now, I will never call you Wolfy."

The three of them took off their heavy coats as they entered the café and took a seat right next to the café's large front window. They gave the waitress their orders. While Rosa and Wolfy slid into the bench seats opposite one another, Charlie remained standing.

"Well, if you two will excuse me," Charlie said, "I will go outside to smoke a few puffs of my cigar before our order arrives." He went back to the front door and put on his heavy coat before exiting the café.

"Well, go ahead then, Wolfgang," she said, "tell me your story." Wolfy looked at her with open eyes. "Quickly, before our coffee arrives," she added.

Wolfy began. "To start with, my story is no different from any other German after losing a second world war. My generation of Germans had to rebuild a millennia-old nation that their fathers had completely destroyed in a mere six years. After a while, I found a job repairing US Army trucks on their base, where I learned to be a mechanic. Anyway, I was such a talented 'grease-monkey', as the Americans called them, that I soon owned my very own auto repair shop near the American base. Although business was good, I felt my life was idle—it all seemed too easy and repetitious and worse: meaningless. But once I'd heard about the World Premiere of *Tiefland* by Director Riefenstahl, I took a chance that you would be here. And I was right. I can't explain it, but when I saw you and Charlie, I felt alive." Wolfy paused. "It is a feeling I haven't had since the day Peter died."

While Wolfy continued talking, Rosa was still getting over the shock of seeing him. Wolfy looked exactly how Peter would have looked, had he lived. And even though Wolfy was not an identical twin, they looked eerily similar.

"Wolfgang, I have to make a confession. I've felt wrong all these years for not telling you the truth. But Peter's death happened so suddenly, and I never saw you again. Until now."

He looked intensely at her. She pulled out her red scarf from her pocket and laid it out on the table.

"Peter's scarf," he said. "You've kept it all these years?"

"It's not Peter's scarf. It's mine."

"Well, of course, it's yours. Peter gave it to you when he was dying."

"You don't understand. It was my scarf even before Peter returned it to me."

His confused face told Rosa he didn't understand. "It was my scarf. And Peter removed it from my head that day. The day I hit him in his head with a rock."

His face finally registered his understanding. "You are kidding me? You were that little Gypsy girl we surrounded that day?" He paused, taking it all in.

"Of course, I had no idea that it was Peter."

"It wasn't just Peter. I was there. We were all there."

"All of you?"

"Me. Fritz. The Muller brothers."

"What about Gunter? I don't remember seeing him."

"He was still peddling to catch up with the rest of us. He was still big back then."

"But this was in Cologne, and you were all from Berlin?"

"It was a Hitler Youth camp."

"I'm sorry."

"It wasn't your fault. We chased after you. A group of bullies picking on a little girl; it was our fault."

"No. I mean I'm sorry about Peter. I was so relieved to find out that I hadn't killed that boy on that day, ironically at the same time that same boy was dying in my arms. But if I hadn't taken him with us, he wouldn't have been shot by Klaus, and he'd still be alive today."

"It's not just your fault. I bear a huge responsibility for my brother's death too."

"What do you mean?" Rosa asked.

"I was with Klaus when he shadowed the Americans. He was excited, like a kid. He'd never killed an American. I had a bad feeling, but I didn't say or do anything. Not until I realised he'd shot Peter: by then it was too late. Peter must have seen the glint from the scope and stood in front of the GI at the last moment. When I saw the bullet had gone through them both, I shot Klaus. So, you see, I'm as much to blame as you—"

Wolfy's talking was suddenly halted when they heard a commotion erupt outside; everyone looked through the café's large front window. On the footpath, Leni Riefenstahl was arguing with Franz Eichberger, her mother trailing behind. Finally, Leni Riefenstahl stormed across the street and stood outside the Stuttgart Cinema while her mother and Franz departed in a white Volkswagen.

Charlie, who was on the footpath puffing on his cigar, had front-row tickets to the unfolding drama. He stubbed out his cigar and re-entered the café.

"What just happened with the great Gypsy Queen?" asked Rosa.

"Franz Eichberger just told Fraulein Riefenstahl that the distributors are furious with the film and are pulling it from their theatres."

"I can see why she's unhappy."

"She held up some papers saying that she will sue them for breach of contract if they do. And, get this, she said, *when it comes to the courts of law, Leni Riefenstahl always wins.*"

"From what I've read, she often does. That's probably how she paid for her expensive mink coats," Rosa said, looking over at Leni standing outside the cinema with the *Tiefland* signage directly above her. "What is *Director* Riefenstahl doing now?"

"There was supposed to be a celebration party held by the distributors at some swanky hotel in the city, but it's been cancelled. But she didn't believe either Franz or her mother, and she's waiting in the street for the limousine that will never arrive."

"That's the story of Director Riefenstahl's life," said Rosa, looking across the snow-laden street at Leni Riefenstahl, all alone, trying to keep herself warm. The cinema lights blaring her name above the director turned off.

## Chapter 26

August 1960

*Jerusalem, Israel,*

Rosa shielded her eyes from the glare of the setting sun. The rumbling truck bounced and squeaked along the lonely dirt road that led to Jerusalem. The ex-US Army WWII lorry seemed to be held together only by a thick layer of red rust and a prayer from Rosa to get there on time. She held onto her amulet and rubbed her family's stone for luck before kissing it and putting it back under her work shirt.

Rosa had spent all day in the tray-backed vehicle driving down the mountain ranges east of the biblical city. Rosa and her driver had trouble getting through the many checkpoints along the way. There had been troubles recently, and security was stepped up.

The driver reached for a pack of cigarettes from the dusty brown dashboard. He popped the cigarette straight onto the left side of his lower lip as he deftly flicked the silver Zippo lighter, a souvenir from the war, which his American GI captor had given to him.

"You know those things will kill you one day, Wolfy," Rosa gently scolded.

After leaving 'Accursed Europe', Rosa had wandered for months, like a Gypsy caravan-of-one. She somehow ended up in Egypt working with an archaeology team desperate to resume their pre-war work. Her language skills and fearlessness had been invaluable. In 1947, when the war began in Palestine, she answered Israel's call to arms to fight for its independence and become its own nation. Although she was not a Jew, having lived and lost family members in concentration camps alongside Jews, she felt a kindred spirit, and she also vowed: *never again.*

After the war for Israel was won, she decided to stay. She lived and worked in a kibbutz dangerously close to the Arabs who had vowed to drive Israel back into the sea. Her skills with languages became just as valuable as her fighting spirit. In Israel, she was a refugee among the world's refugees. She had finally found her tribe and home.

Not long after they shared a coffee in Stuttgart, Wolfy ended up moving to Israel to be with Rosa. A few years later, he'd told Rosa that the night they were having a cup of coffee, and when he saw the way her eyes lit up talking about Peter, and that she was his kindred spirit—they both knew and loved Peter.

At first, it was a holiday as he'd always wanted to see the pyramids and the city from the Bible, Jerusalem. Then he came back again and again. No-one at the kibbutz complained because his skill with diesel trucks, generators and tractors was an invaluable asset. Slowly, bit by bit, as his visits increased her resistance to him decreased. But she wasn't interested in him even if he was Peter's brother. Wolfy wasn't Peter.

Then, one day when she was awaiting his arrival at the airport, when he didn't get off the plane, was when her heart first sank. She'd tried ringing him. No answer. So, she asked Charlie to investigate. Wolfgang was sick in hospital and had almost died from pneumonia. Apparently, the German cold air and his smoking didn't agree with his lungs, one of the reasons she was trying to get him to quit smoking. And after this event, and in no time at all, he sold up in Germany and moved to Israel to join her.

Suddenly, the truck braked to a halt, jolting Rosa out of her reminiscing.

"We are here," Wolfy proudly announced, as he'd fulfilled his promise that the truck would not break down.

Rosa got out of the truck and slammed the dented door shut so that it would stay closed. She looked up at the sign surrounded by flashing bulbs: MARLENE DIETRICH'S FINAL SHOW, it read in English.

"I won't be long," she said before hurrying away.

"Take your time. I need to give the old girl a service before we head home," Wolfy shouted after her as he got out and reached for his toolbox.

Rosa stopped and looked at Wolfy as though she was about to change her mind.

Wolfy motioned with his bright blue eyes: Go!

Rosa turned and walked up the stairs and entered the tremendous sandstone structure. She walked into the high-ceilinged lobby of the large concert hall: the International Convention Centre. Although they had started building it a decade earlier, the centre still wasn't finished. Rosa had seen the fenced-off works outside, and work areas were also roped off inside. The International Convention Centre was just like Israel itself, she thought—a work in progress. There were photos of Marlene Dietrich's trademarked softly lit images all around the walls. Even at the ripe age of sixty, she was still stunning.

Rosa marvelled as she took in each image. She wasn't in a hurry. She could hear Marlene Dietrich singing a song accompanied by a piano. The first half would be over soon, she thought, as she looked up at the grand clock above the ticket booths. Rosa decided to get nearer the closed doors so she could listen in.

As she approached the doors, two black-suited attendants intercepted her. "Where do you think you are going?" they said harshly in Hebrew.

They were wearing black tuxedos, and Rosa suddenly became aware of her dirty overalls and the faded red scarf that tied her hair back.

Before she could respond, a well-dressed young man stepped up and asked in English, "Are you Rosa?"

Rosa nodded. The pungent smell of his aftershave made her even more self-conscious of her attire. This *was* a bad idea, she thought.

"I'm Miss Dietrich's assistant, and we've been expecting you."

The attendants melted into the background, resuming their security vigil.

"Follow me, please," the assistant said, leading the way.

As Rosa followed him through a side door, the music became louder. They walked through a labyrinth of corridors and stairwells until finally, they walked by the stage curtains. Rosa stopped momentarily and pulled at the heavy cloth until she got a glimpse. There she was—the irrepressible Marlene Dietrich.

Once the highest-paid actor in Hollywood, she was now the world's highest-paid cabaret singer. And she looked every inch the part. She wore a large, white-laced coat that draped behind her like a wedding train as she glided over the stage. Her white-sequined dress sparkled under the bright stage lights, just like the jewellery that hung around her neck. No doubt about it: Marlene Dietrich was still the queen of choreography—choreographing absolutely everything down to the slightest of details, including the posters that Rosa just walked past.

Once Marlene Dietrich finished her song, she walked to the front of the stage.

"Before you go for intermission," she said, speaking into her hand-held microphone, "I want you to meet an extraordinary person. He's my arranger. He's my accompanist. He's my conductor. And I wish I could say he's my composer, but that isn't true. He's everybody's composer. Burt Bacharach!"

A tall young man stood up from behind the piano and came out to accept the applause offered by the very appreciative Israeli crowd.

Miss Dietrich's assistant gently urged Rosa to continue walking and escorted her to Marlene's dressing room. Once Rosa was left alone, she toured the dressing room like she were a tourist in a museum with her hands held behind her back as she looked at all the glitz and glitter that went into making Marlene Dietrich so irrepressible.

After the war, Marlene had gone back to movies, but her film career was never the same. Nevertheless, she was Marlene Dietrich, who always landed on her feet. That was why people called her "irrepressible".

Rosa had read in a recent Israeli magazine article that from her USO days, Marlene had discovered an appreciation and love of performing in front of a live crowd, which she'd never done before the war. After her hugely popular cabaret show in Vegas, she decided to take her tour around the world. Although she sold out everywhere she went, the Berlin leg of her tour didn't go down too well with the Berliners. There had been a small but vocal protest outside the concert hall, and there were reports that some of the Berliners had spat on her, calling her a traitor. Marlene had reportedly vowed never to return to Germany, especially Berlin; despite this, however, Rosa felt certain Marlene Dietrich still loved her beloved Germany.

But what had especially caught Rosa's eye were all the photos of Marlene, which sat on top of dressers like perfectly aligned soldiers on parade. The black and whites were all from her WWII years: Italy, England, France, Holland, and Germany. They were from her USO days during the war with various images: performing on stage, from behind the stage with her looking out at her massive, uniformed crowd, with other entertainers and performers, with soldiers gathered in and around her jeep, eating at the officers' mess, with famous generals, including one of her being dwarfed by the six-foot-plus General George S. Patton.

Then Rosa saw him, not front and centre like Patton, but in the background, almost like a shadow: Sgt. Marion Mayflower. She picked it up, looking at him. She thought the name Marion was a woman's name, which she learned was a sore point with him, but then Marlene explained that Marion was a common boy's name, especially in the American Midwest. Rosa remembered that intense eye that always seemed to follow her. And then, an image flashed of his hook dropping down from the stretcher in front of a devastated Marlene Dietrich.

The song number ended to applause, and Rosa could hear the announcer call intermission.

Marlene rushed into her dressing room, going directly to the drinks cabinet and pouring a long vodka. Her hands shook as she gulped down the clear alcohol. The urgency and trembling ebbed away from Marlene's thin body with every gulp. She didn't appear to notice Rosa standing in a corner.

Rosa coughed to politely announce her presence.

Marlene didn't flinch. She smiled, turned and walked over to Rosa, kissing and hugging her. "Darling, it is so good to see you again." She pointed to a seat, which Rosa took. "I was worried you weren't coming, darling," Marlene said as she casually walked back over to the drinks table. Marlene lifted a bottle of vodka and offered Rosa a drink.

Rosa shook her head, "No."

Marlene poured herself another huge drink, neat, and took a long sip. "Forgive me, but singing is very thirsty work." Marlene moved into a deep soft chair opposite Rosa. "Darling, I have missed you; how long has it been? Four or five years?" she asked.

"Fifteen years," Rosa replied.

The two spoke in German.

"You know my mother died only months after I found her?" said Marlene.

Rosa nodded. "The day of your mother's funeral was the last day we spent together. Not long after that you went back to the States."

"You should have come back with me to work in Hollywood. With all your experience and connections, me, you would have been a gifted director."

"I'm over filming and films, and I've had my fill of directors," Rosa answered. "Besides, I wanted to rebury my parents. I didn't want them forever interred in a Nazi concentration camp. If I couldn't look after them while they were alive, then the least I could do was look out for them after they'd died."

"Where did you rebury them?"

"Alongside my grandmother. It is a beautiful spot overlooking the Rhine."

"Is there a better situated or more beautiful river than the Rhine? If there is, I haven't seen it. And I've travelled the world over." She spoke absent-mindedly holding onto her St. Christopher pendant, which she still wore. "It was as if my mother held on just to see me one last time." She paused, staring at her half-empty glass. "Everybody else was buried in cardboard boxes back then. But not my mother. My mother's casket was made out of discarded school desks constructed by the GIs. Wasn't that thoughtful of the boys?"

Again, Rosa nodded. There was nothing much to say about dead mothers or fathers.

Marlene took another swig and finished her vodka. "School desks—how ironic," she said, laughing to herself. "My mother so loved an education, especially a German one." Marlene looked into Rosa's eyes. "It is so good to speak German again."

Rosa was surprised by Marlene's comment. Since arriving in Israel, Rosa had met thousands of refugees from German-speaking countries.

Responding to Rosa's quizzical look, Marlene continued. "I've been warned by Israel's authorities not to speak or sing in German so as not to offend the Holocaust survivors."

Rosa nodded. Who were two Germans to argue with this simple request by the Israelis?

"What about you? Have you found somebody?"

"Yes. I first met him when I was ten, but about six years ago he found me."

"And is he still around?"

"Yes. He drove me here, and he's waiting for me outside."

"Do you live together?"

"We live in a kibbutz."

"From what I hear, most of them are right on the border—the front lines so to speak."

"What can I say? It's my home."

"Darling, with all your experience, I'm sure I still could get you a job back in the States. Hollywood?"

"Thank you, Miss Dietrich, but I'm happy keeping away from the limelight. I think working and living under the spotlight has its side effects." Rosa gazed at the glass Marlene was still clutching onto.

Marlene looked down at the vodka in her glass and started to swirl it. "Yes, you are right Rosa. Fame does have its *side effects*. But Fame is more addictive than any drug and alcohol combined. It takes just a single drop of pure fame, and you are hooked for life, leaving you loving and resenting it and yourself at the same time."

But, after a long thoughtful pause, she looked up at Rosa. "I suppose you could say that about performing on stage. Once you've performed for thousands of GIs cheering and screaming out your name, there's no going back. That's why I love my cabaret shows. It reminds me of the best and worst time of my life—my USO days during the war. Do you know that when I perform back in the States my shows are full of GI veterans. They've never forgotten me."

"I think you are unforgettable, Miss Dietrich."

There was a knock at the door.

Her assistant called from the other side of the door. "Time, Miss Dietrich."

"You still have nice gams," Rosa said to Marlene.

Marlene smiled. "Stay for the grand finale. I think you'll like it."

They hugged and kissed, and made promises that neither intended to fulfil. Rosa followed Marlene out of the dressing room, and Rosa watched from backstage as Marlene Dietrich took her place on centre stage to a rousing reception. Rosa spent the next hour watching Marlene perform. Wolfy appeared from nowhere and pointed to his watch. It was time to go. Rosa nodded and stood to leave.

Marlene made an announcement. "I have a new song to sing, written by my music arranger and pianist, Burt Bacharach," she said, pointing to him seated at the grand piano. "It's called 'Where

Have All the Flowers Gone?' It's a song about all the lives wasted or lost in a war. The flowers of the next generation lost or stolen from us forever."

The audience applauded louder.

Marlene started to sing it in English, but after a few bars, she stopped. "I have been ordered not to sing in German," Marlene spoke softly into the microphone.

Silence.

"But I think this song was and is meant to be sung in German. So, if no one has any objections?"

The audience stood as they clapped and cheered.

Rosa could see Marlene was visibly shaken by the audience's reaction.

Marlene resumed singing, but this time in German.

Rosa listened: it was a song about the futility of war and the death of youth before they had a chance to bloom. Rosa felt a tingling sensation down her thighs and on the tips of her ears. She could actually see her boys standing in the centre aisle dressed in suits. All the gang were there—none had aged a day since 1945: Little Charlie, Wolfgang, Gunter, Fritz, Hans, the three Muller brothers and Peter. They were all smiling and giggling and pushing one another. They spotted her and waved at her, and she waved back at them. Peter was beaming as he stared at her, and he gave Wolfy, who was standing next to him, a big hug. Rosa's heart galloped on seeing Peter hug his brother. Peter mouthed *I love you* to her and blew her a kiss. She caught his flying kiss and put it in her pocket— for later. She wiped away her tears and left. Rosa could still hear Marlene singing as she exited the building.

"How was she?" Wolfy asked as he gunned the engine.

"Like all of us survivors, taking it one minute at a time."

She slid over the green-vinyl bench seat and cuddled Wolfy, who wrapped an arm around her.

"Remember that question you asked me at the beginning of the trip?" she said. "The answer is yes."

He pulled the truck over to the side of the road. Wolfy pulled out a small silver ring with the tinniest of diamonds embedded in the circular top. With hands shaking, he tenderly put it on her ring finger. She held her ring in front of him. "Is this it? Is this all I'm worth? The smallest engagement ring in all of Israel," she said.

His mouth opened in horror. "There were bigger ones... I mean, I could afford bigger rings, but..."

"But?"

"But I knew you would never wear it. It would get in the way of doing work back at the kibbutz."

She looked down at her new piece of *pragmatic* jewellery, and she loved it. She knew she would never take it off again.

"Rosa Haussmann?" she finally said, looking in the rear-view mirror, trying on the new name as she would a new wedding dress. "That seems a good fit," she smiled.

Wolfy heaved a great sigh of relief. He put the stick into gear and left the blinking theatre lights behind as the truck rumbled up the brightly lit road. Rosa looked at the poster of Marlene Dietrich, and then she removed Peter's worn-red scarf. She looked at the scarf, remembering her childhood hero. But she no longer needed to identify as Little Red Riding Hood, or anyone else for that matter as she was her own person. Regardless of whether it was wartime or peacetime, there were always wolves to battle. But she'd learned that she could handle them either one at a time or all at once. She shook her long glowing hair, which only shone brighter after years of living underneath the desert sun. There was no longer any need to hide from who she was. She kissed Peter's red scarf and dropped it outside the window, letting the wind carry it away.

The lyrics of 'Where Have All the Flowers Gone?' snaked their way out of the theatre and chased after them, but Rosa didn't want to hear them. She didn't have time for any more sad songs; she was happy, happy because she finally had a home, and she finally knew who she was: Rosa Haussmann of Israel, born in Berlin, Germany, formerly a resident of Europe and still, always and forever, a proud world Romani.

THE END

Jericho J. Johnson will return with 'Time To Say Goodbye'

# Postscript

## Rosa the Romani

Although Rosa is fictional, she was inspired by the Gypsy children who were used in the filming of *Tiefland*, in particular Rosa Winter (see Rosa Winter below). The Gypsy or Romani Holocaust is called the Porajmos (devouring or destruction). Although the number of Gypsies murdered in the Holocaust was initially numbered in the hundreds of thousands (300-500,000, from a pre-war population estimated to be around 1-1.5 million European Roma/Romani, but it is impossible to know as nations tended not to record their actual numbers. When this is compared to over six million Jews, the percentage of Gypsies killed is believed to be higher than most of the groups persecuted by the Nazis from 1933-1945.

Travelling Sinti and Roma have lived in Austria since medieval times. From the end of the 19th century, the development of modern national states made nomadic lifestyles increasingly difficult. Government policies forced the Sinti to settle down, and if they didn't, they were deported from their country. From 1918, there was international cooperation for a solution to "the gypsy problem". Until 1938, about 3,000 travelling Sinti lived in Austria. After the "Anschluss" (the entry of Austria into the German Reich), the "detention decree" (Festsetzungsbescheid) came into force. It became illegal for Sinti to move from their temporary "places of residence". Most of them were detained in the Maxglan/Leopoldskron collection camp in Salzburg and were forced to do hard labour. In 1943, the camp was closed, and most inmates were deported to Auschwitz.

According to Project Group Wege nach Ravensbrueck, Rosa Winter was born in Königswiesen (Upper Austria) in 1923. She was the fourth child of a travelling Sinti family. Her parents and their twelve children moved from market to market in their caravan, selling goods all over Austria. Rosa Winter did not go to school. She helped in the household and took care of her younger siblings. When the family stopped off at Salzburg in the autumn of 1939, the police detained them, commandeered their wagon, horses and goods, and took them to a collection camp on the grounds of the trotting course.

In September 1940, she was sent to the Maxglan camp, and shortly afterwards, the film director Leni Riefenstahl picked out extras, including Rosa, for her movie *Tiefland*. Rosa Winter was also taken to Mittenwald in Germany for the shooting of the film. When she heard that her family was going to be deported, she fled but was rearrested in Rosenheim and imprisoned at the Salzburg police prison. In the cell there, she saw her mother for the last time. In 1941, she was deported to the Ravensbrück concentration camp.

In the autumn of 1940 and the summer of 1941, 40-60 prisoners were taken to Krünn in Mittenwald/Germany to the film location in police custody. The extras' salaries were paid to the camp cashier. In the contract, an immediate reporting of escape attempts was agreed upon. Rosa survived the war, and she remained in Austria until her death.

### Leni Riefenstahl

As for Leni Riefenstahl, immediately after the war, she lived in the courts, firstly to successfully fight allegations that she was a Nazi and then in a number of libel cases that she also won. She filed for divorce from Peter Jacob, a notorious womaniser, in May, 1947, and she never married again or had any children. Despite several attempts at a comeback career in the film industry, they all came to naught, as she was never able to shake off the Nazi stigma despite her numerous court victories. Although believed to be a consummate liar at the time, there was never any proof to convict her of any specific wrongdoing.

I have applied far less fiction to my character Leni Riefenstahl than the reader should assume. She did burn down her own set. According to Steven Bach in his excellent book *Leni: The Life and Work of Leni Riefenstahl*, Leni was at Hitler's Berghof mountain retreat when they were planning the invasion of Poland during her 37th birthday. She spent considerable time in and out of mental institutions during the war and in the years following.

In Ray Müller's illuminating documentary, *The Wonderful, Horrible Life of Leni Riefenstahl* (1993), she steadfastly believed that she never did anything wrong and instead saw herself as a benefactor to the Gypsy children under her care. However, subsequent to the fall of the Berlin Wall, certain documents surfaced, including eyewitnesses of her "auditions" at a Gypsy concentration camp in Salzburg. Leni Riefenstahl escaped any successful prosecution, mainly because several incriminating documents, which have since come to light, weren't available or known about at that time.

Up until her dying day, she maintained ignorance of Nazi atrocities. She said that all the Gypsy children referred to her as "Aunt Leni". She even claimed she had seen all the Gypsies used in her film alive and well long after the war, which was an impossibility, as most had been sent to Auschwitz, where they were murdered along with thousands of other Gypsies, Romani, Roma or Sinti.

Later, in old age, she simply refused to discuss her use of Gypsy children in *Tiefland*. Eighteen days after her 101st birthday, on 8 September 2003, she died peacefully in her bed, with her much younger lover by her side, holding her hand. On Friday, 12 September, she was cremated in Munich.

I have never done anything I didn't want to, and nothing I've ever been ashamed of.

– Leni Riefenstahl

No one would deny that with her talent, she developed cinematic methods that have since become part of an aesthetic canon. Her career also shows that one cannot lead an honest life in service of the false and that art is never apolitical.
– German Culture Minister, Christina Weiss 2003

## *Tiefland (1954)*

Twenty years after Leni Riefenstahl purchased the film rights for 40,000 reichsmarks in 1934, and 14 years after the first camera had rolled a single frame of footage in 1940, the world premiere of the 99-minute *Tiefland* took place in Stuttgart on 11 February 1954. It was estimated to cost seven million marks (one of the most expensive war movies ever made) but was a spectacular failure. Leni herself said that the most agonising disappointment of her life was observing herself on-screen as the Gypsy Queen, Martha.

But the film did garner some minor notoriety, as *Tiefland* was in the *Guinness Book of Records* as having the longest-ever production period for any movie. There have been subsequent films that have taken longer to film; however, *Tiefland* was a Titanic disaster in which the movie's lead star, executive producer, director and screenwriter, Leni Riefenstahl, was her very own iceberg.

## Marlene Dietrich

After the spitting incident during her 1960 tour of Berlin, she vowed never to return to Germany. However, upon her death on 6 May 1992, aged 90, she was buried in Germany and is interred in Berlin.

Pre-war, Marlene Dietrich was a staunch and vocal anti-Nazi. She donated her salary from her films to help Jewish refugees escape pre-war Nazi Germany (Jean Gabin, who would become her lover, also helped smuggle Jews out of Nazi Germany). Marlene Dietrich is said to have performed for over half-a-million servicemen while touring overseas for the USO. And, by all reports, if indeed there were a kissing category in the *Guinness Book of Records* of most men kissed, then Marlene Dietrich would undoubtedly win the world record, hands (or lips) down.

As a result of her performances for the GIs, she became addicted to live performances. Once her Hollywood career seemed over, she returned to cabaret shows, which she toured for many years until 29 September 1975, when she fell off a stage on Sydney, Australia and broke her leg.

In the final years of her life, she became an alcoholic and pain-killing drug addict and secluded herself in Paris. She was awarded several medals for her wartime service, for which she was immensely proud.

Her song 'Lili Marlene' was enjoyed by soldiers fighting on either side, American GIs and the German Wehrmacht alike. Despite Goebbels banning the song as not being "military enough", the German soldiers of the Afrika Korps demanded the song be played on the German radio. The Allies also heard the song, becoming a hit with the American Eighth Army. When the OSS got Marlene Dietrich to record the song in German and English in 1943, it topped the frontline charts for both sides.

Although Marlene and her mother did speak via radio (in English), Marlene wasn't reunited with her mother until mid-September 1945. She arrived in Berlin to finally be present with her mother in front of the foreign press. Shortly afterwards, while in Paris, Marlene received a telegram stating that her mother had had a fatal heart attack on 6 November 1945. Josephine Felsing Dietrich von Losch died just days short of her sixty-ninth birthday. The casket was made of discarded school desks, thoughtfully constructed by GIs, who knew it was for the mother of the irrepressible Marlene Dietrich, whom they would never forget. With the death of her much-beloved "general" of a mother, her last bond to her former Fatherland had been cut. Her mother's words were words that Marlene Dietrich would live by her entire life: "Do something!"

Berlin Memorial Plaque
"Where have all the flowers gone"
Marlene Dietrich
27 December 1901 - 6 May 1992
Actress and Singer


She was one of the few German actresses who attained international significance. Despite tempting offers by the Nazi regime, she emigrated to the USA and became an American citizen.

In 2002, the city of Berlin posthumously made her an honorary citizen.

"I am, thank God, a Berliner."

### Sgt. Mayflower (American GI)

The word GI refers to General Infantry or the army term "General Issue", as the soldiers believed themselves were General Issue along with their equipment. Sgt Marion Mayflower represents the heroic valour of the American GI who gave his life in far-off countries to free several nations from tyranny. On 12 April, 2000, the US House of Representatives voted 397-0 that the American GI was the "Person of the Century" [the 20th century].

... Whereas, in large measure, due to the heroic efforts of the American GI, more people around the world enjoy the benefits of freedom at the end of the 20th century than at any other time in history. ...

[from *House Concurrent Resolution 282*]

## Author's Note

Although real people and actual events inspired this work, nonetheless, it is a novel. Fact and truth have been carefully interspersed with the glue of my sweat, tears and imagination. This story may not be how things unfolded precisely, but rather how they should have been, at least from my point of view.

Historians have a single duty to serve the truth, whereas storytellers have the sole duty to serve the story. However, it would not have been possible for writers of historical fiction to bring history to life if it weren't for the dedicated work of historians.

I am indebted to Donna Cohen of Westport, Connecticut. Reference is often made to six degrees of separation to anyone famous. On 28 August, 2010, Donna, the CEO of the Holocaust and Human Rights Education Center at the Manhattanville College in Purchase, New York, had already introduced me to a handful of Holocaust survivors, including a Holocaust Hero: Dr Tina Strobos. Due to the part she played in the Dutch underground rescuing Jews in Holland during the war, Israel declared Dr Tina Strobos a hero.

While we were having tea at Dr Tina Strobos' place, Donna told Tina about my work of historical fiction that I had worked on since late 2004, which was set in the Second World War.

"Oh, who is it about?" she asked.

"My story centres on a Gypsy girl called Rosa and German-US actress Marlene Dietrich," I replied.

"Oh, I knew Marlene," she answered.

"You did?" I said, stunned. "How? Where?"

"As a child, we always skied in the Swiss Alps, and Marlene Dietrich was often there."

"What was she like?"

"Oh, she was her usual self. A diva. She acted like she was above us all, but we didn't care [about her snooty attitude]; she was *the* irrepressible Marlene Dietrich."

In a long, isolated journey, we aspiring writers often need reassurance that we're on the right path, or at least I did, and this was like a giant neon sign, like one of those bright screens flashing on New York's Broadway; the city where I was studying writing at the time. And, just like that, as an aspiring writer, I had only one degree of separation from the Hollywood star and GI poster girl: the lovely and irrepressible Miss Marlene Dietrich.

# Timeline

## *1933*

| 30 Jan | Adolf Hitler appointed Chancellor of Germany |
| 20 Mar | Germany's first concentration camp, Dachau, opens |
| 23 Mar | Hitler decreed Dictator of Germany |
| 01 Apr | Gestapo established |
| 10 May | Nazis start massive book burnings |

## *1934*

| 25 Jul | Adolf Hitler becomes Führer of Germany |

## *1935*

| 26 Nov | Hitler classifies the nationless Romani or Roma as "enemies of the state" |

## *1936*

| 07 Mar | Germany reoccupies the Rhineland |
| 16 Jul | 500 Roma and Sinti rounded up and sent to Berlin-Marzahn (Camp for Roma) |
| 01-16 Aug | Berlin 1936 Summer Olympics (Berlin won the bid to host the games in 1931) |
| 01 Dec | Compulsory Hitler Youth for all males aged 10-18 |

## *1938*

| 12 Mar | Austria annexed by Germany (Anschluss) |
| 30 Sep | Sudetenland was given to Germany (Munich Agreement) |
| 09/10 Nov | Crystal Night, an anti-Jewish pogrom starts (Kristallnacht) |

## *1939*

| 15 Mar | Germany invades Czechoslovakia (Prague is the Capital) |

| | |
|---|---|
| 03 Apr | "Fall Weiss" planning for the invasion of Poland begins |
| 23 Aug | Germany and the Soviet Union sign a non-aggression pact |
| 01 Sep | Berlin Peace Rally scheduled but never happens (Nazi ruse to invade Poland) |
| 01 Sep | Germany invades and declares war on Poland |
| 3 Sep | As a result, France and Britain (and their allies) declare war on Germany |

## *1941*

| | |
|---|---|
| 22 Jun | The German invasion of the Soviet Union |
| 07 Dec | Pearl Harbor attacked by the Japanese (declaration of war by Japan) |
| 08 Dec | USA declares war on Japan |
| 11 Dec | Adolf Hitler declares war on the USA |

## *1942*

| | |
|---|---|
| 20 Jan | "The Final Solution" of exterminating European Jews is formalised |

## *1944*

| | |
|---|---|
| 06 Jun | D-Day Invasion of Europe, 155,000 troops, landed at Normandy |
| 13 Jun | The first V1-Flying Bomb bombs England (one of Hitler's many wonder weapons) |
| 20 Jul | Hitler assassination attempt & Alfred Riefenstahl funeral |
| 24 Jul | Russians liberate the first concentration camp in Maidanek |
| 19-25 Aug | "The Battle for Paris" |
| 26 Aug | Paris Liberation (parade) |
| 30 Aug | Germans abandon Bulgaria to the coming Soviets |
| 08 Sep | V-2 Rockets first bombing of Paris |

| | |
|---|---|
| 09 Sep | V-2 Rockets first bombing of London |
| 12 Sep | US 1st Army enters Germany |
| 15 Sep | American forces reach the German Siegfried Line |
| 1 Oct | Soviet Union troops enter Yugoslavia |
| 5 Oct | Soviet Union Red Army enters Hungary (Budapest is the Capital) |
| 13 Oct | US 1st Army enters Aachen (near Cologne) |
| 18 Oct | Volksturm, the last-ditch people's army created in Germany |
| 21 Oct | The US 1st Army occupies Aachen after the local Germans surrender |
| 25 Oct | The Soviet Army liberates Romania |
| 28 Oct | Women relocated from Auschwitz to Bergen-Belsen |
| 30 Oct | Last gassings in Auschwitz concentration camp |
| 12 Nov | The Americans capture the V-weapon factory at Wittering |
| 29 Dec | Soviets launch "The Battle of Budapest" |
| 31 Dec | Hungary declares war on Germany |

## 1945

| | |
|---|---|
| 15 Jan | Hitler and Eva Braun move to the Bunker |
| 16 Jan | Soviet troops lay siege to Budapest |
| 25 Jan | "The Battle of the Bulge" officially ends (most American casualties in WW2) |
| 27 Jan | Auschwitz concentration camp liberated by the Soviets |
| 31 Jan | The Soviet Army crosses the Oder River (<50 miles from Berlin) |
| 11 Feb | Soviets overrun Budapest and push northwards to Dresden |
| 13 Feb | "Battle of Budapest" finally ends with a Soviet victory |

| | |
|---|---|
| 13/14 Feb | The Firebombing of Dresden (100,000 German civilians killed) |
| 14 Feb | Accidental bombing of Prague (mistaken for Dresden) |
| 05 Mar | Cologne captured by the US armies |
| 07 Mar | The Americans cross over the Rhine River at Remagen Bridge |
| 16 Mar | The Soviets defeat Germans in Hungary |
| 20 Mar | General Patton's troops capture Mainz, Germany |
| 20 Mar | Hitler awards medals to Hitler Youth in Chancellery Garden |
| 23 Mar | Germany surrounded and attacked from all borders |
| 11 Apr | Buchenwald concentration camp liberated by the American 3rd Army |
| 12 Apr | President Roosevelt dies aged 63, during his fourth term |
| 15 Apr | Bergen-Belsen concentration camp liberated by the British |
| 16 Apr | "The Battle of Berlin" begins between Germany and the Soviets |
| 19 Apr | Soviet forces reach Berlin suburbs |
| 20 Apr | Hitler celebrates his 56th birthday in the Berlin Bunker |
| 23 Apr | Soviets enter Berlin |
| 25 Apr | Soviet and American forces meet at Elbe River near Torgau, Germany |
| 26 Apr | Storch light plane flight lands in Berlin by female aviator Hanna Reitsch |
| 28 Apr | Last flight out of Berlin by Hanna Reitsch in an Arado Ar 96 |
| 27 Apr | Berlin completely surrounded by the Soviet Army |
| 29 Apr | Dachau concentration camp liberated by the Americans |
| 29 Apr | Hitler marries Eva Braun |
| 30 Apr | Hitler and Eva Braun commit suicide |
| 01 May | Goebbels and his wife kill their six children before their suicides |
| 02 May | "The Battle of Berlin" ends |

| 07 May | Germany surrenders unconditionally to the Allies |
| 08 May | VE Day (Victory in Europe) |
| 31 May | Berlin Zoo audit (91 of 3715 survive the war), including Asian elephant, Siam |
| 01 Jul | American, British and French Troops officially enter Berlin |
| 17 Jul | The Potsdam Conference begins near Berlin (to 2 Aug 1945) |
| 20 Nov | Nuremberg trials begin |

## 1948

| 14 May | The State of Israel is declared |

## 1954

| 11 Feb | Leni Riefenstahl releases *Tiefland* in Stuttgart, Germany |

## 1960

Marlene Dietrich tours Germany and Israel

## 1969

(Private) Kurt Vonnegut publishes his book *Slaughterhouse 5*, which is inspired by his POW experiences (he was caught by the Germans during "The Battle of the Bulge"), where he hid in Slaughterhouse 5 during the Dresden fire-bombings (in his book, he mentions an alien, time-travelling race called the Tralfamadorians).

.

Printed in Great Britain
by Amazon

52180024R00166